Criminal Recidivism in
New York City

Robert Fishman

The Praeger Special Studies program—utilizing the most modern and efficient book production techniques and a selective worldwide distribution network—makes available to the academic, government, and business communities significant, timely research in U.S. and international economic, social, and political development.

Criminal Recidivism in New York City

An Evaluation of
the Impact of
Rehabilitation
and Diversion Services

PRAEGER SPECIAL STUDIES IN U.S. ECONOMIC, SOCIAL, AND POLITICAL ISSUES

Praeger Publishers   New York   London

Library of Congress Cataloging in Publication Data

Fishman, Robert.
    Criminal recidivism in New York City.

    (Praeger special studies in U.S. economic, social,
and political issues)
    Includes bibliographical references.
    1. Recidivists—New York (City) 2. Rehabilitation
of criminals—New York (City) 3. Pre-trial intervention—
New York (City) 4. Criminal justice, Administration
of—New York (City) I. Title.
HV6795.N5F57 1977   364.3'2   76-12850
ISBN 0-275-23580-7

A grant from the City of New York through the
auspices of the Criminal Justice Coordinating Council
provided the funds for the preparation of the report,
but the City of New York disclaims all responsibility
for the contents thereof.

PRAEGER PUBLISHERS
200 Park Avenue, New York, N.Y. 10017, U.S.A.

Published in the United States of America in 1977
by Praeger Publishers, Inc.

789   038   987654321

Printed in the United States of America

To my beloved wife Henrietta,
for her inexhaustible patience,
interest, and support.

ACKNOWLEDGMENTS

This book is an updating and revision of the report, "An Evaluation of the Effect on Criminal Recidivism of New York City Projects Providing Rehabilitation and Diversion Services, A Final Report to the Mayor's Criminal Justice Coordinating Council," March 31, 1975. The evaluation was supported by grants to the Graduate Center and Research Foundation of the City University of New York from the New York State Division of Criminal Justice Services and the Mayor's Criminal Justice Coordinating Council (CJCC) using Law Enforcement Assistance Administration funds. I thank these agencies as well as the staff of each of the CJCC projects and cooperating city agencies, particularly the New York City Police Department which provided the arrest histories of the project clients for the evaluation.

The staff of the evaluation were, of course, responsible for the bulk of the work that resulted in the final report. I appreciate their work very much. Felicisimo Llacuna's dedication to the supervision of the processing and reporting of data was only exceeded by the quality of his effort. Hari R. Shiledar Baxi, Director of Statistics for the evaluation, was responsible for innovative applications of statistics which made it possible to answer the difficult question of whether differences among projects affected the arrest recidivism rates of their clients. His contributions have been invaluable. Irving Wexler wrote parts of the appendix on method (Appendix A). The parts were chapters 4 and 5 on collecting and processing data from the police department and part of chapter 6 on the measurement of the severity of prior arrest history. As office manager Marie Hoffmeister's formidable charm, good humor, and competence made the pressures of the project more bearable for all.

The planning and funding of the evaluation project were in response to requests by Henry S. Ruth, Jr., then Director of the CJCC. Mr. Ruth left the CJCC before the evaluation completed and turned in its final report. His special contributions and support will always be remembered and appreciated.

Marvin E. Wolfgang and Robert M. Figlio deserve special thanks for their assistance with the task of the measurement of the severity of arrest histories. Professor Wolfgang also contributed very helpful criticisms of the draft of the original report, and a lot of moral support when it was most needed.

David Rudenstine of the New York Civil Liberties Union represented me in negotiations with the CJCC, on issues which included CJCC permission to publish the final report. He also critiqued parts of the draft of this book. I am extremly indebted to Mr. Rudenstine and the NYCLU.

I thank Richardson White, Jr. for a very constructive critique of the draft of this book.

There were many others who contributed to the evaluation and this book in valuable ways which included typing and editing. I can't name each of them so rather than slight anyone I will name none. However, each of their contributions is appreciated.

Finally, it is stressed that the conclusions and recommendations in this book are solely the responsibility of the author and do not necessarily reflect the views of the agencies or individuals acknowledged. I emphasize this because some of those acknowledged here disagree strongly with certain of my views such as the possible use of mandatory sentences and preventive detention to deter and prevent violent crime. Under the circumstances, their assistance, particularly in obtaining release of the final report to the general public, is both appreciated and admired.

THE STAFF OF THE EVALUATION PROJECT

Director

Mr. Robert Fishman

Assistant Directors and Senior Staff

Dr. Hari R. Shiledar Baxi
Mr. Wayne Goldberg
Dr. Irving Kweller
Dr. Sheldon Litt
Mr. Dale Ordes
Dr. Philip Taylor

Full-Time, Permanent, Research, Administrative, and Clerical Staff

Mrs. Emma Baines
Mr. Roger Borgen
Miss Karen Codrington
Mr. George Goldschmied
Miss Marie Hoffmeister
Mr. Felicisimo Llacuna
Mrs. Katherine Lynn
Mrs. Caralee Roberts
Miss Fayge Shuldman
Mr. David Wenger

Temporary and Part-Time Research Staff

Mr. Serban Andronescu
Mr. William Cahill
Mr. Cleveland Da Costa
Mr. Carlos Hernandez
Miss Margaret Konefsky
Mr. Ansley La Mar
Miss Kate Liebhold*
Mr. Fazal-ur Rehman
Mrs. Joyce Scott
Mr. Leslie Spector
Mr. James Thomas

---

*She assisted during the development of the proposal.

CONTENTS

LIST OF TABLES

INTRODUCTION

This book is an adaption of the final report by the evaluation project about the impact of rehabilitation and diversion services on criminal recidivism. All of the statistical data presented in the report have been included here without change. Additional information has been included from the literature and other sources.

The first of the book's three major parts consists of descriptions of the evaluation of and the findings on the effects of rehabilitation and diversion services, provided by 18 projects, on the criminal recidivism of 2,860 men and boys.

These findings led to the conclusions in the second part that the amount and type of criminal recidivism are so high in their cost to victims that the rehabilitation services fail as approaches to the prevention and control of crime, particularly violent crime. Further, differences among the projects such as the amounts or types of rehabilitation services provided or environmental factors such as unemployment did not appear to be related to the failure.

The implications of the findings for approaches to the problem of violent crime are discussed in the last part. Since neither rehabilitation (by job training and placement, remedial education, and varieties of mental health counseling) nor current criminal justice system approaches appear to work, few options remain. Mandatory sentences of incarceration for those convicted of violent crimes against strangers are discussed, illustrated, and recommended as the most promising and important approach. Preventive detention of those charged with violent crimes and the application of both of these approaches to juveniles are also recommended.

The first part of this book is intended primarily for behavioral scientists. The second and third parts are intended for use in public policy decision making and are written, therefore, mainly for non-scientific readers.

The final report, from which this book stems, was considered controversial by many from the time it was turned into the CJCC, the evaluation project's sponsor. [1] Although there were some criticisms of aspects of the evaluation methodology (These are discussed in the book.), I believe that the controversy occurred mainly for other reasons.

There is probably at this time in America no more controversial or emotionally charged topic then the problem of crime and its possible resolution. Violent crime and its consequences affect, directly or indirectly, almost every resident of our large cities. The reactions of many persons to violent crime and their ideas of what constitutes the best response to it by society are influenced strongly by their moral or ethical beliefs. Many civil libertarians argue that the safeguarding of the constitutional rights of those accused or convicted of a crime must be society's primary consideration in its reaction to crime. In most cities, more violent crimes are committed by blacks and Hispanics, proportionally, than by whites. On the one hand, this generates and reinforces racial prejudice. On the other hand, there is resentment of this prejudice and anxiety about its possible consequences. For many, the pervasive poverty of these offenders seems to be the main cause of their criminal behavior; thus their preexisting beliefs in the need for sweeping political and socio-economic changes are strengthened. Attempts to explain the causes and dynamics of criminal behavior also draw into confrontation those who espouse differing positions on the nature of personality and mental illness.

In the opinion of this author, the dominant philosophical position on crime prevention and control, among New York City political decision makers, criminal justice court officials, and the staff members of the CJCC, favors the same rehabilitation approaches which the evaluation considered failures. Moreover these officials strongly oppose such approaches as mandatory sentencing and preventive detention which the evaluation recommended. Under the circumstances, controversy is not very surprising and may be beneficial in that it may force a more objective and open examination of these views by both public officials and the public.

Most of the controversy has been expressed in the form of a legal, advocacy-adversary argument. Within a court of law an advocate, such as a defense attorney, is expected to consider the interests of his client as paramount. In furthering those interests he is expected to present facts in support of his client's case, attack the validity of potentially harmful facts presented by an adversary, but not volunteer facts that might help the other side. Both the goal and the method of argument are inappropriate and may result in serious error when used to choose from two alternatives such as continuation of existing sentencing policies or their modification by use of mandatory sentencing. Advocacy is inappropriate because it argues (by a selective marshalling of the facts) for a choice on the basis of consequences to the welfare and rights of one of the groups affected by the decision without presenting fully—or at all—the consequences to the other group affected. (Both the offenders and their potential victims are examples of such groups.)

Since a decision obviously affects both groups, from a public policy standpoint the method of analysis must be empirical. This method requires objective assessment of the benefits and of the costs to the offender group and to the potential victim group of each of the policy alternatives. In my view, advocacy is as unsuitable to the choice among alternative approaches to the control and prevention of crime as it is to the control and prevention of bubonic plague.

One of the objectives of the book was to maximize the use of this empirical approach in analyses of the issues, both to enable more accurate decisions and to defuse some of the more emotionally-charged issues. (To effect the latter I have used medical model analogies in presenting some of the analyses.)

Mandatory sentences and preventive detention are not, to me, the most palatable of approaches to the problem. I must confess that I would have been delighted if the data had shown that the rehabilitation and diversion services were successful. But they did not, and the effects of violent crime on the population of New York City and other large American cities are, in my view, unpalatable.

The sheer numbers of victims of murder, rape, robbery, and assault, as presented later in this book, are staggering. Any lessening of the rate of increase which may occur is generally hailed thankfully by criminal justice officials and by the media. Yet the existing level of crime is almost unbearable. The statistics, although bleak, reflect only partially and imperfectly the actual nature and consequences of violent crime. Their reality is far bleaker.

NOTES

1. New York Times, August 10, 1975 pp. 1, 24.

Criminal Recidivism in New York City

THE PROBLEM OF CRIME

In New York City in 1974, there were 519,825 complaints of serious crimes, or one complaint for every 16 persons in the city. * Among the four violent crimes, 1,554 were non-negligent homicides, an average of about four a day. In addition, there were 4,054 rapes (about 11 a day), 77,940 robberies (about 214 a day), and 41,068 aggravated assaults (about 112 a day). [1] Except for homicide, the numbers of these crimes might actually be twice as large if unreported crimes were included. [2] From 1968 to 1974, the rate of non-negligent homicide increased 67 percent, forcible rape 122 percent, robbery 43 percent, and aggravated assault 44 percent. [3]

Although the deaths and injuries are the highest cost of these urban crimes, pain and suffering are only one component of this cost; public fear and a sense of vulnerability have affected the life-style of almost every city resident.

These factors have contributed to a change in the population of the city. Many of those, who can afford to, move out. Primarily white and middle-class, they have numbered over a million in New York City. In the 1960s the number of whites in New York City declined by 900,000, and there was an additional decrease of 400,000 from 1970 to 1973. The gap was filled by blacks, who increased from 1970 to 1973 by 5.6 percent to a total of 2 million, and by Hispanics,

---

*The Uniform Crime Reporting system (UCR) divides the seven most "serious" crimes into violent crimes (homicide, forcible rape, robbery, and aggravated assault) and crimes against property (burglary, larceny, and auto theft).

whose increase in that period was 11.5 percent to a total of 1.2 million. Blacks now compose 25 percent of the city's population and Hispanics 16 percent; the bulk of them are in the lower socioeconomic class.

Accompanying these developments, the city's tax base has steadily shrunk. Each municipal budget becomes more of a crisis, in which a substantial part of the solution is to cut city services, including threatened reductions in the number of police and fireman. A serious cut in such services might well accelerate the out-migration of taxpayers and further depress the tax base.

THE CRIMINALS

In New York City, the violent crimes of murder, forcible rape, robbery,* and aggravated assault are committed primarily by young males, black or Hispanic, who are poor and undereducated. In 1974, there were 260,739 arrests in New York City.[4] Of these, 43,831 were for violent crimes.

Sex. Males represented 89 percent of these arrests.

Age. Among those males arrested for violent crimes, 43 percent were 7 to 20 years old, while 30 percent were aged 21 to 29.

Race.† In 1974, among the 1,140 males arrested for murder, 52 percent were black, 32 percent were Hispanic, and 15 percent were white.[5] For 1,642 of the 1,972 persons arrested in 1975 for forcible rape, 63 percent were black, 23 percent were Hispanic, 13 percent were white, and 1 percent were yellow and "other."[6] Zeisel, deGrazia, and Friedman[7] reported on the race of those arrested for robbery, using a sample of 1,888 arrests picked at random from arrest registers in Manhattan, Brooklyn, the Bronx, and Queens. Of these arrests, 15 percent (about 289) were for robbery. Within this sample, blacks composed 71 percent; Hispanics, 16 percent; and whites, 13 percent.

The racial composition of arrests for murder, rape, and robbery indicates that blacks and Hispanics represent 84, 86, and 87 percent, respectively, of arrests for these crimes. As in other

---

*This includes most "muggings."

†With the exception of homicide arrests, New York City Police Department policy prohibits the release of data about the race or ethnicity of the arrest population. This policy is to be changed in 1977.

large cities, the bulk of blacks and Hispanics are undereducated and from the lowest socioeconomic class.

A RESPONSE TO THE PROBLEM

The Criminal Justice Coordinating Council (CJCC) was set up by the City of New York as one response to the problem of crime. The CJCC was to administer, at the local level, national funds channeled to it through the state's Office of Crime Control Planning from the Law Enforcement Assistance Administration (LEAA), created by Congress in 1968.

In addition to supporting such institutionalized elements of the criminal justice system (CJS) as police, courts, and prisons, the CJCC found itself heavily committed, through a variety of projects, to a strategy of rehabilitation programs. The emphasis in these was on services to offenders, ex-offenders, and in some cases "pre-offenders."

Target Groups. The target groups of clients for these "people programs" were described in the CJCC annual plans of 1971-73. They were principally the types of offenders described in the preceding section. The CJCC placed particular emphasis on males: juveniles, youths, and young adults; blacks and Hispanics; ex-convicts; the poor and undereducated; drug addicts; and, for preventive purposes, some first offenders.

Rehabilitation and Diversion. Rehabilitation relied primarily on combinations of remedial education: job referral, training, or placement; counseling; and legal aid and drug addiction treatment. Municipal or voluntary agencies and community groups either provided these services to the clients themselves or they referred them to others who could help. Many of the projects also provided "diversion" from the processes of the criminal justice system. Under this concept, offenders (mainly juveniles and young adults) who are thought to be better suited for "people projects" than for the conventional CJS are remanded or released to such programs. Some are conditionally released without service, as on bail or probation.

Agency Evaluation Needs. For purposes of orderly administration, the CJCC found that it had to know a variety of things about these programs:

- To make decisions about modifying, re-funding and institutionalizing them, it had to know their individual and collective criminological effects on their clients.

- To make the same or similar decisions, it needed information that would enable it to compare the criminological effect of different projects on the same types of clients.
- To monitor the programs and to be able to make program adjustments in midstream, it needed information about how criminological impact was related to such program characteristics as type, mix, and quality of services offered, staff-client ratio, and the proportion of professional to paraprofessional staff.
- To make policy and broader programmatic decisions, it had to know the relationship between a client's criminal history and his criminal behavior after he entered a project.

To satisfy these needs, a part of a project's gross budget—usually 5 to 10 percent—was set aside for evaluation, generally by academics or consulting firms on subcontracts. Since these evaluators were responsible to the individual project directors rather than to the CJCC, their objectivity, in some cases, was questionable. Moreover, the natural and inescapable outcome was an enormous variety of evaluation goals, designs, methods, resources, and competence among the individual evaluators. This made it virtually impossible for the CJCC to compare the criminological effectiveness of different program models in serving similar types of clients. An evaluation that defined recidivism as reincarceration, for instance, could not be compared with evaluations that defined it as rearrest, reconviction, or change on an attitude scale.

In response to these problems (and some of the agency's management information needs) an evaluation plan was proposed for a centrally conducted, standardized effort. It was funded in July 1971 and completed in March 1975 at a cost of approximately $800,000.

NOTES

1. Personal communication with John Getting, Crime Analysis Section, New York City Police Department, December 6, 1976.

2. "Crime in the Nation's Five Largest Cities," LEAA, National Criminal Justice Information and Statistics Service, April 1974.

3. Rates per year are from the Crime Analysis Section, New York City Police Department, 1975. The evaluation computed the differences between the rates per 100,000 for 1968 and 1974 on a population base of 7,894,862.

4. Crime Analysis Section, New York City Police Department, November 1976.

5. Personal communication with Philip McGuire, Crime Analysis Section, New York City Police Department, December 3, 1976.

6. Personal communication with Dennis Butler, Sex Crimes Analysis Unit, New York City Police Department, December 4, 1976.

7. Hans Zeisel, Jessica deGrazia, and Lucy Friedman, "Criminal Justice System Under Stress: A Study of the Disposition of Felony Arrests in New York City," Vera Institute of Justice, August 1975.

CHAPTER

2

THE DESIGN
OF THE EVALUATION

The design of the evaluation, from the proposal stage, stipulated that there would be one basic goal of CJCC and its projects, and a common measure of that goal.

THE COMMON GOAL—REDUCING CRIME

Title I of the Omnibus Crime Control and Safe Streets Act of 1968 established the Law Enforcement Assistance Administration (LEAA) to address the problem of "the high incidence of crime."[1] Thus, the basic goal has been the reduction of crime. In the 1973 amendment of that act, the goal of reducing the incidence of crime was articulated into crime reduction, crime prevention, reducing juvenile delinquency, and ensuring the greater safety of the people.[2] Therefore, it was evident that the basic goal of all CJCC's LEAA-funded "people projects" would be to reduce the incidence of crime, and that they would be evaluated with that goal as a basic criterion.

The services provided by the projects (and the projects themselves) thus became methods by which the goal was to be achieved. For projects providing some combination of remedial education and job training, for example, such outcomes as an increased ability to read, or employment, became methods by which the projects proposed to reduce the criminal behavior of their clients. These outcomes could not be justified as ends in themselves. *

---

*If, on the other hand, the projects were funded by the Department of Labor or the Department of Health, Education, and Welfare, then employment or increased reading ability might logically and legally have been considered as the project goals. This was not the case for funds from LEAA.

An important evaluation implication of this distinction was that a measure of criminal behavior had to be the dependent variable in this design, while project service outputs would be independent variables (to the extent that the service outputs could be measured adequately). This distinction between dependent and independent variables was important in that its effects ranged from allocation of evaluation resources to methods of analysis. *

THE COMMON MEASURE—ARRESTS

The most reasonable interpretation of the intent of Congress when it spoke about reducing the "incidence of crime" is a literal one. In other words, Congress was not restricting itself to a technical meaning in terms of formal, recorded complaints. It also meant crimes that are never reported, or what social scientists would refer to as criminal behavior. It was this behavior, as it affects the population of the country, that Congress meant to reduce.

This focus on behavior is emphasized here because often there is confusion about the difference between a legal and an empirical or behavioral definition of crime. A person who has in fact shot someone in the head during a robbery may not legally have committed a crime if a court finds him to be psychotic, or if his confession was obtained illegally. Nevertheless, the victim remains shot in the head, and criminal behavior did take place. The very broad legal definition of this event includes factors such as competence and due process, which have no logical or factual relationship whatsoever to the empirical question of whether the event occurred and who did it. Rather, these legal criteria, in the example of the "innocent" psychotic killer, would entail incorrect answers to the empirical questions. (It should also be obvious that there is no violation of constitutional rights when the criminal behavior of unidentified individuals is measured by arrests.)

The evaluation had to settle on some common measure of incidence of crime, and the alternatives available were complaints, convictions, incarcerations, and arrests. †

---

*In the initial proposal the evaluation had anticipated that its primary emphasis would have to be on measuring validly and accurately the criminological outcomes of the projects. A next step, to the extent possible, would be measuring relationships between criminological outcomes and project services or other project characteristics.

†It had already been clear that in terms of time and money, one had to be able to measure adequately criminological outcomes; otherwise measurement of service outputs alone would not be particularly meaningful within the intent of the LEAA legislation.

Complaints. In theory, complaints are the most accurate measure
of crime of these four, but they were not considered appropriate.
They are primarily useful as a measure of crime in a geographic area,
but many CJCC projects were not restricted to standard areas, for
example, precincts or boroughs, while those which were had too few
clients to allow assessment of the relationship of project outcomes
to the incidence of crime.

Convictions. Many arrests may be dismissed prior to conviction for
reasons such as insufficient or improper evidence, when in fact the
person charged did commit a criminal act. The prevalence of plea
bargaining suggests that a measure of criminal behavior based on
convictions will be systematically skewed toward a more benign
representation of criminal behavior than is actually the case. * In
1974, for example, 80 percent of all felony arrests in New York City
were disposed of by lower courts empowered to adjudicate only misdemeanors. [3] Further, conviction on a given charge ("copped" or not)
may represent additional crimes that also were charged at the time
but were not included in the conviction. This leads to additional understatement of criminal behavior.

Incarcerations. The rate in New York City is so low that this measure
was deemed the weakest (discussed later).

Arrests. Arrests were considered closest to complaints in ability to
reflect criminal behavior. In New York City, arrest records are
relatively complete, accurate, and retrievable. Measuring by arrest
records allows comparability of results with other evaluations in or
out of New York City which use the same measure. It was concluded
after the review of the other measures that arrests were the most
accurate measure of criminal behavior that this evaluation could use.
  But arrests have some weaknesses as a measure. Some
proportion of those arrested are arrested mistakenly in that they did
not participate in any criminal behavior. Others may be uncharged,
mischarged, overcharged, or undercharged. Therefore, the evaluation
had to attempt to determine the extent to which arrests measure
accurately the criminal behavior of the project clients. The discussion

---

  *"Plea bargaining" occurs when a defendant pleads guilty to a
lesser offense than that with which he is charged (and in most cases
did commit) in order to obtain a lesser sentence. Harried and
underbudgeted courts, in turn, save the cost of prosecuting and
trying the defendant on the initial charge.

to follow is based on nonjuvenile clients, but the conclusions are applicable to juveniles.

VALIDITY OF ARRESTS

The accuracy of arrests would be affected by: arrests of persons who had not committed a crime and arrests on wrong charges, which would have resulted in overstatement of the magnitude and severity of criminal behavior respectively; and arrests that did not occur, but should have, which would result in understatement of actual criminal behavior in the same two ways.

Overstatement of Magnitude

What was being looked for was an estimate of the proportion of clients who had been arrested but who, as defined by the New York State penal law, had not done anything criminal at all (as opposed to being overcharged or mischarged). These were classified as false arrests.

Reasons for which a person might be arrested without having engaged in any criminal behavior include false complaints, or simply gross error on the part of the arresting officer.

The best approach to estimating the proportion of false arrests would have been a self-report study of an appropriate sample of project clients. For reasons of confidentiality, the evaluation was not able to conduct such a study. The question to be addressed by a self-report study was: "Did criminal behavior occur for which that arrest was made?" The false arrest rate would have to be determined for a group of individuals, but only with respect to one arrest for each individual. We could not find any self-report studies which had done this.

Consequently, a somewhat hurried and less than rigorous attempt had to be made to provide some factual basis for at least a tentative estimate. The evaluation settled on an informal poll of New York City attorneys familiar with the nature of arrests. An attorney with both prosecution and defense experience asked 21 defense attorneys and 26 prosecutors to estimate, from their experience, the proportion of all clients arrested who had actually done nothing criminal in relation to that arrest.

Clearly, this was not going to be "hard" statistical data. The selection of the sample of attorneys had not been controlled, nor was the question asked in a standardized form and fashion, since it required careful qualification. Nevertheless, the results permitted a rough estimate.

The estimates by the prosecutors of the proportion of false arrests averaged 5 percent. The estimates of the defense attorneys averaged about 8 percent. The evaluation's estimate, from these data, was that approximately 7 percent (give or take 2 percent) of those arrested for an event actually did not engage in any criminal behavior. The percentage would be lower for serious crimes. *

The evaluation therefore decided to estimate generously that, in magnitude, false arrests overstated criminal behavior by no more than 10 percent.

Overstatement of Severity

The police may overcharge or "puff" an arrest† to give the prosecutor more leverage in plea bargaining, to make the arrest seem more important for departmental or personal reasons, because they are angry with the arrested person, or because of error.

Overcharging could have affected the evaluation's measurement of the severity of the arrest rate for violent crime, and the analysis by types of crime. What was needed was an estimate of the percentage of arrest charges, whether single charges or the most serious of multiple charges, which were overcharges and not the actual criminal behavior that had taken place.

It was not possible to get estimates of the percent of arrest charges which were overcharges by the police. It was necessary to make a ballpark estimate. So it was decided, somewhat arbitrarily, to estimate overstatements of severity as also 10 percent.

Understatement of Magnitude

Understatements of the magnitude of criminal behavior, using arrests as the measure, would stem entirely from the police not making arrests for criminal behavior that did occur. The result would be expressed in terms both of persons (unapprehended recidivists) and of crimes (criminal events for which no one was arrested).

An understatement of severity would be an arrest charge less severe than the criminal event that took place. It was not possible to get estimates on this, but the evaluation submits that this proportion

---

*The results were also interesting in that they did not conform to or even suggest support of the much higher estimates of false arrests made by people less familiar with the phenomenon.

†An example might be a case of picking pockets charged as a robbery rather than a larceny.

of arrests would be less than the 10 percent estimated for overstated
severity.

To estimate the extent of understatement of magnitude, the
evaluation needed to know the proportion of clients classified as
nonrecidivists who were really unapprehended recidivists. It is
known that only a portion of reported crimes result in apprehensions.
For example, there were 77,940 complaints of robberies in New York
City during 1974, and 19,648 arrests for that crime, or about one
in four. [4] Further, the findings of a National Crime Panel survey of
victimization indicated that there are approximately twice as many
robberies in New York City as complaints. [5] This would make the
arrest-to-robbery ratio about one to eight.

It was concluded, therefore, that there is a substantial proportion
of crime in New York City for which the perpetrators are not
apprehended. Given the criminal history of the group of project
clients evaluated, it is submitted that some proportion of those
unapprehended criminals would be among the group; some of them,
by virtue of arrests for other crimes, would already have been
classified as recidivists; and some of them would not have been
arrested, and would be classified falsely as nonrecidivists.

With little better basis than these sorts of indications and
impressions to go on, and after informal discussions with law
enforcement and court officials, the evaluation selected the somewhat
conservative* figure of 20 percent as a tentative estimate of the
proportion of those reported to be nonrecidivists who actually
committed unapprehended crimes after project entry. This would
result in an understatement of criminal behavior by the arrest
recidivism rate.

Conclusion

Because of a paucity of data, the estimates that were made are
tentative and somewhat speculative. They are meant to be used as a
framework for a conclusion about the accuracy of the arrest measure
and not as "significant results" of the evaluation. Nevertheless, they
are the best estimates that we were able to make on the basis of the
data available. Therefore, it is submitted that balancing false and
overcharged arrests against unapprehended crimes yields a net
result in which the magnitude and severity of criminal recidivism
findings in this report understate actual criminal behavior.

---

*Some persons can commit a remarkable number of crimes
before being apprehended. There are cases on record of confessions,
after an arrest, of from 60 to more than 100 robberies.

CLIENT CHARACTERISTICS AND CRIME

The study, from the very outset, was designed to allow measurement of the projects' criminological effects (individually and comparatively)* on the primary CJCC target groups of clients described earlier. [6] In so doing, it had to control for those client characteristics most related to recidivism. It was important, for example, to be able to ascertain separate recidivism rates for a project's 7- to 12-year-old male juvenile first offenders and for 19- to 20-year-old male serious offenders among its clients, since the project might be effective with one group but not the other. This was, of course, even more essential in comparing the project's criminological effectiveness with 7- to 12-year-olds or 19- to 20-year-olds with those age groups in other "competing" projects. The three client characteristics selected were age, sex, and prior criminal history. Heroin addiction was to have been a fourth characteristic, but it could not be used, primarily because police arrest records did not distinguish between heroin and other drugs. Many other personal characteristics might affect criminal behavior and reactions to it by the criminal justice system—including, for example, socioeconomic background, intelligence, ethnicity, and motivation. But the evaluation had to select only the most important and measurable. IQ, for example, may be a determinant of recidivism, but it is very expensive to measure adequately for the large number of clients in the study. Motivation is also of great importance, but there is no known standard test for it that is recognized by the testing community as a whole.

Age, in New York State, is a key deciding factor in arrest, type of court, dispositions available, and conditions of release or incarceration. The four basic age groups were 7 to 15 for juveniles, 16 to 18 for youthful offenders, 19 to 20 for adults, and 21 or older for a second adult category. † Only males were analyzed, since

---

*Comparatively among themselves and/or a "control" group.

†As a rule, for similar crimes, juveniles aged 7 to 15 are arrested less frequently and detained or incarcerated for much shorter periods than nonjuveniles. Juveniles are not arrested but are given a summons called a "YD-1" card for minor violations such as subway turnstile jumping and some misdemeanors for which an adult could be arrested. Youthful offender status for 16- to 18-year-olds may apply at the time of sentencing if a Class A felony or a previous felony conviction is not involved. If granted this status, they receive very short sentences.

females make up a relatively small proportion (approximately 10 percent) of those who commit serious crimes, and since the number of females in most of the projects was too low for valid statistical analysis. Severity of criminal history before project entry is generally considered an important predictor of recidivism after entry.

NOTES

1. Declaration and Purpose, Law Enforcement Assistance, Act of June 19, 1968, P. L. 90-351, Title I, § 100; 82 Stat. 197.

2. Declaration and Purpose, Law Enforcement Assistance, Act of August 6, 1973, P. L. 93-83, 2, 87 Stat. 197.

3. New York Times, February 11, 1975.

4. Crime Analysis Section, New York City Police Department, 1975.

5. "Crime in the Nation's Five Largest Cities," LEAA, National Criminal Justice Information and Statistics Service, April 1974.

6. Robert Fishman, "A Proposal for Individual and Comparative Evaluation of Diversion Projects for the Criminal Justice Coordinating Council," May 15, 1971 (proposal at the Mayor's CJCC, New York City).

3

METHOD

Following is a brief summary description of the collection and processing of the evaluation data from the projects and the police. Appendix A provides an extensively detailed description of these processes.

DATA COLLECTION

Because the unit of measurement was to be arrests, it was necessary to collect and prepare the data about project clients to allow accurate matching with official arrest records. This created many problems, since the projects not only differed from each other in programmatic format but also enjoyed considerable autonomy. Their record-keeping systems and their records were as individual as their programs. Records ranged from "homemade" forms in community-based projects to elaborate information systems in agencies.

A first evaluation step was to design and implement a Standard Intake Form for the projects that would, among other things, yield data necessary to retrieve arrest records. In addition, the evaluation had to create an entire system for making that form a practical instrument and for checking constantly to see that it remained so. Initially, there was a very high error rate on important items of the form, such as misspelled names and incorrect ages. In some projects, there was resistance to providing any data. The problems and resistance were encountered for such reasons as lack of competence in record keeping by community-based project staff and objections related to the principle of confidentiality.

To cope with these problems the evaluation launched an extensive training program for project staffs and became more closely involved in the projects' record-keeping operations.

To maximize the accuracy of the project data after they were received, two steps were taken. First, The Intake Forms were scrutinized for certain types of errors and, if necessary, sent back for correction. Forms that could not be corrected were not used.

Second, validation resulted from the awareness that seemingly correct Intake Forms during scrutiny might in fact contain false information, for example, misspelled names. The errors might result from misinterpretation by project staff of an Intake Form item, or they might simply be errors in reporting or transcribing information given by a client. The solution was to check each Intake Form intended for analysis against the actual records in those projects for the "index" items—name, sex, date of birth, address, date of project entry, and client admission status.

Other data-retrieval problems had to be solved in obtaining arrest records from the police. Juvenile and adult records were kept in different places and in different ways and required different methods of identification for retrieval. Matching accurately a project client and his police arrest history required the development of a complex set of procedures and tests to achieve the desired level of accuracy.

After resolving problems of implementation, the evaluation achieved one of its intended goals by establishing an on-going system of collecting standardized demographic data from all projects and measuring the criminological effects of larger projects.

THE PROJECTS

As Table 3.1 shows, 4 out of the 53 projects under the CJCC did not submit intake forms; the remaining 49 submitted a total of 27,733 intake forms.* Data from 31 of the 49 projects were not analyzed, either because there was not enough time to process their records, because they did not contain enough clients to permit analysis, or because their clients were female.†

To clarify more fully the reasons for the lack of time and clients, it should be noted that for a client to be included in the

---

*Numbers 7, 11, 17, and 43 (Table 3.1).
†Numbers 3, 6, 8, 9, 10, 12, 13, 14, 15, 18, 20, 24, 25, 26, 27, 28, 35, 36, 37, 38, 39, 40, 41, 42, 44, 46, 48, 49, 50, 51, and 53 (Table 3.1).

TABLE 3.1

Summary of Information Retrieval, Processing, and Reporting

Project Name	Acronym For Analysis	Contract Number	Monthly Case Activity Report	CLIENT INTAKE FORMS			
				Number Received	Number Punched	Validation At Project	Analyzed For Report
1. Addict Diversion Program	ASA	57798	+	1,772	979	+	333
2. Addicts Rehabilitation Center	ARC	56964	+	2,040	477	+	264
3. Altern School for Excp Children		62964	+	151	41	-	-
4. Altern to Detention - HRA	ATD-HRA	50411	-	938	401	+	117
5. Altern to Detention - Probation	ATD-PROB	50411	-	602	529	+	220
6. Bed-Stuy Ex-Offender		56965	+	210	79	-	-
7. Corrections Educ Career Dev Prog		69838	+	-	-	-	-
8. Co-Workers Cooperative Project		64558	+	178	47	-	-
9. East Harlem Halfway House		73300	+	79	-	-	-
10. Encounter		59315	-	116	-	-	-
11. Family Court Rapid Intervention		59895	+	-	-	-	-
12. Fortune Society Employment Unit		68313	+	372	-	-	-
13. Frontiers for Families		62012	+	458	249	+	-
14. Harlem Probation		62762	+	175	144	+	-
15. Holy Apostles Center		72177	+	103	-	-	-
16. Independence House	INDH	61685	+	569	321	+	56
17. Juvenile Employment Ref		74937	+	-	-	-	-
18. Legal Aid Soc - Juvenile Services		67752	+	1,409	622	+	-
19. Legal Propinquity	LPQ	60372	+	207	150	+	55
20. Mobilization for Youth - Juv Court Div		66559	+	178	51	-	-
21. Morrisania Youth Serv Center	MLA	55332	+	410	379	+	166
22. NAACP Project Rebound	NAACP	56445	+	795	541	+	190
23. Neighborhood Youth Diversion	NYD	57871	+	702	598	+	133
24. N Y Lawyers Com for Cvl Rts - Supv Rel		57980	-	84	-	-	-
25. The Osborne Residence		62418	+	100	29	-	-

No. Program	Code	ID					
26. Positive Altern - Univ of the St		63977	+	138	71	-	-
27. Pre-trial Services Agency		66635	+	236	-	+	-
28. Private Concerns, Inc	PUL	73298	+	76	-	-	-
29. Probation - Urban League		60785	+	372	336	+	92
30. Project BYCEP	BYCEP	50803	+	559	469	+	63
31. Project Manhood	MANHD	49764	+	1,787	1,135	+	185
32. Project Second Chance	SCH	59545	+	733	539	+	160
33. Project Share	SHARE	58945	+	346	160	+	31
34. Protestant Board of Guardians		57872	+	839	532	+	172
35. Puerto Rican Assoc for Com Action	PBG	70723	+	157	-	-	-
36. Puerto Rican Forum Offender Prog		72027	+	96	-	-	-
37. Queens Probation Reading Clinic		65715	+	374	207	+	-
38. QUERER		72179	+	324	-	+	-
39. Richmond Probation Reading Clinic		70724	+	183	-	-	-
40. SERA Manpower Unit		73092	+	215	-	+	-
41. Sloane House YMCA - Dept of Corr		68176	+	171	-	-	-
42. St. Peter's Youthful Offender Prog		74538	+	46	-	-	-
43. Theatre for the Forgotten		63710	+	-	-	-	-
44. United Neighborhood Houses		66466	+	268	124	-	-
45. Vera Supportive Work Program; Wildcat	VERA	62914	+	1,712*	815*	+	219*
46. Vocational Remedial Educ Trng Proj		70473	+	155	-	+	-
47. VOI - Bronx Com Counseling	BCC	56446	+	1,260	882	+	283
48. Wiltwyck Bklyn Com Care		55722	+	225	192	-	-
49. Wiltwyck School Group Homes		56870	+	19	10	-	-
50. Women's Diversion		58498	-	38	-	-	-
51. Women's Education		55161	+	180	165	-	-
52. Youth Counsel Bureau		57933	+	5,281	2,288	+	121
53. Youth Services Bureau - Bushwick	YCB	61463	+_	295	180	-	-
		TOTAL	48	27,733	13,742		2,860

*Includes a control group.

<u>Source:</u> Compiled by the evaluation project.

17

TABLE 3.2

Project Summaries

PROJECT-COMPONENT	LEAA FUNDS	DURATION	CLIENT TYPES	SERVICES PROVIDED	FUNDING
1. ADDICTS REHABILITATION CENTER (ARC) Resident and Non-Resident Day Care	$ 971,000	01.01.72 to 06.30.74	Narcotics Addicts Male and Female Ages 9+	Residency, drug-free treatment, counseling emergency referrals	CJCC ended Picked up by NIMH
2. ASA ADDICTS DIVERSION (ASA)	$ 2,032,000	01.22.71 to 11.30.74	Narcotics related court cases; Male and Female; 17+	Diversion, screening, & placement in treatment; follow up	CJCC ended Picked up by ASA
3. VERA SUPPORTIVE WORK (VERA) Wildcat Control Group	$ 2,000,000	07.01.72 to 06.30.75	Ex-addicts and ex-offenders; Male-Female; Ages 18+	Supervised work and training in Wildcat Corp; counseling	CJCC extended to 06.30.75
4. INDEPENDENCE HOUSE (INDH) Long-Term Service Short-Term Service	$ 561,000	07.01.72 to 06.30.74	Ex-offenders and YSA referrals; Male only; Ages 17-21	Residency, vocational and educational counseling	CJCC extended to 06.30.75
5. MORRISANIA YOUTH SERVICES CENTER (MLA) Legal Services	$ 760,000	09.07.71 to 03.26.74	Criminal Court & Fam Court cases; M-F; Ages 9-21	Diversion, Legal assistance, counseling and referral	CJCC ended Not picked up
6. PROBATION-URBAN LEAGUE (PUL)	$ 1,546,000	04.26.72 to 04.15.74	Probation cases; Male & Female; Ages 14-21	Diversion, Probation supervision; counseling and recreation	CJCC ended NOT picked up
7. PROJECT BYCEP (BYCEP)	$ 498,000	04.01.71 to 11.30.73	Ex-inmates Adol Remand Shelter; Males; Ages 16-21	Counseling, referral, and follow up	CJCC ended Not picked up
8. LEGAL PROPINQUITY (LPQ)	$ 127,000	05.01.72 to 04.30.74	Misdemeanor or low felony arrest; M-F; Ages 15-20	Legal assistance, counseling and referral	CJCC ended Not picked up

Program	Dates	Amount	Target Population	Services	Status
9. YOUTH COUNSEL BUREAU (YCB) Long-Term Parole	12.01.71 to 04.26.74	$ 298,000	First offenders & DA referred cases; M-F; Ages 16+	Diversion, supervision, counseling, follow up	CJCC ended City continues
10. VOI BRONX COMMUNITY COUNSELING (BCC) Day, Evening, Teenage	06.01.70 to 07.15.73	$ 873,000	Addicts and ex-offenders; Male-Female; Ages 13+	Diversion, Counseling, remedial ed, job training, addiction treatment	CJCC ended Picked up by NIMH
11. PROJECT SHARE (SHARE) Resident Non-Resident	03.01.72 to 06.30.75	$ 533,000	Ex-offenders; Males; Ages 18+	Counseling, job prep and referral, emergency residence	CJCC extended to 6.30.75
12. SECOND CHANCE (SCH)	02.01.72 to 10.31.74	$ 283,000	Ex-offenders; Males; Ages 21+	Job counseling and referral; follow up	CJCC ended Picked up by MCDA
13. MANHOOD (MANHD) Counseling Sessions only Job Referral	01.01.71 to 07.31.73	$ 617,000	Ex-offenders; Male-Female; Ages 16+	Job counseling and referral	CJCC Funded as Operation Upgrade
14. NAACP REBOUND (NAACP) Intensive Non-Intensive	09.15.71 to 07.31.74	$ 322,000	Ex-offenders; Male-Female; Ages 21+	Job and educational counseling, job referral	CJCC ended Picked up by MCDA
15. NEIGHBORHOOD YOUTH DIVERSION (NYD)	10.01.70 to 11.30.73	$ 1,016,000	Probation; Male-Female; Ages 7-15	Diversion, supervision, counseling, remediation, recreation	CJCC ended Picked up by HRA
16. ALTERNATIVES TO DETENTION – PROBATION (ATD-PROB) Sup. Det. Release & Day-Evng. Ctr.; Pre-Court Inten. Serv.	11.01.70 to 06.30.73	$ 462,000	Probation, parole case pending, DC, PINS; Male and Female; Ages 8-17	Diversion, counseling referral, supervision	CJCC ended Picked up by NYC
17. ALTERNATIVES TO DETENTION – HRA (ATD-HRA) Family Boarding Home Group Home	11.01.72 to 02.28.74	$ 852,000	DC & PINS, Family Court; Male and Female; Ages 10-16	Diversion, Family & group boarding homes, supervision, counseling	CJCC ended Picked up by HRA
18. PROTESTANT BOARD OF GUARDIANS (PBG)	11.15.71 to 06.30.75	$ 839,000	Probation, Family Court, Youth AID; Male and Female; Ages 7-17	Diversion, Short term crisis intervention, family aid, counseling, referral	CJCC extended to 6.30.75
	TOTAL	$14,590,000			

Source: Compiled by the evaluation project.

analysis there had to be a minimum of 12 months after project entry, during which criminal behavior would be measured. For any project, there had to be enough male clients of the required ages who met these criteria, at the time of selection, to satisfy statistical requirements for analysis (initially 100, finally 50). Furthermore, the 53 projects were funded and became fully operational at widely differing times during (and prior to) the evaluation. Thus, newer projects generally did not have enough clients who met evaluation criteria at the time of selection.

Because the evaluation had to meet a deadline for a final report, the clients who met the criteria had to be identified in time for use in that report. The interaction of these factors made it impossible to analyze 31 of the projects, as mentioned above. *

This left 18 projects, with a total of 20,924 intake forms. The 18 projects were not a "sample" selected from the 53 at one point in time, but constituted the universe of all projects that had enough clients to satisfy evaluation criteria at the time of selection.

The 18 projects were similar in that they all provided rehabilitative or diversion services primarily outside prison. However, they varied enormously in such important characteristics as sponsors (community-based groups, private foundations, or city agencies); staffing (by paraprofessionals and professionals); status (new projects versus existing ones); nature of service (diversion and nondiversion); and funding (a few hundred thousand dollars versus several million) (Table 3. 2). In addition to some combination of services toward remediation, jobs, counseling, or diversion, residence was provided by three, recreation by three, and legal assistance by two. The total LEAA funding for the 18 projects, which varied in duration, was $14,590,000.

It appeared, upon careful inspection of the projects and their records, that the 18 projects were basically representative of most nonprison approaches to rehabilitation of this type in New York City and elsewhere (see Appendix B for project descriptions).

THE CLIENTS

As with the projects, there was no "sampling" of the standard intake forms for clients. † Sampling implies the use of only a portion

---

*The evaluation was unsuccessful in receiving additional funds to extend its duration so that it could evaluate 8 of the 31 projects which had provided sufficient data too late for data processing to be completed for the final report (numbers 13, 14, 18, 27, 37, 38, 40, and 46 in Table 3. 1).

†Except for one, YCB, which submitted over 1,300 forms, from which a simple random sample of 150 was selected (no. 52, table 3. 1).

TABLE 3.3

Client Intake Forms Included (or Excluded) at Points During Data Processing for the 18 Projects

| | | PRIOR TO PUNCHING | | | | | | | AFTER PUNCHING | | | | | |
Project Col.#(1)	Received (2)	Non-admits (3)	Info Incomplete (4)	Processing Terminated (5)	Pending Admission (6)	Total Punched (7) =2-(3,4,5,6)	Admits After Cut-off Date or Females (8)	Submitted for Validation (9) =(7-8)	Deleted During Validation (10)	Arrest Records Not Retrieved (11)	Clients With Arrest Records (12) =9-(10+11)	Arrest History of Less Than 12 Months (13)	Components or Age Groups Not Analyzed (14)	Total Analyzed (15) =12-(13+14)
P#,Final Report	30	A26	A26	29	A26	30	29	A27-A28	A27-A28	A59	A59	A121	A125	30
1. ASA	1772	538	51	28	176	979	227	752	326	48	378	-	45	333
2. ABC	2040	-	-	956	507	477	110	367	30	73	264	-	-	264
3. ATD-HRA	938	502	7	28	-	401	240	151	8	22	131	12	2	117
4. ATD-PROB	602	-	24	45	4	529	217	312	25	46	241	11	10	220
5. INDH	569	-	56	192	-	321	241	30	1	19	60	4	-	56
6. LPQ	207	1	7	44	5	150	76	74	7	5	62	7	-	55
7. MLA	410	6	4	19	2	379	177	232	6	21	175	6	3	166
8. NAACP	795	216	36	-	2	541	207	334	52	46	236	46	-	190
9. NYD	702	-	15	89	-	598	384	214	18	27	169	22	14	133
10. PUL	372	1	16	19	-	336	212	124	18	4	102	10	-	92
11. BYCEP	559	1	40	32	17	469	291	178	95	1	82	19	-	63
12. MANHD	1787	1	30	620	1	1135	890	245	6	22	217	20	12	185
13. SCH	733	-	17	177	-	539	364	195	7	14	174	3	11	160
14. SHARE	346	32	6	111	37	160	52	68	15	3	50	-	19	31
15. PBG	839	1	1	304	-	532	250	232	25	53	204	32	-	172
16. VERA	1712	1	144	667	81	815	323	492	8	52	432	178	35	219
17. BCC	1260	129	74	165	10	882	430	452	94	69	289	-	6	283
18. YCB	5281	19	22	2718	234	2288	1888	150*	11	11	128	-	7	121
TOTAL	20924	1452	550	6214	1076	11531	6599	4582	752	536	3394	370	164	2860

*A simple random sample of 150 Intake Forms was drawn from the 400 forms that were submitted for validation (2288-1888).

Source: Compiled by the evaluation project.

TABLE 3.4

Age of Clients at Project Entry

Legal Status	Age	Clients	Percent	Cumulative Percent	Age Group In Report
Juvenile	7-10	41	1.4	1.4	1
	11-12	87	3.0	4.5	
	13-15	559	19.5	24.0	2
Youthful Offender	16-18	606	21.2	45.2	3
Adult	19-20	234	8.2	53.4	4
	21-24	567	19.8	73.2	5
	25-29	397	13.9	87.1	
	30-34	184	6.4	93.5	6
	35-39	130	4.5	98.1	
	40-44	33	1.2	99.2	7
	45-49	10	0.3	99.6	
	50-54	10	0.3	99.9	
	55-71	2	0.0	100.0	
	TOTAL	2860	100.0	100.0	

Source: Compiled by the evaluation project.

of all forms which meet criteria. The universe of all forms was used for all clients from the 18 projects who met the evaluation project's strict criteria for age, sex, 12-month duration after project entry by the analytic cut-off dates, and availability of all data needed for police record retrieval at the times clients were selected for evaluation. Thus, from the total of 20,924 intake forms from the 18 projects, only 2,860 arrest records were used for analysis. The unused balance of the 20,924 forms are analogous to unreturned, incomplete, or incorrect forms in an election survey. See Table 3.3 for details of exclusions of forms during data processing.

Age. The 2,860 clients spanned a wide age range, from 7 to 71, but most were young. Three-fourths were under 25, including one-fourth who were legally juveniles (7 to 15) and one-fifth in the 16 to 18 age range to which youthful offender treatment may be given. Only 2 percent were 40 or older. See Table 3.4.

Race and Ethnicity. The overwhelming majority of the clients, 93 percent, were black (68 percent) or Spanish surnamed. Nearly all the others were white (see Table 3.5). The preponderance of blacks and Hispanics occurred within each of the seven age groups. It also occurs among the criminal justice system population of New York City, but to a lesser degree than among the study clients.

Education. An individual 18 or older is expected to have completed high school. Among study clients of this age range, only one-third had completed 12 or more years of school or received high school equivalency diplomas (Table 3.6). Most clients 18 or older had completed 9 to 11 years of school, a few had completed less, and only 4 percent had gone beyond high school.

Prior Criminal History. More than 90 percent of the clients had been arrested at least once before entering the projects, and most

TABLE 3.5

Race or Ethnicity of Clients

Race-Ethnicity	Number of Clients	Per Cent	Cumulative Per Cent
Black	1860	67.6	67.6
Spanish surnamed	701	25.5	93.1
White	184	6.6	99.7
Other (Oriental, American Indian, Other)	7	0.3	100.0
TOTAL	2752	100.0	100.0

Note: There were 108 clients for whom information on race-ethnicity was not available.

Source: Compiled by the evaluation project.

TABLE 3. 6

Highest Year of School Completed
by Clients 18 or Older

Highest Year of School Completed	Number of Clients	Per Cent	Cumulative Per Cent
1-4	7	0.4	0.4
5-8	132	8.3	8.7
9-11	944	59.3	68.0
12*	451	28.3	96.3
13-17	59	3.7	100.0
TOTAL	1593	100.0	100.0

*Includes high school graduates and clients with high school equivalency diplomas.

Source: Compiled by the evaluation project.

of the remainder had other types of police records before project entry (usually YD-1 contacts). Table 4. 2 shows that the average number of arrests before project entry ranged from 0. 8 to 4. 6 for those 20 and younger, while clients 21 and older ranged from 3. 3 to 18. 7 arrests. * For both juveniles and adults these arrests included many serious charges.

Representativeness. These clients clearly appear to be representative of the young, male, undereducated, poor blacks and Hispanics who account for the major share of violent crime arrests in New York City. Nevertheless, it could be contended that the 2, 860 clients in the evaluation may not be a representative sample of the total

---

For clients 21 and over, there was no relationship between severity of criminal history and recidivism. These arrest rates are descriptive only for those 21 and over.

population of the criminal justice system, or of the 53 projects. Such a sampling was never intended or possible.

The study was specifically designed to assess the criminological effects of the projects on certain important subgroups of clients, according to age and severity of arrest history, for example, young black and Hispanic males of various ages with severe prior arrest histories (Table 4.1) and not on others such as females. Given the selection method of the evaluation (all who met the criteria were included), each of the 16 types of clients shown in Tables 4.1 and 4.6 is—in the author's view—representative of clients of the same age, criminal history, race or ethnicity, and education in the 18 projects evaluated and of clients in the 35 projects not evaluated, as well as in the criminal justice system as a whole. (And as stated in Chapter 1 this is particularly the case for the most important types of criminals in the CJS insofar as violent crime arrests are concerned.)

In other words, in comparing the effectiveness of projects, it appears far more useful and accurate to ask how they affect specific types of clients (by assessing each type separately) than to get one recidivism rate for a "representative sample" of all clients, which for such a sample may be composed of different proportions of males and females of differing ages and criminal histories. This sample is a poor measure because it understates the actual higher recidivism rate of the more difficult clients, for example, young males with long records, by masking them with the far lower rates of young male or female first offenders. This type of error can be gross and is not controlled by comparisons with control groups. For example, in the measurement of projects containing small numbers of different types of clients it is sometimes impossible to determine whether differences between projects and control groups are due to treatment or to the effects of the different types of clients.

Possible unrepresentativeness can be ascribed to any sample. But for the assertion to be meaningful, the following three questions must be carefully answered: How is the method of selection biased? What kind of unrepresentativeness does this cause? How could the possible unrepresentativeness have resulted in the findings and conclusions presented?

A related point is that if the clients in each of the subgroups (see Table 4.1) in the study are unrepresentative, it is unlikely that they are more recidivistic than a comparable population in the criminal justice system, since most projects, the courts, and the probation department tried to keep out those with more severe criminal histories. If they are less recidivistic than comparable types in the criminal justice system, then the findings, conclusions,

and recommendations of the evaluation are even more
significant.

In any case, the study was able to evaluate separately the
recidivism rates of those with severe histories, first offenders,
and each of the other types of clients among the 16 shown in Table
4.1,* as classified by age and severity of arrest history. It is
more appropriate, therefore, that the three questions about the
representativeness of the 2,860 be addressed to each of these
types.

SEVERITY OF ARREST HISTORY

Since the prior arrest histories of these clients were to be
controlled in assessing the comparative effectiveness of the 18
projects, it was important to obtain a method of measuring their
severity. Such a measure was thought to require a resolution of the
problem of combining the frequency of an individual's arrests with
the nature of the arrest charges. †

The Sellin-Wolfgang Index was the best standardized measure
available for the task. [1] The scale could not be used in its original
form because the information required was not available within the
fiscal and time restraints of the study, but an alternative approach
was suggested by Wolfgang and Figlio. †† This consisted of using
mean seriousness scores (MSS) for each of the 26 Uniform Crime
Reporting (UCR) categories based on data collected in the Philadelphia
"cohort" study. [2] It was necessary, therefore, to test the predictive
and concurrent validity of the MSS for a New York City population.

Validation of a Measure of Severity

Validation of the MSS was guided by its intended use, which was
to permit comparison only of client groups with similar severity of
prior criminal history. The predictive validity would be shown by
how well the MSS predicted arrest recidivism after project entry: a
higher severity before entry should have indicated a greater likelihood
of recidivism, and more severe recidivism, after project entry. The
concurrent validity would be demonstrated by correlation between the
MSS and other related measures of severity. Two possible alternative

---

*Or 13 types of clients if, as discussed on p. 31, the levels of
severity of prior arrest history are collapsed for the age groups
21-29 and 30-39.

†See Appendix A, pp. 139-68, for details.

††At a meeting with staff of the evaluation project in 1972.

measures were number of arrests before project entry and type of
arrest charges, such as violent crimes. (The MSS synthesized both
and contained more information than either.)

The relationship between prior criminal history and
recidivism (the dependent variable) was assessed by a number of
analyses using stepwise linear regression. For most of these analyses,
the independent variables were combinations of total MSS, number
of arrests before project entry, the year of age at project entry,
and the interactions.

In almost all cases, the F-value was highly significant for the
independent variables and their interactions. However, this may have
stemmed from the large numbers of degrees of freedom for the
residual sum of squares, which ranged from approximately 100 to
600 for age subgroups used. Surprisingly, the total variance
accounted for by the independent variables was generally less than
15 percent for each analysis—an outcome without a ready explanation.

In the testing of predictive validity, the inconclusive results
of the regression analyses and analysis of variance suggested that
any relationship between severity of prior criminal history (both
MSS and number of arrests prior to project entry) and recidivism
was not linear.

However, it was decided that for evaluation purposes both the
MSS and the number of arrests before project entry were sufficiently
valid predictively for use as measures of severity of criminal history
before project entry. The decision was reached because the results
of t-tests, Kolmogorov-Smirnov tests, and chi-square trend analyses
supported a significant relationship between both measures of severity
and recidivism for clients 13 to 15, 16 to 18, and 19 to 20, and
marginally for clients 21 and older (although the relationship might
not be linear). Since the MSS predicted recidivism as well, and in
a similar manner as the average number of arrests, the concurrent
validity requirement appeared to be satisfied.

However, although the average number of prior arrests and the
MSS appeared to be equally effective as measures of severity in
predicting recidivism, the former was easier to use, far less
expensive, and more easily understood by readers. Therefore, it
was selected as the evaluation's measure of severity. *

----

*Note that the MSS is not a Sellin-Wolfgang score. It is a
mean derived from Sellin-Wolfgang scores solely for use by this
evaluation. The validity of the Sellin-Wolfgang score was not
tested directly by this study.

Levels of Severity

The method of determining levels of severity used the Duncan Multiple Range Test, as adjusted by the method of Dalenius. [3]

One purpose of using the Duncan test and the Dalenius method of forming homogeneous groups was to identify mutually exclusive and exhaustive levels of severity of criminal history before project entry for each age group to be used in the analysis.

This was a two-step process. First, the Duncan test was used to see if, within each age group, the projects could be arranged in clusters in such a way that, in a given cluster, the project with the lowest mean number of client arrests (MNA) before project entry would not be significantly different from the project with the highest MNA. Further, the Duncan test determined for each age group the clusters of projects that were significantly different from each other— that is, there was at least one project with an MNA in one cluster significantly different from the MNA of at least one project in a different cluster in that age group.

Given the criteria above, when the Duncan test was applied to the projects within an age group, the clusters that resulted might not have been mutually exclusive. In other words, there might have been some projects in more than one cluster. This overlap among the clusters could have created confusion in interpreting the outcomes.

Therefore, as a second step, the method of Dalenius was applied to the clusters of projects in each age group in order to make the clusters mutually exclusive. The clusters that resulted were then defined as levels of severity for that age group (see Appendix A, p. 160).

Categorization of the clients by the levels of severity of their prior arrest history has two functions. For those 20 and younger, the levels are related to recidivism and are also a descriptive characteristic. For clients 21 and older, the levels of severity are not related to recidivism but are descriptive characteristics only. This should be noted in interpreting Tables 4.1, 4.2, and 4.6.

ANALYSIS

Several evaluation questions stemmed from the CJCC evaluation needs described in Chapter 1, and a variety of analytic methods was used to answer them.

Magnitude and Seriousness of Criminal Recidivism

The arrest recidivism rate was the ratio of clients arrested one or more times during the 12 months after project entry to all clients, arrested or not.

The magnitude was measured by the recidivism rates and a ratio of the total number of arrests of recidivists to the total number of clients (recidivists and nonrecidivists).

Seriousness was measured by the types of crimes charged as classified by the Uniform Crime Reporting (UCR) system into seven serious (index) crimes composed of the violent crimes against persons (homicide, rape, robbery, and assault) and the crimes against property (burglary, larceny, and auto theft) (Table 4. 3).

The relationship of these measures to the client characteristics of age and severity of prior criminal history was then assessed. It should be noted that no significant relationship was found between race or ethnicity and arrest recidivism, or violent crime arrest rates, for six of the seven age groups when tested by the x^2 (chi square). The relationship was significant only for the 16- to 18-year-olds on both measures, probably because the whites had less severe criminal histories than the blacks and Hispanics of those ages.

The relationship between heroin addiction and recidivism could not be evaluated, mainly because the type of drug used could not be determined from charges on arrest records. But some evidence suggested that there were fairly high proportions of users or ex-users of heroin in all the projects with clients 21 and older.

Project Impacts on Crime

Project impacts were addressed in three ways.

First, the "classic" control group frequently is proposed because this is the ideal method of assessing whether treatment works. This model requires that an untreated group, with clients of equivalent characteristics, be compared with the treated or experimental group. But the probability of the materialization of such a control group in an action program is virtually nil. Lipton, Martinson, and Wilks comment: "Only rarely, outside of a laboratory, can the requirements of this design be fulfilled. "[4] For Vorenberg and Ohlin, the problem of establishing adequate control groups (much less classical control groups) "has been the greatest obstacle to successful evaluation research in social action programs. "[5]

The format of an analysis based on classic control groups was rejected as impractical in action programs. [6] Truly random assignment is rarely possible, and ethical questions arise. Matching is equally difficult. Finally, the assumption that in a city like New York the controls will actually remain "untreated" is highly questionable. One possibility that the evaluation hoped to explore was a post-hoc control group, selected and matched after one project group of young clients had been identified and selected. This effort did not work because of the difficulty of obtaining the data necessary to select the control group.

But a valid control or comparison group was obtained by one of the projects, Vera Wildcat, and was used by the evaluation for clients 21 and older.[7] The 105 male Vera control clients were compared with the male clients of eight other projects.* The recidivism rates of 21- to 29-year-old clients were compared by the Duncan Multiple Range Test, and those of the 30- to 39-year-olds by the X^2 test.

Next, the projects were assessed to see if they decreased the criminal behavior of clients. This was done by comparing the arrest rates of the second year before project entry with the rates during the year after. The second year before entry was used because most of the projects, particularly diversion projects, required arrest as a condition of project entry. But during the 12 months after project entry, clients had the opportunity to be arrested or not. Therefore, comparing that 12 months to the first year prior to project entry would be invalid since the arrest requirement in that first year would artificially inflate the arrest rate. Comparisons were made by applying the X^2 test to the arrest rates by age groups.

Finally, projects were compared in their criminological effects on similar types of clients, for example, male 13- to 15-year-olds with severe arrest histories, to see which projects lowered recidivism rates most. This effort sought to determine whether project characteristics—differences among projects—affected the recidivism rates of similar clients.

The goals and priorities of this evaluation did not make it possible to measure directly project characteristics or to link, for individual projects, differences in arrest-recidivism rates and such project characteristics as services delivered, types of staff, and staff-client ratios (see Appendix B). Moreover, the statistical methods used in assessing the effect of project characteristics on recidivism could determine only whether or not a significant difference existed among the projects. But if there was such a difference, the method could not be used to specify which project characteristics were related to different effects of the projects on recidivism.

The application of the statistical methods to assess the relationship between differences among projects and recidivism occurred in three stages.

---

*This is not a true control group but a comparison group. The control group was "unserviced" in the sense that it was not provided with subsidized employment or other supportive services by the project; the members of the control group had to find their own jobs or services. At least some, therefore, may have received services.

First, the 18 projects were classified by clients' age and by the seriousness of their clients' arrest history before project entry. (The classification by levels of seriousness was by the method described on p. 28.)

The tests of the predictive validity of the severity measures showed a relationship between the severity of prior arrest history and arrest recidivism for clients 20 and younger and no relationship for those 21 and older. Therefore, clients 20 and younger were classified into ten groups: ages 7 to 12 at one level of severity; ages 13 to 15 at three levels of severity; ages 16 to 18 at four levels of severity; and ages 19 to 20 at two levels of severity (see Table 4. 6). The three age groups 21 to 29, 30 to 39, and 40 to 71 were not classified by levels of severity. * The overall classification was of 13 groups of clients classified by age and severity. Each of the 13 groups contained clients classified by the 18 projects and their service components. There was a total of 46 such subgroups.

The second step was to apply the Duncan test to determine whether there were significant differences between arrest recidivism rates of projects within each of the 13 levels of severity and/or age.

The final step was to estimate the overall probability of the 13 outcomes observed. This was estimated with a statistic similar to the binomial expansion. This statistic was applied to each level of severity and/or age in order to compute the probability of each of the 13 outcomes observed. This was followed by computation of the overall probability of the occurrence of no more than the observed number of differences for the 13 outcomes (in case of no differences, at least one such difference was assumed).

The overall probability was computed under the following assumptions: (1) the test of the null hypothesis implied determining the probability of no more than the observed number of differences between recidivism rates as the ones that occurred; (2) within each group, the probability of difference between any two arrest recidivism

---

*Except for the 10 groups of clients 20 and younger, Table 4. 6 does not represent the 13 groups of clients (by age or severity) discussed here. Table 4. 6 represents 16 groups of clients (by age and severity) that result from the assumption that there is a relationship between severity and recidivism at all ages, including 21 and older. The analysis of the 16 groups (and the construction of Table 4. 6) was done before the analysis of the 13 groups which was the primary study of whether differences between projects affect recidivism. Unfortunately, a table representing the analysis of the 13 groups was not prepared.

rates was . 05 (since . 05 was the level of confidence used in the
second step); (3) each of the groups formed by age and/or level of
severity was considered independent.

The relationship between project characteristics and recidivism
was also tested by the same statistical method for an alternative
assumption about the relationship between the severity of arrest
history and recidivism. The assumption was that there was a
relationship between severity and recidivism for all clients, including
those 21 and older. As shown by Table 4. 6, this resulted in the
classification of the 18 projects by 16 groups composed of ages
7 to 12, 13 to 15, 16 to 18, and 19 to 20 at 1, 3, 4, and 2 levels of
severity, respectively; and ages 21 to 29, 30 to 39, and 40 to 71 were
classified at 3, 2, and 1 levels of severity, respectively.

The statistical method described above was also applied to
test the relationship between project characteristics and recidivism
for only those clients 21 and older by the six levels of age and
severity and for only those clients 20 and younger by the ten levels
of age and severity (Table 4. 6).

Violent Crimes Before and After Project Entry

The t-test was used to determine the difference between the
rates of violent crime arrests after project entry of clients who had
no history of violent crime arrests before project entry, and the rate
of violent crime recidivism of clients who had a history of violent
crime arrests before project entry.

CAVEATS

There follow general considerations to aid in interpreting the
results of the evaluation. For a detailed discussion, see Appendix
A, pp. 169-72.

For these analytic methods, the 2, 860 clients were divided
into seven age groupings—7 to 12, 13 to 15, 16 to 18, 19 to 20,
21 to 29, 30 to 39, and 40 to 71. (For details about the combining
of project service components described below see Table 3. 7.) For
each age group, the outcomes of clients in different service
components in a project would be combined for use in an analysis
if there was reason to believe that clients in one component had also
received services from another component. This would result in
double counting by overlap. The remaining service components
were combined if their respective clients' average numbers of
arrests before project entry were not significantly different, and
were analyzed separately if they were different. For combined and
separated components, if a group of project clients, classified by

TABLE 3.7

Project and Component Names and Acronyms

Project and Component Names	Acronym	Component Status
1. ASA – ADDICTS DIVERSION PROGRAM	ASA	–
None	–	–
Service Unverified	–	X
2. ADDICTS REHABILITATION CENTER	ARC	
Resident and Non-Resident Day Care	r/nrd	O
3. ALTERNATIVES TO DETENTION – HRA	ATD-HRA	–
Family Boarding Home	fbh	N
Group Home	gh	N
4. ALTERNATIVES TO DETENTION – PROBATION	ATD-PROB	–
Supervised Detention Release and Day-Evening Center	sdr/dc	O
Pre-Court Intensive Services	pcis	N
5. INDEPENDENCE HOUSE	INDH	–
Long-Term Service and Short-Term Service	lts/sts	O
6. LEGAL PROPINQUITY	LPQ	–
None	–	–
7. MORRISANIA YOUTH SERVICES CENTER	MLA	–
Legal Services	ls	Y
8. NAACP PROJECT REBOUND	NAACP	–
Intensive	i	N
Non-Intensive	n	N
Intensive and Non-Intensive	i/n	S
9. NEIGHBORHOOD YOUTH DIVERSION	NYD	–
None	–	–
Interviewed Only	–	X
10. PROBATION – URBAN LEAGUE	PUL	–
None	–	–
11. PROJECT BYCEP	BYCEP	–
None	–	–
12. PROJECT MANHOOD	MANHD	–
Counseling Sessions Only and Job Referral	co/jr	S
13. PROJECT SECOND CHANCE	SCH	–
None	–	–
14. PROJECT SHARE	SHARE	–
Resident and Non-Resident	r/nr	O
15. PROTESTANT BOARD OF GUARDIANS	PBG	–
None	–	–
16. VERA SUPPORTIVE WORK PROGRAM	VERA	–
Wildcat	w	Y
Control Group	c	–
17. VOI – BRONX COMMUNITY COUNSELING	BCC	–
Daytime, Evening and Teenage	d/e/t	O
18. YOUTH COUNSEL BUREAU	YCB	–
Long-Term Parole	ltp	Y

Note: O = Components combined because some clients were in more than one component; X = Dropped by error; Y = The only project component measured in multi-component project; N = Significant difference between components in average number of arrests of clients prior to project entry; S = Components combined because of no significant difference between the average number of arrests of their respective clients prior to project entry.

Source: Compiled by the project evaluation.

age and/or severity of arrest history, contained fewer than 20 members, it was dropped from the analysis. For the juveniles, aged 7 to 15, YD-1 cards were not included as arrests in the analysis (see Chapter 2, note 8). The arrest recidivism was measured over the period of 12 months after project entry although a client may not have been in the project during that entire period. Throughout this book the term "significant," unless otherwise qualified, means that P is equal to or is less than . 05.

Arrest recidivism rates can be expected to increase over time, along with total number of arrests. After 18 months or 24 months they would be higher than after the 12 months measured by the evaluation.

Strictly speaking, recidivism means recurrence and, in criminological terms, recurrence of criminal behavior or a CJS reaction to it, such as rearrest. There were a very few clients arrested after project entry for whom no record of arrest before project entry was found. Analysis indicated that even some of these had probably been previously arrested, so the likelihood of actual first arrests occurring after project entry was very small.

Some of the recidivism rates are reported for subgroups of clients within projects. These subgroups are defined by sex, age, and severity of previous criminal history. A reported rate applies to other clients similar in age and severity, whether included in the analysis or not. The rates cannot be applied to any subgroup of clients from a project that is not the same in age, severity, and sex as the group for which the rate was determined.

For instance, the rate for males 16 to 18 years old at a severity level in a project may be generalized to other males of that age at the same severity level in the same or another project or the CJS. It does not apply to females, to males at some other level of severity but of the same age, or to males at the same level of severity but a different age.

When data are reported in units of arrests, charges, complaints, victims, or clients, the number of units almost always exceeds the number of individuals. For example, a total number of arrests reported annually includes as separate cases individuals who are arrested more than once.

In this evaluation, it was estimated that of the 2, 860 individuals included in the analysis, 1. 3 percent were enrolled in more than one project. The effect (if any) of the double count on the analytic questions was considered negligible.

NOTES

1. Thorsten Sellin and Marvin E. Wolfgang, The Measurement of Delinquency (New York: John Wiley and Sons, 1964).

2. Marvin E. Wolfgang, Robert M. Figlio, and Thorsten Sellin, Delinquency in a Birth-Cohort (Chicago: University of Chicago Press, 1972).

3. T. Dalenius and J. L. Hodges, Jr. , "Minimum Variance Stratification," Journal of the American Statistical Association 54 (1959): 85-101; W. G. Cochran, "Comparison of Methods for Determining Stratum Boundaries," Bulletin of the International Statistics Institute 38, no. 2 (1961): 345-58; and W. G. Cochran, Sampling Techniques, 2d ed. (New York: John Wiley and Sons, 1963), pp. 128-33.

4. Douglas Lipton, Robert Martinson, and Judith Wilks, "Treatment Evaluation Survey," 1971, p. 54.

5. John Vorenberg and Lloyd Ohlin, "Draft of a Proposal Submitted to the National Institute of the LEAA for the Evaluation of the Addiction Research Treatment Center (ARTC) in Brooklyn, N. Y. ," 1971.

6. For a detailed discussion of control groups see Robert Fishman, "A Proposal for Individual and Comparative Evaluation of Diversion Projects for the Criminal Justice Coordinating Council," May 15, 1971 (proposal at the Mayor's CJCC, New York City).

7. Lucy N. Friedman and Hans Zeisel, "First Annual Research Report on Supported Employment," Vera Institute of Justice, 1973.

4

MAGNITUDE AND SEVERITY
OF CRIMINAL RECIDIVISM

The magnitude of criminal recidivism was high. The majority of the crimes represented by the arrests were serious. More clients aged 20 or younger recidivated, with a greater number of arrests, and with crimes that were more serious, than did clients who were 21 or older. This was particularly true for juveniles in the 13 to 15 age group who were in five diversion projects. That group had the highest and most serious criminal recidivism of any of the age groups measured.

Magnitude

The magnitude of criminal recidivism was measured in two ways: by the proportion of clients arrested one or more times during the 12 months after project entry (the arrest recidivism rate), and by the number of times those recidivists were arrested. These measures were applied to 2,860 clients, 53 percent of whom were 20 or younger.

The recidivism rates (across projects and levels of severity) ranged from 51 percent for the 13 to 15 age group, to 24 percent for the 40 to 71 age group (Table 4.1).

Among clients 20 or younger, close to half—47 percent—were arrested one or more times after project entry. Among clients 21 or older, 35 percent, or about one-third, were rearrested.

Those with higher levels of severity of criminal history prior to project entry, in the age groups 13 to 15 and 16 to 18, had recidivism rates as high as 60 percent.

Among projects, the highest recidivism rate—72 percent—was for clients from Independence House in the 19 to 20 age group at the highest level of severity. The lowest recidivism rate—19 percent—was for the 7 to 12 age group in the Protestant Board of Guardians project (Table 4. 2).

Since the recidivism rate understates the amount of criminal behavior, the number of arrests was converted into a ratio of the total number of arrests to the total number of clients (Table 4.1, col. 8). For the 13 to 15 age group at the second level of severity, for example, 55 of the 100 clients had one or more arrests after project entry (see table 4.1, column 4). This yielded a 55 percent recidivism rate. The total number of arrests for these 55 recidivists, however, was 107, or more arrests than there were clients in the project. The ratio was 1.1. If the 55 recidivists had each been arrested only once, the ratio would have been 0.5. For the 1,527 clients 20 and younger, the ratio of arrests to clients was 0.9, or almost as many arrests as clients (Table 4.1, col. 8).

The ratio of arrests to clients appeared to be related to the level of severity of prior arrest history for those 20 and younger. All of the higher levels of severity had ratios over 1.0. For those 21 and over there appeared to be no relationship between level of severity and ratio.

Severity

The seriousness of recidivism after project entry was measured by the types of serious or index crime classified as violent crimes—homicide, forcible rape, robbery, and aggravated assault—and crimes against property—burglary, larceny, and auto theft (see Table 4. 3). *

Sixty-seven percent of the total number of arrests of the recidivists were for index (serious) crimes. For index crimes, arrests ranged from 82 percent for 7- to 12-year-olds to 56 percent for those 30 to 39. For violent crimes, arrests ranged from about one-third for 7- to 15-year-olds to 19 percent for those 30 to 39.

---

*It should be noted that the term "violent crime recidivism" should not be used, since some clients arrested for violent crimes after project entry had no arrests for any prior to project entry. Robberies and to a lesser extent aggravated assaults include most "muggings." Aggravated assault is defined as an attack by one person upon another with the intent of inflicting severe bodily injury, usually accompanied by the use of a weapon or other means to produce death or serious bodily harm.

TABLE 4.1

Measures of Criminal Recidivism by Age and Severity of Prior Arrest History

Age (1)	Severity Level (2)	Total No. of Clients (3)	No. of Clients One or More Arrests (4)	% Client Arrest Recidivism (4)÷(3) (5)	No. of Arrests (6)	Ratio of Arrests to Recidivists (6)÷(4) (7)	Arrests to Clients Ratio (6)÷(3) (8)	No. of Clients One or More Arrests for Violent Crime (9)	% Client Arrest for Violent Crime (9)÷(3) (10)	No. of Arrests for Violent Crime (11)	Violent Crime Arrests As % of Total Arrests (11)÷(6) (12)	Ratio of Violent Crime Arrests to Clients Arrested for Violent Crimes (11)÷(9) (13)	Ratio of Violent Crime Arrests to All Clients (11)÷(3) (14)
7-12	1	128	39	30	74	1.9	0.6	20	16	26	35	1.3	0.2
13-15	1	187	69	37	116	1.7	0.6	33	18	39	34	1.2	0.2
	2	100	55	55	107	1.9	1.1	26	26	36	34	1.4	0.4
	3	272	162	60	329	2.0	1.2	82	30	109	33	1.3	0.4
16-18	1	121	29	24	45	1.6	0.4	11	9	12	27	1.1	0.1
	2	182	73	40	142	1.9	0.8	33	18	43	30	1.3	0.2
	3	93	56	60	110	2.0	1.2	27	29	32	29	1.2	0.3
	4	210	118	56	223	1.9	1.1	46	22	61	27	1.3	0.3
19-20	1	104	47	45	61	1.3	0.6	14	13	18	30	1.3	0.2
	2	130	70	54	129	1.8	1.0	33	25	46	36	1.4	0.4
21-29	1	303	105	35	172	1.6	0.6	35	12	47	27	1.3	0.2
	2	309	118	38	191	1.6	0.6	44	14	55	29	1.2	0.2
	3	352	136	39	203	1.5	0.6	39	11	47	23	1.2	0.1

30–39	1	137	42	31	71	1.7	0.5	10	7	15	21	1.5	0.1
	2	177	50	28	76	1.5	0.4	12	7	13	17	1.1	0.1
40–71	1	55	13	24	23	1.8	0.4	5	9	6	26	1.2	0.1
	TOTAL	2,860	1,182	41	2,072	1.8	0.7	470	16	605	29	1.3	0.2
7–12		128	39	30	74	1.9	0.6	20	16	26	35	1.3	0.2
13–15		559	286	51	552	1.9	1.0	141	25	184	33	1.3	0.3
16–18		606	276	46	520	1.9	0.9	117	19	148	28	1.3	0.2
19–20		234	117	50	190	1.6	0.8	47	20	64	34	1.4	0.3
21–29		964	359	37	566	1.6	0.6	118	12	149	26	1.3	0.2
30–39		314	92	29	147	1.6	0.5	22	7	28	19	1.3	0.1
40–71		55	13	24	23	1.8	0.4	5	9	6	26	1.2	0.1
	TOTAL	2,860	1,182	41	2,072	1.8	0.7	470	16	605	29	1.3	0.2
7–20		1,527	718	47	1,336	1.9	0.9	325	21	422	32	1.3	0.3
21–71		1,333	464	35	736	1.6	0.6	145	11	183	25	1.3	0.1
	TOTAL	2,860	1,182	41	2,072	1.8	0.7	470	16	605	29	1.3	0.2

Note: The 16 types of clients classified by age and severity in column 2 reduce to 13 types when the severity levels for ages 21 to 29 and 30 to 39 are collapsed. See p. 31.
Source: Compiled by the project evaluation.

TABLE 4.2

Measures of Criminal Recidivism by Projects

			BEFORE PROJECT ENTRY			DURING TWELVE MONTHS AFTER PROJECT ENTRY							
			Severity Level			All Crime				Violent Crime			
PROJECT AND COMPONENT	REPORT ACROYNM	AGE	No of Levels for Age	Level of Group	Average No of Arrests	Total No of Clients	No of Clients One or More Arrests	% Clients Recidv (8)÷(7)	No of Arrests	No of Clients One or More Arrests for Violent Crime	% Clients Arrest for Violent Crime (11)÷(7)	No of Arrests for Violent Crime	Violent Crime Arrests as % of Total Arrests (13)÷(10)
(1)	(2)	(3)	(4)	(5)	(6)	(7)	(8)	(9)	(10)	(11)	(12)	(13)	(14)
1. PROT BRD OF GRDNS None	PBG	7-12	1	1	0.8	43	8	19%	13	5	12%	7	a%
		13-15	3	1	1.0	129	52	40	93	25	19	30	32
2. ALT TO DET - PROB	ATD-PROB												
Pre-Court Int Serv		7-12	1	1	1.0	25	10	40	17	4	16	5	a
Pre-Court Int Serv		13-15	3	2	1.4	55	34	62	60	15	27	19	32
Sup Rel&Day Evg Ctr		13-15	3	3	2.4	140	82	59	183	46	33	66	36
3. ALT TO DET - HRA	ATD-HRA												
Family Brdg Home		7-12	1	1	1.2	28	8	29	15	5	18	6	a
Family Brdg Home		13-15	3	1	1.2	58	17	29	23	8	14	9	39
Group Home		13-15	3	3	2.9	31	17	55	30	8	26	9	30
4. NGHBRHD YTH DIVERSN None	NYD	7-12	1	1	1.1	32	13	41	29	6	19	8	28
		13-15	3	3	1.8	101	63	62	116	28	28	34	29
5. MORISAN YTH SV CTR Legal Services *	MLA	13-15	3	2	1.5	45	21	47	47	11	24	17	36
		16-18	4	2	2.1	95	39	41	69	18	19	25	36
		19-20	2	1	2.7	26	12	46	18	5	19	7	a
6. YOUTH COUNSEL BUREAU Long-Term Parole	YCB	16-18	4	1	1.6	121	29	24	45	11	9	12	27
7. PROB-URBAN LEAGUE None	PUL	16-18	4	3	3.1	62	37	60	81	21	34	26	32
		19-20	2	1	2.8	30	14	47	20	4	13	5	25
8. PROJECT BYCEP None	BYCEP	16-18	4	4	3.6	63	37	59	72	17	27	22	31

Program	Code	Age											
9. LEGAL PROPINQUITY	LPQ												
None		16-18	2	4	2.1	55	23	42	47	10	18	12	26
10. INDEPENDENCE HOUSE	INDH												
Long-Term Service * &		16-18	3	4	2.9	31	19	61	29	6	19	6	21
Short-Term Service *		19-20	2	2	3.8	25	18	72	37	9	36	11	30
11. VOI-BRONX COM CNSEL	BCC												
Daytime, Evening &		16-18	4	4	3.4	100	56	56	98	20	20	25	26
Teenage *		19-20	1	2	2.7	48	21	44	23	5	10	6	26
		21-29	1	3	3.3	115	38	33	55	13	11	14	25
		30-39	1	2	6.5	20	2	10	6	0	0	0	0
12. ADDICTS REHAB CTR	ARC												
Resident & Non-Resident		16-18	2	4	2.8	32	11	34	26	5	16	6	23
Day Care *		19-20	2	2	3.0	52	26	50	53	13	25	24	45
		21-29	2	3	5.2	131	58	44	109	22	17	27	25
		30-39	1	2	9.9	29	10	34	24	1	3	1	4
		40-71	1	1	12.8	20	3	15	3	2	10	2	a
13. ASA - ADDICT DIV PROG	ASA												
None		16-18	4	4	4.6	47	25	53	53	9	19	14	26
		19-20	2	2	4.3	53	26	49	39	11	21	11	28
		21-29	3	3	6.2	182	65	36	102	17	9	19	19
		30-39	2	2	11.4	51	16	31	30	5	10	6	20
14. VERA SUP WRK-Wildcat	VERA												
Wildcat		21-29	3	3	5.6	76	25	33	34	8	10	8	24
		30-39	2	2	10.6	38	8	21	8	3	8	3	a
Control Group		21-29	2	3	5.5	62	27	44	38	10	16	10	26
Control Group		30-39	2	2	11.8	43	11	26	14	2	5	2	a
15. PROJECT SHARE	SHARE												
Resident & Non-Resident		21-29	3	3	5.7	31	9	29	14	4	13	5	a
16. NAACP PROJECT REBOUND	NAACP												
Intensive		21-29	1	3	4.3	47	17	36	24	7	15	8	33
Non-Intensive		21-29	3	3	5.6	63	37	59	53	10	16	15	28
Int & Non-Int		30-39	2	2	10.6	45	15	33	24	2	4	2	8
Int & Non-Int		40-71	1	1	18.7	35	10	29	20	3	9	4	20
17. PROJECT SECOND CHANCE	SCH												
None		21-29	2	3	4.8	116	33	28	44	12	10	18	41
		30-39	1	2	7.7	44	14	32	16	3	7	4	a
18. PROJECT MANHOOD	MANHD												
Counseling Sessions		21-29	1	3	4.7	141	50	36	93	15	11	25	27
& Job Referral *		30-39	1	2	7.7	44	16	36	25	6	14	10	40
TOTAL						2860	1182	41%	2072	470	16%	605	29%

* Component(s) apply to all age groups; a. Less than 20 arrests in column (10), No. of Arrests.

<u>Source</u>: Compiled by the project evaluation.

Homicide accounted for 4 percent of all arrests for violent crimes, forcible rape for 4 percent, robbery for 69 percent, and aggravated assault for 23 percent. There appeared to be little difference between each of the seven age groups in the proportions of their arrests for each of the four types of violent crime.

The highest proportion of arrests for burglary, 27 percent of all arrests, was for the 39 juvenile recidivists aged 7 to 12 (Table 4.3). The highest proportion of arrests for larceny, 20 percent, was in the age group 30 to 39. The proportion of arrests for auto theft was about even across the age groups, with the exception of the 40 to 71 age group, which had a much higher percentage of its arrests, 26 percent, in that category.

Of the clients arrested for violent crimes, 95 percent had one or two arrests, while 4 percent had three (Table 4.4). The remaining 1 percent consisted of one client with four arrests, three clients with five arrests, one client with eight arrests, and one with nine arrests. *

Inspection of each of the four violent crimes showed that two clients were arrested for two rapes each. For robbery, 13 clients (4 percent) were arrested for three robberies, while five clients had four to eight robbery arrests each.

Overall, clients 20 and younger appear to have a higher magnitude and severity of criminal recidivism by every measure used. The highest was for the 559 juveniles, 13 to 15, from five diversion projects, whose recidivism rate was 51 percent during the year after project entry. Their ratio of arrests to all clients was 1.0; 75 percent of their arrests were for serious (index) crimes, and 33 percent were for violent crimes. For the age group 7 to 12, the percentage of arrests for violent crimes totaled 35 percent and for serious crimes, 82 percent (Table 4.3).

The relationship between average number of arrests before project entry and criminal recidivism was positive for those 20 and younger. The relationship did not appear to exist for those 21 and older. For those 20 and younger, the higher the average number of arrests before entry, the higher the magnitude of recidivism.

---

*It should be noted that the police records of each of the six extreme cases with four or more arrests were reviewed by the evaluation. Most, at the time of their initial arrest after project entry, were charged with or arrested for other crimes which occurred during that 12-month interval. The point here is that these clients generally were not arrested and released four to nine times each during the 12-month period.

TABLE 4.3

Arrests by the 26 Types of Crimes of the Uniform Crime Reporting (UCR) System

CLASS	NO.*	TYPE	ALL AGES 1182 CLIENTS No. of ARRESTS	%	CUM. %	AGE 7-12 39 CLIENTS No. of ARRESTS	%	CUM. %	AGE 13-15 286 CLIENTS No. of ARRESTS	%	CUM. %	AGE 16-18 276 CLIENTS No. of ARRESTS	%	CUM. %	AGE 19-20 117 CLIENTS No. of ARRESTS	%	CUM. %	AGE 21-29 359 CLIENTS No. of ARRESTS	%	CUM. %	AGE 30-39 92 CLIENTS ARRESTS	%	CUM. %	AGE 40-71 13 CLIENTS ARRESTS	%	CUM. %
VIOLENT	1	HOMICIDE	23	1.1	1.1	-	-	-	3	0.5	0.5	6	1.2	1.2	2	1.1	1.1	12	2.1	2.1	-	-	-	-	-	-
	2	RAPE, FORCIBLE	26	1.3	2.4	1	1.4	1.4	7	1.3	1.8	4	0.8	1.9	7	3.7	4.7	4	0.7	2.8	3	2.0	2.0	-	-	-
	3	ROBBERY	416	20.1	22.4	21	28.4	29.7	137	24.8	26.6	104	20.0	21.9	42	22.1	26.8	97	17.1	20.0	13	8.8	10.9	2	8.7	8.7
	4	ASSAULT, AGGRAV.	140	6.8	29.2	4	5.4	35.1	37	6.7	33.3	34	6.5	28.5	13	6.8	33.7	36	6.4	26.3	12	8.2	19.0	4	17.4	26.1
PROPERTY	5	BURGLARY	336	16.2	45.4	20	27.0	62.2	121	21.9	55.3	96	18.5	46.9	27	14.2	47.9	55	9.7	36.0	16	10.9	29.9	1	4.3	30.4
	6	LARCENY	301	14.5	59.9	10	13.5	75.7	73	13.2	68.5	65	12.5	59.4	27	14.2	62.1	95	16.8	52.8	29	19.7	49.7	2	8.7	39.1
	7	AUTO THEFT	149	7.2	67.1	5	6.8	82.4	37	6.7	75.2	50	9.6	69.0	7	3.7	65.8	34	6.0	58.8	10	6.8	56.5	6	26.1	65.2
NONINDEX	8	ASSAULT, OTHER	126	6.1	73.2	3	4.1	86.5	27	4.9	80.1	27	5.2	74.2	12	6.3	72.1	39	6.9	65.7	18	12.2	68.7	-	-	-
	9	ARSON	3	0.1	73.4	-	-	-	1	0.2	80.3	1	0.2	74.4	-	-	-	1	0.2	65.9	-	-	-	-	-	-
	10	FORGERY, COUNTERFEIT	9	0.4	73.8	-	-	-	-	-	-	1	0.2	74.6	4	2.1	74.2	3	0.5	66.4	1	0.7	69.4	-	-	-
	11	FRAUD	5	0.2	74.0	-	-	-	1	0.2	80.4	1	0.2	74.8	2	1.1	75.3	1	0.2	66.6	-	-	-	-	-	-
	13	PROPERTY, STOLEN	78	3.8	77.8	1	1.4	87.8	14	2.5	83.0	16	3.1	77.9	7	3.7	78.9	30	5.3	71.9	9	6.1	75.5	1	4.3	69.6
	14	VANDALISM	50	2.4	80.2	2	2.7	90.5	23	4.2	87.1	12	2.3	80.2	2	1.1	80.0	9	1.6	73.5	2	1.4	76.9	-	-	-
	15	WEAPONS	98	4.7	84.9	1	1.4	91.9	27	4.9	92.0	19	3.7	83.8	11	5.8	85.8	34	6.0	79.5	6	4.1	81.0	-	-	-
	17	SEX OFFENSES	23	1.1	86.1	1	1.4	93.2	4	0.7	92.8	8	1.5	85.4	1	0.5	86.3	7	1.2	80.7	2	1.4	82.3	-	-	-
	18	NARCOTICS	151	7.3	93.3	1	1.4	94.6	7	1.3	94.0	39	7.5	92.9	17	8.9	95.3	70	12.4	93.1	15	10.2	92.5	2	8.7	78.3
	19	GAMBLING	3	0.1	93.5	-	-	-	-	-	-	2	0.4	93.3	-	-	-	-	-	-	1	0.7	93.2	-	-	-
	21	DRUNKEN DRIVING	3	0.1	93.6	-	-	-	-	-	-	-	-	-	1	0.5	95.8	1	0.2	93.3	1	0.7	93.9	-	-	-
	23	DRUNKENNES	7	0.3	94.0	-	-	-	-	-	-	1	0.2	93.5	1	0.5	96.3	4	0.7	94.0	1	0.7	94.6	-	-	-
	24	DISORDERLY CONDUCT	21	1.0	95.0	-	-	-	6	1.1	95.1	8	1.5	95.0	1	0.5	96.8	3	0.5	94.5	3	2.0	96.6	-	-	-
	25	VAGRANCY	23	1.1	96.1	-	-	-	2	0.4	95.5	7	1.3	96.3	1	0.5	97.4	10	1.8	96.3	2	1.4	98.0	1	4.3	82.6
	26	OFFENSES, OTHER	81	3.9	100.0	4	5.4	100.0	25	4.5	100.0	19	3.7	100.0	5	2.6	100.0	21	3.7	100.0	3	2.0	100.0	4	17.4	100.0
		TOTAL	2072	100.0	100.0	74	100.0	100.0	552	100.0	100.0	520	100.0	100.0	190	100.0	100.0	566	100.0	100.0	147	100.0	100.0	23	100.0	100.0

Note: Percents and cumulative percents may be off by .1% due to rounding errors; * UCR rank.

Source: Compiled by the evaluation project.

TABLE 4.4

Number and Percent of Clients with One, Two, or More Arrests
for Violent Crimes during the 12 Months after Project Entry

TYPE OF VIOLENT CRIME	NO. OF ARRESTS	AGE 7-12			AGE 13-15			AGE 16-18			AGE 19-20			AGE 21-29			AGE 30-39			AGE 40-71			ALL AGE GROUPS		
		CLIENTS	%	CUM.%	CLIENT	%	CUM.%	CLIENTS	%	CUM.%	CLIENTS	%	CUM.%	CLIENTS	%	CUM.%	CLIENTS	%	CUM.%	CLIENTS	%	CUM.%	CLIENTS	%	CUM.%
1 HOMICIDE	1	–	–	–	3	a	a	6	a	a	2	a	a	12	a	a	–	–	–	–	–	–	23	100	100
	Total	–	–	–	3	a	a	6	a	a	2	a	a	12	a	a	–	–	–	–	–	–	23	100	100
2 RAPE	1	1	a	a	7	a	a	2	a	a	5	a	a	4	a	a	3	a	a	–	–	–	22	92	92
	2	–	–	a	–	–	a	1	a	a	1	a	a	–	–	a	–	–	a	–	–	–	2	8	100
	Total	1	a	a	7	a	a	3	a	a	6	a	a	4	a	a	3	a	a	–	–	–	24	100%	100%
3 ROBBERY	1	10	a	a	83	78	78	69	82	82	23	79	79	63	85	85	7	a	a	2	a	a	257	80	80
	2	4	a	a	17	16	94	10	12	94	4	14	93	7	10	95	3	a	a	–	–	a	45	14	94
	3	1	a	a	5	5	99	5	6	100	1	3	96	1	1	96	–	–	a	–	–	a	13	4	98
	4	–	–	a	–	–	99	–	–	100	–	–	96	1	1	97	–	–	a	–	–	a	1	b	98
	5	–	–	a	1	1	100	–	–	100	1	3	99	1	1	98	–	–	a	–	–	a	2	1	99
	8	–	–	a	–	–	100	–	–	100	–	–	99	1	1	99	–	–	a	–	–	a	2	1	100
	Total	15	a	a	106	100	100	84	100	100	29	99	99	74	99	99	10	a	a	2	a	a	320	100%	100%
4 ASSAULT, AGGRAV.	1	4	a	a	33	94	94	30	94	94	13	a	a	36	100	100	8	a	a	4	a	a	128	96	96
	2	–	–	a	2	6	100	2	6	100	–	–	a	–	–	100	2	a	a	–	–	a	6	4	100
	Total	4	a	a	35	100%	100	32	100	100	13	a	a	36	100	100	10	a	a	4	a	a	134	100%	100%
ALL VIOLENT CRIMES	1	15	75	75	108	76	76	95	81	81	37	79	79	100	84	84	17	77	77	4	a	a	376	80	80
	2	4	20	95	25	18	94	15	13	94	8	17	96	14	12	96	4	18	95	1	a	a	71	15	95
	3	1	5	100	7	5	99	6	5	99	1	2	98	1	1	97	1	5	100	–	–	a	17	4	99
	4	–	–	100	1	1	99	–	–	99	–	–	98	1	1	98	–	–	100	–	–	a	1	b	99
	5	–	–	100	–	–	100	1	1	100	1	2	100	1	1	99	–	–	100	–	–	a	3	1	100
	8	–	–	100	1	1	100	–	–	100	–	–	100	–	–	99	–	–	100	–	–	a	1	b	100
	9	–	–	100	–	–	100	–	–	100	–	–	100	1	1	100	–	–	100	1	a	a	1	b	100
	Total	20	100%	100%	141	100%	100%	117	100%	100%	47	100%	100%	118	100%	100%	22	100%	100%	5	a	a	470	100%	100%

Note: Percents may total to more or less than 100 due to rounding errors.

a. Percent not computed because the total number of clients is less than 20.

b. Less than 1 percent.

Source: Compiled by the evaluation project.

Of the 2,860 clients, 1,182, or 41 percent, were arrested 2,072 times, an arrest-to-client ratio of 0.7. Of the arrests, 605, or 29 percent, were for the violent crimes of homicide, forcible rape, robbery, and aggravated assault.

PROJECT IMPACTS ON CRIME

There were three approaches to measuring project impacts.

Control Group Comparisons. There was no significant difference between the Vera control or comparison group and the 21- to 39-year-old clients of eight projects with clients of that age. Specifically, the rates for the Vera control group for the 21- to 29-year-olds were statistically equal to those of projects Second Chance, SHARE, Vera Wildcat, BCC, Manhood, ASA, NAACP (Intensive), ARC, and NAACP (Non-intensive). When the Vera control's recidivism rate for 30- to 39-year-olds was compared to those of the projects, there were no significant differences for those projects and components: BCC, Manhood, Second Chance, ARC, Vera Wildcat, NAACP (Intensive and Non-intensive), and ASA.

Recidivism Before and After Project Entry. Comparing the year after project entry and the second year before project entry showed the recidivism rates significantly higher for those 18 and younger, no different for those 19 and 20, lower for those 21 to 39, and no different for those 40 to 71 (Table 4.5).

Comparison of Recidivism among the Projects. Differences among projects did not significantly affect their ability to lower the recidivism rates. The overall estimated probability was 0.56 for the outcomes observed for the 13 groups of projects classified to ten levels of age and severity of prior arrest history for those 20 and younger, and three levels of age across levels of severity for those 21 and older.

The probabilities of the outcomes observed for the test of project differences on recidivism were: 0.56 when clients of all ages were classified by 16 levels of age and severity (Table 4.6); 0.69 when classified by the 10 levels of age and severity for only those clients 20 and younger; and 0.52 when classified by the three age groups for only those clients 21 and older.

It can be concluded not only that there was no significant relationship between project characteristics and client recidivism, but that there was also no difference regardless of which of four assumptions was used about the relationship between severity of

TABLE 4.5

Comparison of Arrest Rates during Second Year
before Project Entry and during One Year after
Project Entry by Age Group across Projects

| | ARREST RATE DURING | | | x^2 |
AGE	SECOND Year BEFORE Project Entry	FIRST Year AFTER Project Entry	Change	Value
7–12	7	30	+	21.564*
13–15	18	51	+	137.057*
16–18	30	46	+	29.680*
19–20	46	50	+	0.548
21–29	48	37	–	23.366*
30–39	40	29	–	7.210*
40–71	40	24	–	2.682

Source: Compiled by the project evaluation.

prior arrest history and recidivism at different ages to assess the
effect of project characteristics.

The quantity, quality, types, and mix of services provided by
the projects to their clients—as well as their staff-client ratios,
proportions of paraprofessional staff, per capita funding, and other
project characteristics—had no apparent effect on the projects'
ability to influence the arrest recidivism of their clients. Overall,
no project was better than another.

VIOLENT CRIME BEFORE AND AFTER
PROJECT ENTRY

The relationship existed across ages, for each of the seven
age groups except 19 to 20 and 40 to 71. An examination of the
relationship between a prior and subsequent history of violent
crimes (homicide, forcible rape, robbery, and aggravated

TABLE 4.6

Projects Grouped by Statistically Equivalent or Different Arrest Recidivism Rates within Each Level of Severity of Mean Number of Arrests Prior to Project Entry

AGE of Client	LEVEL OF SEVERITY By Mean Number of ARRESTS Prior to Project Entry	PROJECT AND COMPONENT	ARREST RECIDIVISM Rates By Per Cent	PROJECTS GROUPED BY ARREST RECIDIVISM RATES Within the Level of Severity
7-12	1	PROTESTANT BOARD OF GUARDIANS	19	Same
		ALTERNATIVES TO DETENTION – HRA Family Boarding Home	29	
		ALTERNATIVES TO DETENTION – PROBATION Pre-court Intensive Service	40	
		NEIGHBORHOOD YOUTH DIVERSION	41	
13-15	1	ALTERNATIVES TO DETENTION – HRA Family Boarding Home	29	Same
		PROTESTANT BOARD OF GUARDIANS	40	
	2	MORRISANIA YOUTH SERVICE CENTER Legal Services	47	Same
		ALTERNATIVES TO DETENTION – PROBATION Pre-court Intensive Service	62	
	3	ALTERNATIVES TO DETENTION – HRA Group Home	55	Same
		ALTERNATIVES TO DETENTION – PROBATION Supvd Deten Release & Day/Eve Ctr	59	
		NEIGHBORHOOD YOUTH DIVERSION	62	
16-18	1	YOUTH COUNSEL BUREAU Long-term Parole	24	Same
	2	ADDICTS REHABILITATION CENTER	34	Same
		MORRISANIA YOUTH SERVICE CENTER Legal Services	41	
		LEGAL PROPINQUITY	42	
	3	PROBATION – URBAN LEAGUE	60	Same
		INDEPENDENCE HOUSE	61	
	4	ASA – ADDICTS DIVERSION PROGRAM	53	Same
		VOI – BRONX COMMUNITY COUNSELING	56	
		PROJECT BYCEP	59	
19-20	1	VOI – BRONX COMMUNITY COUNSELING	44	Same
		MORRISANIA YOUTH SERVICE CENTER Legal Services	46	
		PROBATION – URBAN LEAGUE	47	
	2	ASA – ADDICTS DIVERSION PROGRAM	49	Same
		ADDICTS REHABILITATION CENTER	50	
		INDEPENDENCE HOUSE	72	
21-29	1	VOI – BRONX COMMUNITY COUNSELING	33	Same
		PROJECT MANHOOD	36	
		NAACP PROJECT REBOUND Intensive	36	
	2	PROJECT SECOND CHANCE	28	1
		VERA SUPPORTIVE WORK PROGRAM Control Group	44	2
		ADDICTS REHABILITATION CENTER	44	
	3	PROJECT SHARE	29	1
		VERA SUPPORTIVE WORK PROGRAM Wildcat	33	
		ASA – ADDICTS DIVERSION PROGRAM	36	
		NAACP PROJECT REBOUND Non-Intensive	59	2
30-39	1	VOI – BRONX COMMUNITY COUNSELING	10	Same
		PROJECT SECOND CHANCE	32	
		ADDICTS REHABILITATION CENTER	34	
		PROJECT MANHOOD	36	
	2	VERA SUPPORTIVE WORK PROGRAM Wildcat	21	Same
		VERA SUPPORTIVE WORK PROGRAM Control	26	
		ASA – ADDICTS DIVERSION PROGRAM	31	
		NAACP PROJECT REBOUND Intensive and Non-Intensive	33	
40-71	1	ADDICTS REHABILITATION CENTER	15	Same
		NAACP PROJECT REBOUND Intensive and Non-Intensive	29	

Source: Compiled by the project evaluation.

TABLE 4. 7

t-Test Values for Outcomes of Differences Between
Violent Crime Arrest Rates After Project Entry

Age Group	Homicide	Rape	Robbery	Aggravated Assault	All Violent Crimes
7–12	a	a	−2.15*	a	−1.69*
13–15	a	a	−3.19*	−1.00	−3.38*
16–18	a	a	−4.82*	−2.19*	−4.39*
19–20	a	a	−1.37	−1.34	−1.21
21–29	−1.05	a	−1.79*	−3.16*	−3.07*
30–39	a	a	−0.60	−2.03*	−2.19*
40–71	a	a	−1.86*	a	−0.36
Across Ages	−0.84	−2.56*	−5.31*	−3.97*	−5.25*

Notes: 1. Since arrests for robbery accounted for 69 percent
of all arrests for violent crimes, it was not surprising that these
results tended to parallel those for all violent crimes.
    a Number of clients less than 20.
    * Arrest rates after project entry are significantly higher for
clients with one or more arrests for a violent crime before project
entry as opposed to clients with no violent crime arrests before project
entry. P is equal to or less than .05, by a one-tailed test.
    Source: Compiled by the project evaluation.

assault) found that the relationship held across age groups for rape,
robbery, and assault, but not for homicide (Table 4. 7).
    A stepwise linear regression analysis was done on the
independent variables (1) year of age at project entry, and (2) a
history of at least one arrest for violent crime before project entry. *

---

    *The analysis was done initially as part of the effort to
validate a measure of severity.

The prediction was of the dependent variable of one or more arrests for violent crimes during the twelve months after project entry.

The results indicated that any relationship between violent crimes before and after project entry was not linear. The F values and r values were significant for the age groups 13 to 15, 16 to 18, 19 to 20, 21 to 24, and 35 to 39. However, the degrees of freedom were quite high for each of the age groups tested. The correlation of year of age to the dependent variable was only significant for the age group 16 to 18. The total variance accounted for by the independent variables did not exceed 0. 08 for any of the age groups.

ADDENDUM: NONCRIMINOLOGICAL OUTCOMES

In addition to its basic objective of determining the criminological outcomes of the project services, the evaluation had some noncriminological objectives. The first was based on a desire to fill CJCC's need for individual and comparative measures of the project services of remedial reading and job placement as an aid to programmatic and administrative decisions about projects. In order to be comparable, the statistical measures would have to be standardized, and it was the identification of standard measures that the evaluation undertook, even though other evaluators would be doing the measuring. In order to supplement statistical measures, the second effort focused on qualitative, nonstatistical evaluations of individual projects' programmatic features and accomplishments. This was to be done by other evaluators hired by the CJCC or the projects who would follow standardized guidelines. With both of these efforts, the evaluation (as part of its technical assistance to the CJCC) specified and negotiated the terms of many of the evaluations which were done by outside evaluators.

The objective became the development of means whereby the individual projects could measure their own service outputs, in a standardized fashion; and the effort was concentrated on two basic services, job placement and remedial reading. With the measures standardized, it was thought, CJCC would be able to make comparisons between projects.

A first step was a review of project proposals so that proposed individual evaluation goals and methods could be made uniform. A secondary gain would be that the criminological investigation being performed centrally by the evaluation would not be duplicated by the projects. Only a few first proposals were reviewed in this fashion. More proposals became available when the projects reached the stage of first re-funding, but by then it was usually too late to establish or modify internal evaluation goals or methods to the extent necessary.

Job Placement. This task was meant to include all such vocational services as job training, job development, and job placement. The hope was that comparisons of services could be achieved if the projects would, on the basis of accurate records, answer five questions: What proportion of those clients referred to jobs are placed? At what entry-level wage? By what Department of Labor DOT classifications? For how long? If they have left, why?

In those projects which provided job placement services, primarily Second Chance, Manhood, and NAACP, the big stumbling block was the availability and accuracy of records. The projects were community-based and staffed by paraprofessionals whose experience generally did not include record keeping. When outside evaluators were employed by these projects, either to assess results or to provide technical assistance in the form of staff training, the results were little better. The research results tended to be academic and tangential; the staff training did not address the accuracy or standardization of records. As a result, it generally was not possible to determine validly what the project job placements had been, or to establish the standard measures.

Remedial Reading. This was the most common service offered in CJCC-funded projects that undertook to provide remedial education. A standard measure of reading achievement was available for projects with school-age children in the Metropolitan Reading Achievement Test (standard in New York City schools at the time).

There was little success in the attempt to make the use of that test standard in CJCC projects and in the evaluation of those projects by outside evaluators. The test was required by the evaluation for several Probation Department remedial reading projects with school-age children, along with the CAT and ABLE tests for Department of Corrections projects with clients older than school age.

There was great resistance on the part of the projects, particularly those under the Probation Department. Their staffs stated concern that the tests are culturally biased and unfair to the projects' predominantly black and Hispanic populations. Each project, and its outside evaluators, wanted to use a "better" test, existing or newly created, to measure each project's success in remedial reading.

The evaluation's position was that so long as the projects dealt with New York City children, the test used by the city's public schools for their own decision making was the most pertinent. If the projects could achieve service results that the test could not measure, such results could be counted as not very important so far as the children were concerned.

The possibility of bias in the test, for the use intended, was not a significant issue. The intention was to measure projects comparatively, not individual children. A project evaluation can control for bias. (Since almost all clients were black or Hispanic, if the test was "unfair," it would be equally so for all.) If, however, each project used its own test, and if they all were different from the test used by the city schools, there would never be a way to compare used by the city schools, there would never be a way to compare projects. If at some point the schools changed to some other, presumably less biased test, the projects could all then change to the use of that test, also.

Finally, it was pointed out repeatedly that the projects could, for whatever reasons they felt important, administer as many additional tests as they wanted. The comparative evaluation, however, was to have been based on the one test used by local schools.

The project staff and their CJCC monitors continued to resist the test. The final outcomes of the issue or of the individual or comparative accomplishments of the remedial reading services are not known to the evaluation.

Other Services. The most important additional service provided by projects was legal assistance and screening for recommendations of diversion or nondiversion. The outcomes of legal services appear to be quite good in terms of the provision of defense attorneys to project clients. The outcomes (other than criminological) of the diversion services provided to the courts, particularly by the juvenile projects, were considered good by the courts, funding agencies, projects, and outside evaluators. The courts released large numbers of clients to the projects, even in cases where the clients had severe and lengthy prior criminal records. Sometimes this was because of enthusiastic advocacy on the part of project staff.

General Outcomes. Most projects were not able to provide services to the number and types of clients contracted for during their first year of operation. This was due to problems of implementation during that year and, in many cases, to overstated project goals.

Following implementation during the second funding period, the projects were generally better able to meet their contractual goals in terms of the number and types of clients to whom services would be provided.

This problem is not restricted to the LEAA-funded projects, but is endemic nationally and has characterized most new projects funded by OEO, DOL, and HEW.

Standard Project Monitoring Service. In addition to the quantitative measures, the uniform monitoring system was to be supplemented by the addition of standardized nonquantitative impressionistic reports based on site visits by senior evaluators with program experience and observational skills.* Such reports can be produced more quickly than statistical ones and can assist program administration as well as CJCC decision making on such issues as re-funding—particularly if statistically based evaluations are inadequate or late. The evaluation prepared standard outlines for such reports and participated in the selection of evaluators.

The plan had mixed success. There were too few qualified evaluators of this type available, and too little central coordination and supervision by CJCC or the evaluation project. A number of such evaluations were undertaken and completed, however, and their findings were used by CJCC in re-funding decisions.

---

*The unique ability, personality, and charisma of a project director, for example, may greatly affect a program's effectiveness. As a matter of fact, this may be one of the single most important determinants of project effectiveness during the first year of implementation. Therefore, it is helpful to identify and apply such nonquantifiable factors in interpreting most usefully the meaning of statistical analyses of project effectiveness.

5

An introductory point that needs to be made is an observation about rehabilitation and diversion as project services. Given the reduction of crime as the ultimate objective of the projects which are the subject of this report, rehabilitation is a method by which most of them hoped to accomplish that objective. The means of providing rehabilitation were such project services as job placement, remedial education, or counseling.

Diversion, as that term has been used so far in this report, has stressed the concept of an alternative through which the criminal justice system could dispose of a case without resorting to either detention or incarceration. Diversion is also used as an alternative to the prosecution of charges against an arrested person. As a result of this alternative, no determination is made about the person's guilt or innocence. A period of satisfactory conduct while receiving the project's rehabilitative services is usually considered sufficient basis for dropping the charges.

Another point that may not have been clear from previous discussion of rehabilitation and diversion as project services is that they are in no way comparable to each other. A project is not either a rehabilitation project or a diversion project. Diversion is merely a means by which some projects come by their clients (or just have them released from the courts, for example, bonds or probation). Rehabilitation is a method by which some projects hope to reduce or eliminate the criminal behavior of their clients.

Some projects provided only rehabilitation (Manhood), both rehabilitation and diversion (Neighborhood Youth Diversion), and almost nothing other than diversion (Alternatives to Detention-Probation). Some projects which incorporated both rehabilitation and diversion services in their programmatic format did not provide both to all their clients. Some clients received only diversion, others only rehabilitation.

In addition, it should not be overlooked that the primary provider of diversion services to a court is its probation arm, which has available to it forms of diversion in addition to the services offered by such projects as those studied in this evaluation. Probation departments usually retain legal jurisdiction over a diverted client, even when both the recommendation of diversion and the rehabilitative services are provided by a project. In some cases, such as Neighborhood Youth Diversion, the distinction between the status of projects and probation departments may have become blurred because the diversion might not have been made if the project had not recommended it.

Finally, we repeat that the orientation of the evaluation places major emphasis on violent crimes. Within this orientation, the focus is on crimes against strangers, victims who are neither related to nor more than casual acquaintances of the person charged. This orientation and focus probably also was the intent—as implied by the title—of the original Safe Streets Act.

REHABILITATION BY THE PROJECTS
JUDGED A FAILURE

The failure of the projects was particularly evident with young clients, and in relation to violent crime. This judgment is based on the criminal recidivism of project clients. It resulted in great cost to both society and the victims because of the magnitude and severity of the criminal behavior.* The criteria used to make the determination were: the cost of the outcomes of the recidivism, which is by far the most important, and the comparison of project outcomes with those of available comparison (control) groups.

Cost of Recidivism to Society and Victims. Of the 2,860 clients from 7 to 71 years of age, 1,182, or 41 percent, were arrested a total of 2,072 times during the 12 months after project entry. These arrests reflect several thousand victims and many millions of dollars in the cost to victims of theft, property damage, and injury.

---

*As discussed earlier, the net benefits of rehabilitation by the projects must be determined solely in relation to crime: the possible provision of jobs and other services to clients is not a pertinent benefit, because the projects were funded by LEAA, whose intention is the prevention and control of crime. The same service outcomes might be judged beneficial, however, if funded by such non-crime-control sources as HEW or the Department of Labor.

Of these arrests, however, 29 percent, or 605, were for violent crimes. This understated measure of criminal behavior means that there were at least 605 victims, of whom about 50 were killed or raped and 555 robbed or severely assaulted. Just this portion of the outcome leads strongly to the judgment that the cost of the recidivism both to society and to the victims is too high (Table 4. 1).

Nor does the conclusion change if the cost is examined for each of the 13 types of clients shown on Table 4. 1 by age or prior arrest history. For example, the comparatively "good" 29 percent recidivism rate of the 314 clients aged 30 to 39 reflects that of the 147 arrests, about one out of five was for violent crimes (Table 4. 1). When the results of representatives of the primary target groups of young males under 21 with severe prior criminal histories are examined, most outcomes are worse than the summary statistics for all 2, 860 clients cited above (Table 4. 1). *

It could be asserted that if there was a 41 percent recidivism rate, then 59 percent of the clients were clearly successes or nonrecidivists. This argument would not be acceptable, because success or failure, in terms of recidivism to serious and violent crimes, obviously is qualitatively different in its consequences from other measures, such as failing to pass a test in reading achievement or gaining job skills. Failure or recidivism in this context implies victims. To illustrate, assume that we are discussing the effects of a new medication for treating disease in a group of 2, 860 persons. If a side-effect of curing, say, 59 percent of the disease cases were infecting more than 600 outsiders with a mutation of the disease—with even a fraction of the fatalities, injuries, and suffering of the victims of violent crimes—there is little question that the extent of adverse side-effects would be considered too high a price to pay.

The judgment of failure does not stem from direct comparisons. Assume it could be shown that other types of projects, or no projects at all (a control group), or the existing CJS, yields recidivism and victimization rates 20 percent higher than the outcomes of the projects studied. The actual rates and numbers, now relatively

---

*In addition, these summary statistics understate the actual criminal behavior because: (1) the higher recidivism rates of the most important target groups (clients under 21 with more severe criminal histories) are masked by inclusion (see Chapter 3, note 4), and (2) some findings suggested that crimes by project clients for which they were not apprehended were greater than the number of clients who were arrested but who did not commit any crimes.

low, would still be judged a failure because of the cost to
victims. *

For a behavioral scientist to judge an outcome such as this
recidivism rate as a success solely because it was statistically lower
than that of a hypothetical control group—without assessing the
consequences of the recidivism in terms of victims—would be
difficult to justify either empirically or ethically. It would also be
difficult to understand a denial of the empirical validity and pragmatic
importance of some recidivism outcomes solely on the basis of the
absence of a control comparison, for example, the recidivism
findings for juveniles. †

<u>Control Group Comparisons</u>. It should be stressed, however, that
there were no significant differences between a "control group" and
eight of the projects for the 1, 270 clients aged 21 to 39. Moreover,
the somewhat forced assumption that a control or comparison group
necessarily consists of clients who are only unserved by being
either on the streets or in the existing CJS, prevents comparisons

---

*If, in another year of operation, these projects could improve
their record by 25 percent, reducing to 450 the 600 or so possible
victims of violent crime, the number would still be too high to be
judged by the evaluation as other than a failure.

†A basic and valid commandment within the sciences is that
the effect of a treatment is determined by comparing the outcomes of
the treated group with those of an equivalent untreated control or
comparison group. But this does not mean that the findings of a
study without a control or comparison group constitute no findings
at all. Some evaluation outcomes, with or without comparisons, may
be high enough—or low enough—to be essential for policy decisions
affecting the health, safety, and welfare of the public—particularly
in the prevention and control of crime. The extent of recidivism and
violent crime among the 1, 527 clients 20 and younger in this study,
for example, has obvious policy implications, regardless of whether
these results are compared with those of a control group.

Yet, in the important survey by Lipton, Martinson, and Wilks
of the effectiveness of correctional rehabilitation treatment, only
studies which had control or comparison groups were considered for
inclusion. Studies which did not have such groups, but which may
have met the other survey criteria, were excluded. [1] Since the
survey was intended and used for policy decisions in crime control,
the question arises as to how this survey criterion can be reconciled
with excluding valid data that may be important in making such
decisions.

with other alternatives. * Some important alternatives may be the testing of the possible CJS approaches of mandatory minimum sentencing and preventive detention for their ability to reduce violent crime.

Before-and-After Comparisons. The before-and-after project entry comparisons showed significant increases in arrests for younger clients and decreases for older ones. These results were congruent with nationwide reports for these ages. Since the reports represent many who do not receive rehabilitation services, they may act as a weak control comparison. If one accepts the control comparison, then the projects' rehabilitation services probably did not cause either the increase or decrease in arrests. † If one does not accept the comparisons, then the relationship of the rehabilitation services to the outcomes is not analyzable.

Conclusion. Ultimate criteria for judging "high" and "low," or success and failure, are left up to the reader; but precedents may be found in federal and state controls over drugs and foods, which consider very limited pain, injury, or death too high a price for the benefits of certain products.

    In these projects, however, the costs of criminal recidivism, especially for violent crime, are judged to be so high to victims and society that it appears to be unjustified to continue to use governmental crime control funds for rehabilitation services to achieve the objectives of the Crime Control Act as amended in 1973, to "reduce and prevent crime and juvenile delinquency and [particularly!] to insure the greater safety of the people. "[2]

FAILURE NOT FROM PROJECT
ELEMENTS OR OTHER FACTORS

    That there was no significant difference in effect on recidivism among projects as varied as the 18 was very surprising. Generously funded, well-planned, and well-administered "model" projects such as Vera Wildcat Supportive Work Program, ASA Court Diversion, and Neighborhood Youth Diversion were really expected to do better than their less well-endowed competitors (Table 3. 2). But even if

_____

    *Of course clients physically confined by the CSS can only be used as a comparison group during a period after release when they have an opportunity to recidivate.
    †Aging or maturation is probably one important determinant of the outcomes.

the differences between projects had been significant, the actual
outcomes would have been too costly in terms of amount and type
of recidivism to be judged as other than failures. In any case, the
findings raise obvious questions about, and implications for, the
LEAA, the CJCC, and other New York agencies for decisions about
funding or program revisions. For example, can funding anything
except the least expensive of these project types be justified? Why
fund projects whose outcomes are no different from that of a control
group?

Project Elements

The evaluation considered a variety of factors that might have
undermined the projects' efforts, even if their models were valid,
thus leading to their apparent failure. It could be argued, for example,
that these programs were measured during an atypical year, one in
which they were plagued by start-up and implementation problems.
While there were new programs in the study (for example, BYCEP
and NAACP), there were others that had been operational for years
before receiving LEAA funding (for example, Bronx Community
Counseling and Manhood), and the arrest rates for the two categories
were not statistically different.

Perhaps the available funds, staff, or services were not of
sufficient magnitude to effect change, but this was not supported by
the equivalent arrest rates of such massively funded projects as
Probation-Urban League or Vera Wildcat and such lesser-funded
ones as Independence House and Manhood.

Another possibility is that a more positive effect would have
been found if the recidivism measurement had been made from the
twelfth to the twenty-fourth month after project entry, rather than
from entry to the twelfth month. But the unacceptable criminal
recidivism magnitude and severity that was found in the first year
could not possibly have been affected or outweighed by anything that
occurred afterward.

While time in a program was not measured in the evaluation,
arrest rates of projects with relatively long service periods (such as
Vera Wildcat and ARC) did not differ from those of projects with
short service periods (such as Vera Control and Manhood).

Generalizing the Conclusions

It is fair to ask whether it is appropriate to generalize the
findings on these 18 projects and their types of service to other
rehabilitative efforts locally and nationally. From a statistical
standpoint, 18 projects are not very many; at least 20, and preferably

over 200 or 2,000 would certainly be better. However, the question is not being asked in an academic context. Decisions about funding and modifying projects must be made by the CJCC, LEAA, and other agencies regardless of the number in a sample. Important decisions affecting many projects are, in fact, made on the basis of evaluations of as few as one "model" project. Furthermore, evaluations have ranged from subjective site visit reports to measuring program criminological effectiveness by Rorschach tests or self-reports (and even these provide more information if a decision must be made than no evaluation at all). Nevertheless a funding agency may wish to postpone generalizing findings of failure to other projects and trying alternative approaches until larger numbers of projects are evaluated, "classic" control group comparisons are accomplished, or a commission reviews the issues and makes recommendations. This is certainly the agency's prerogative. But it should be noted that in reality the decision has not been postponed. In effect the agency has decided to continue the existing programs. This point is important because the decision to continue the programs also continues the high recidivism rates, and the consequently high rate of violent crime. Such a decision is difficult to justify on academic grounds alone. It is submitted, therefore, that if decisions must be made, and if there are no better comparable data with different results, then the findings from the 18 projects are indeed the best estimate of the outcome to be predicted for a universe of projects.

Assistance to CJCC's decision making about re-funding or institutionalizing of individual projects through the provision of criminological data was not successful during the evaluation. Most of the projects had not accumulated enough clients to permit evaluation by the end of their first funding period, usually from 12 to 18 months after they began. Some did not have enough clients when their LEAA funds ran out, and institutionalization was the issue.

It took the evaluation from two to three years to know with confidence the reasons for most of the delay in criminological assessment. As a project in its own right, it shared with the service projects general problems of implementation, staffing, and the development and perfection of procedures which led to delays. It took two years to resolve satisfactorily the myriad methodological problems connected with the collection of project data and the retrieval and processing of arrest histories (see Appendix A). During that entire period it was not clear whether these methodological road-blocks, or the insufficient numbers of project clients, were the basic cause of delay.

As an interim measure, six-month recidivism figures were reported to CJCC, with the strong admonition that these were to be treated as preliminary. It was not until the June 1974 Interim Report that both six-month and twelve-month recidivism rates were reported for 15 of the 18 projects. Even then, CJCC and division personnel were cautioned not to compare projects with each other, since their clients' levels of severity of prior criminal history had not yet been established, and there were no figures on the seriousness and types of crimes reported by most of the arrest rates.

No recommendations were made in these reports to the city or the state about re-funding or institutionalizing any of the projects on the basis of the criminological results. For their part, the city and state staffs were hesitant to base re-funding or institutionalization decisions on the raw arrest rates that were provided to them, nor were there many cases in which they could have been used. Six-month rates, for example, were obviously lower than annual rates, and the meaning of an arrest rate after six months was difficult to determine with no standard of comparison and no knowledge of the types of criminal behavior represented. Although some of the annual arrest rates for a project were "high" by any reasonable criteria— for example, 60 percent—by the time these were reported in the interim report, most re-funding decisions and some of the decisions about institutionalization had already been made.

By 1973 it had become apparent that the evaluation, when debugged, would still not be able to provide criminological assessments for most projects funded by CJCC in time for re-funding and institutionalization decisions. At that point it was understood that most projects would be unable to accumulate enough clients for evaluation by the time re-funding or institutionalization decisions fell due.

The focus of the evaluation shifted to questions that would make possible decisions about CJCC policy across projects. For example, we included in our extension of our contract at that time the goal of relating the severity of a client's prior criminal history to the likelihood of criminal behavior after project entry.

All the rehabilitative efforts measured were in projects substantially removed from conventional correctional settings, and none of them used such approaches as intensive individual psycho-therapy, operant conditioning, or medical treatment with drugs. In a summary of a major study by Lipton, Martinson, and Wilks[3] in which all English-language reports on rehabilitation efforts were screened and 231 (covering the period 1945-67) were judged valid enough to be analyzable, Martinson stated: "With few and isolated exceptions, the rehabilitative efforts that have been reported so far have had no appreciable effect on recidivism."[4] This evidence— that most rehabilitation programs and program efforts (in the sense of independent variable categories)[5] both similar to and different from the ones in the evaluation's study also did not work—led the evaluation to conclude with more confidence that generalization to similar types of programs was valid and that it also appeared to be applicable to models that had not been evaluated by us.

Unemployment, Poverty, and Mental Illness

Environmental pressures on the projects were also considered. Given the unfavorable economic conditions- particularly the unemployment rate for minorities- it might be asked whether it was reasonable to consider the effectiveness of service programs, particularly vocational programs.

Wilson[6] has made the point ably that so long as crime is more attractive and more remunerative than work, even available employment may not offer an effective alternative to crime:

> One works at crime at one's convenience, enjoys the esteem of colleagues who think a "straight" job is stupid and skill at stealing is commendable, looks forward to the occasional "big score" that may make further work unnecessary for weeks, and relishes the risk and adventure associated with theft. The money value of all these benefits—that is, what one who is not shocked by crime would want in cash to forgo crime—is hard to estimate but is almost certainly far larger than what either public or private employers could offer to unskilled or semi-skilled workers.

Wildcat, a Vera supportive work project, provided jobs with subsidized wages at prevailing rates to its clients. Yet its recidivism rates were not significantly different from those of a control or comparison group that was not provided with these services. Moreover, the rates of Vera Wildcat clients did not differ significantly from comparable clients in seven other projects whose vocational services—some did not have any—consisted almost entirely of job referral.

The job itself has to be desirable to the young blacks and Hispanics among the target groups, and not just available. Many will not accept such unattractive jobs as dishwasher, although such jobs are often available in New York City even during high unemployment. Further, with few exceptions, they are not qualified for the white-collar jobs that they do find attractive when those are available.

At the time of this writing, unemployment rates are almost at a post-World War II high for everyone—criminal and noncriminal.

The rates may get worse. It is apparent, however, that neither the government, business, nor anyone else has been able to do very much about it. Therefore, even if employment were criminologically effective, it may be beyond the practical ability of the society to provide sufficient and satisfactory employment to make an appreciable impact on violent crime in the near future.

Poverty and undereducation, which also might have stood between the rehabilitation services and the reduction of crime, were also considered by the evaluation; but the severity of both within the target groups had been relatively stable over the five years prior to 1975, while crime had grown. It has frequently also been pointed out that the majority of poor, unemployed, undereducated, and otherwise deprived minority group members do not commit violent crimes.

As with unemployment, the question of whether sufficient changes are feasible and not just appropriate is moot. Clearly, one cannot realistically expect in the near future to provide all the poor with an adequate standard of living. "Adequate" might be several times higher than the present somewhat arbitrary definition of poverty-level income.

Finally, there is a prevalent assumption that most criminal behavior is attributable to mental pathology, that the pathology has been imposed on a basically sound individual by environmental factors such as poverty, and that the process is reversible—that the criminal, now a victim, can be "cured."

The curative methodology usually called for is, depending on the preference of the prescriber, either one of the many mental health techniques ranging from group or individual therapy or counseling to conditioning, or one of the many social work or sociological prescriptions ranging from guaranteed income to "advocacy," or some blend.

The evaluation's results show that whichever of the variants the 18 projects selected, it made no significant difference. The summary by Martinson of the Lipton, Martinson, and Wilks study reported the same general lack of results in a much broader range of projects. [7]

The assumption of pathology is hypothetical and based on a definition of mental illness much broader than that used by psychiatry. Since even the psychiatric definition often has proven a difficult base for rigorous studies attempting to link syndromes and possible causal factors, it is clear that the broader definition would be even more difficult to use or test. To that extent it has been irrefutable.

On the other hand, mental health advocates have found it equally difficult to sustain their contention that many pathological syndromes, once in effect, can be reversed in the sense of a "cure." Among the relatively few reported cures for serious mental illness (that is, neurotic disorders),* a substantial number have been attributed to either unique skills and training on the part of the therapist, or facilities that would be prohibitively costly. Neither such facilities, nor such personnel, are generally available to agencies charged with the reduction of crime; nor are they likely to be.

Other Factors—Especially
Sanctions against Crime

Despite the lack of a demonstrable causal relationship between these services and crime reduction (this does not contradict the consistent reports of a positive correlation between factors such as unemployment and crime), it is generally accepted that the relationship has existed in the past and can exist again in the United States in the future. There are countless intricate, unmeasurable causal interactions of factors that may explain why the relationship does not exist at this time.

These factors might include the enormous popularization of violence in television, movies and books; the absence of strong religious or political commitments for most of the criminals in question; the almost universal presence of a pragmatic, relativistic, materially oriented system of ethics, in which ends justify means; the rationalization by some minority group members of such crimes as homicide, rape, or robbery on the basis of an alleged debt owed to them by the white society that exploited their forebears—and, similarly a "politicizing" of these crimes by criminals as alleged reactions to poverty and prejudice; and the greatly increased number and proportion of young males within the population since 1960.

One of the most important factors, however, is the possible ineffectiveness of society's sanctions against crime. To assume that "curing" poverty, unemployment, or undereducation will automatically eliminate crime, without considering interactions with society's sanctions against crime or other factors, is simplistic.

In other words, massive socioeconomic changes which would provide everyone in the target groups with attractive, remunerative jobs, a middle-class standard of living, good housing, and extensive remedial education could contribute to reducing much violent crime. This, in principle, is a desirable and civilized goal. But this goal

---

*The term serious mental illness in this context does not include schizophrenia, character disorders, that is, psychopathy, or certain behavior disorders resulting from brain damage that psychiatrists generally do not consider "curable" at this time.

is not a substitute for effective sanctions against crime. It is naive to think that we have to accept the consequences of countless serious crimes as long as there is unemployment and poverty. As opposed to the naivete of such a position, it is unacceptable to rationalize, overtly or covertly, the cost in victims of violent crime and to oppose alternative approaches to crime in the hope that in some fashion this cost will motivate the society to take the steps necessary to eliminate unemployment and poverty.

EDUCATION AND JOB TRAINING BY OTHER SPONSORS

The finding that these services did not have the desired criminological effect does not mean that they should not be undertaken, continued, or expanded for the population studied. Every effort should be made, for legal, logical, and ethical reasons, to assure that the provision of such benefits is not linked to whether the recipient is a criminal. Society is obliged to provide such service on the basis of need, to criminal and noncriminal alike—in prison or out of it.

But such funding should appropriately be provided by those government departments which exist to manage vocational, educational, and health concerns as opposed to those set up to control and prevent crime. They are also the most appropriate places to determine needs, priorities, and the allocation and management of funds for such purposes— as well as whether such projects are the best way to deliver the services.

NOTES

1. Douglas Lipton, Robert Martinson, and Judith Wilks, The Effectiveness of Correctional Treatment: A Survey of Treatment Evaluation Studies (New York: Praeger, 1975), pp. 4, 5.

2. Declaration and Purpose, Law Enforcement Assistance, Act of August 6, 1973, P. L. 93-83, § 2, 87 Stat. 197.

3. Lipton, Martinson, and Wilks, op. cit.

4. Robert Martinson, "What Works? Questions and Answers About Prison Reform," The Public Interest 35 (1975): 25.

5. Martinson recently stated that the term "efforts" in the quotation above from "What Works?" means "independent variable category." Robert Martinson, "California Research at the Crossroads," Journal of Crime and Delinquency (1976): 184.

6. James Q. Wilson, "Lock 'Em Up and Other Thoughts on Crime," New York Times Magazine, March 9, 1974, p. 11.

7. Martinson, "What Works," op. cit.

6

IMPLICATIONS

Up to this point, the evaluation's conclusions have been based primarily on the findings about the projects and related to project services. One objective of the study, however, was to make practical suggestions as approaches to the major tasks of CJCC. To do this, it became necessary to go beyond the actual data of this evaluation and to consider their implications in the broader context of criminal behavior and possible alternative methods of reducing crime. [1]

At this point it may be useful to consider the possibility that one of the major causes of the increases in the amount and intensity of violent crime is the absence of effective sanctions against crime. As in the conclusions section, most of the following discussions and all of the recommendations about violent crime are restricted to such crimes against strangers, victims who are neither related to nor more than casual acquaintances of the person charged.

SANCTIONS TO PREVENT AND DETER CRIMINAL BEHAVIOR

The study has shown that rehabilitation services outside correctional institutions do not adequately prevent recidivism; other studies have shown that such services within institutions do not work either. The major approach of the criminal justice system is to look for a solution within its own facilities and resources.

The Police. By hiring and deploying more police, for example, prevention and apprehension might be increased. But it is not feasible to carpet the streets with policemen. Further, the police already accounted for $996 million, or 81 percent, of the $1.226 billion New York City 1972-73 criminal justice system budget

TABLE 6. 1

Budget Allocation for New York City
Criminal Justice Agencies

Agency	Budget 1972-73 (in Millions)
Police	995. 6
Correction	115. 2
Probation	23. 0
District Attorneys	18. 2
Courts	64. 1
Defense	9. 6
Total	1, 225. 7

Note: Police includes Housing and Transit Police. Drug treatment and youth services amounting to $128. 3 million are not included. "Defense" includes Legal Aid Society and assigned counsel.

Source: "The Criminal Justice System in the City of New York—An Overview," New York State Commission of Investigation, November 1974.

(see Table 6. 1). Data suggest that the police probably apprehend a much greater proportion of actual criminals than is shown by the ratio of complaint clearances—an individual arrested for a crime may have been responsible for a larger share of crimes than a single complaint may suggest; moreover, many criminals are apprehended several times. Before project entry, for example, approximately 30 percent of the clients had been arrested once or not at all, 37 percent had 2 to 4 arrests, 24 percent had 5 to 10, and 9 percent had 11 or more. In other words, even if the odds of being apprehended for a given crime are low, for example, 1 in 8, the client arrest records before the project indicate that most are apprehended over a period of time for some crime or other. Finally, clearance rates have increased for each of the four violent crimes except homicide from 1968 to 1974; forcible rape from 46 percent to 53 percent; robbery from 17 percent to 25 percent; and aggravated assault from 40 percent to 50 percent. [2] The clearance rate for homicide fell from 93 percent in 1968 to 82 percent in 1974. The

primary problem may not be too few apprehensions, but what happens
after apprehension.

The Courts. After apprehension, if the CJS proceedings result in a
conviction, a defendant is sentenced in the interests of justice. If
the sentence is incarceration, there are four major justifications:
retribution (which has become increasingly difficult to justify in the
current culture), rehabilitation (which this study and others have
shown does not work), prevention or incapacitation (which is
completely effective during the time of incarceration), and deterrence
of others (general deterrence which many court and corrections
officials feel is not an operative factor).

Deterrence by Incarceration. The vast majority of those arrested are
not incarcerated, primarily because of dismissals for legal insufficiency, failure of witnesses to appear, and plea bargaining to
conditional or unconditional release. Of 2,520 felony arrests for
homicide, robbery, narcotics, sex crimes, hijacking, and bribery
during 1972-74, 460 persons—18 percent—were incarcerated as a
final disposition. [3]

The duration of incarceration is shortened greatly by plea
bargaining. As mentioned earlier, in 1974, 80 percent of all felony
cases in New York City were disposed of by the lower courts, which
can only impose a sentence of up to one year of incarceration. [4] The
starkest example of the shortening of sentences by plea bargaining
is that of persons charged with homicide in New York City. A study
by the New York Times of 685 adult suspects in 1973 whose cases
had been adjudicated showed that 80 percent pleaded guilty to a
reduced charge. [5] Of these, 20 percent were released on conditional
discharge, 28 percent received less than five years, and 30 percent
received less than ten years. The remaining 21 percent received
more than ten years. After serving about one-third of their time,
most are eligible for parole. These periods of incarceration for the
most serious crime, of course, suggest that incarceration for such
crimes as car theft are far shorter or even nonexistent.

To explain these findings, officials in the CJS say that the main
reasons for these sentencing practices are the insufficient court and
correctional facilities and personnel for the enormous number of
offenders. This results in plea bargaining by the courts to unsuitably
brief sentences or no incarceration at all.

Other reasons suggested for these practices include the inability
of correctional facilities to rehabilitate or deter and the availability
of alternatives in such noncorrectional projects as those studied in
this report. Some officials say that for first offenders (particularly
from the white middle class or juveniles), arrest and subsequent

processing, including possible detention, has been punishment enough—a position shared by some judges. Many of the blacks and Hispanics, who make up the largest proportion of those arrested, may be victims of an unjust and racist society, some officials add. What is needed, in this view, is not punishment per se, but compensation for the injustice, perhaps in the form of "treatment" (by jobs or remedial education).

Those who justify the present policy assert that there is little if any research evidence to support the position that in this country incarceration deters others. They argue further that the increase in crime in the past decade, despite whatever incarceration has been imposed, demonstrates the absence of any relationship with deterrence other than the possibility of a negative one.

One way to test the assertion that incarceration is not a general deterrent would be to suspend all incarceration and see what effect that would have on crime. It is submitted that crime, committed by others than those released, might increase greatly. The only sustainable inference from the present evidence is that deterrence, as used, has not worked as well as might be desired or needed. It seems just as absurd to assume that the possibility of incarceration will not deter some significant number of potential criminals as it is to assume it will deter all.

There is a relative lack of hard data on general deterrence. Until recently, most studies focused on the death penalty and homicide. These studies had serious weaknesses in method and theory. Within the past few years, however, there have been a number of careful investigations of incarceration and a variety of offenses. Despite some variation in their methods, the findings of these studies indicate a positive relationship between incarceration and deterrence, particularly when punishment is very likely or certain. [6]

It might not be imprisonment itself that is at fault, but the means of its application, that has reduced the effectiveness of the deterrence. The possibility of achieving more effective sanctions by revising CJS applications of incarceration, in the discussion to follow, does not stem from the data-based findings of this study. But the studies cited in note 6 and other evidence suggest that the possibility has enough merit to warrant a test.

Adequacy, Immediacy, Certainty, and Consistency

That the expectation of punishment deters human beings from behaving in certain ways is a relatively noncontroversial fact for many analysts including van den Haag, Wilson, Andenaes, Zimring, and others. [7] Some learning theorists and criminologists suggest,

however, that if incarceration* is to be effective as a general
deterrent, it must be adequate, immediate, certain, and consistent. 8
To maximize effectiveness, all four conditions should interact. The
incarceration policy of the New York City CJS clearly lacks certainty
and consistency, and it applies adequacy and immediacy with mixed
and questionable impact.

Adequacy. Incarceration may be assessed for adequacy by intensity
and duration. Intensity as currently imposed in prisons is probably
more severe than necessary. The loss of liberty, the regimentation,
and the separation from family and friends are punishment enough.
Cruelty, poor food, overcrowding, lack of recreation, and similar
often voiced complaints by prisoners are, to the extent that they
exist, not acceptable punishments and should be corrected. Duration
of the middle and upper range of available sentences as called for
by the penal law for adults is probably sufficient for deterrent
efficacy (but definitely not for youthful offenders and juveniles). As
diminished by the courts and correctional institutions through plea
bargaining, sentencing practices, time off for good behavior, and
parole, that efficacy appears to be seriously undermined.

Immediacy. The quicker that charges of violent crimes can be
adjudicated and, if appropriate, sentence of incarceration imposed,
the more effective the punishment should be. Thus, persons charged
with violent crimes should be given top priority by speeding the
pre-determination processing by the CJS. Time spent in detention
should be greatly shortened, but not by diversion.

Certainty. The evaluation considers the certainty of punishment the
most important deterrent of the four discussed, even though there is
a paucity of research. There is no lack of clarity about the current
certainty of incarceration. There is none. The 18 percent incarceration rate for the 2,520 persons charged with felonies suggests that
persons arrested for such crimes can be reasonably confident (82

---

*Physical confinement during detention before sentencing is
essentially just as punitive as confinement during incarceration after
sentencing. And the duration of detention can be quite long when the
charge is for a serious crime. (Although time in detention can count
against the length of incarceration mandated by the sentence.) These
considerations may complicate analyses of incarceration and its
functions, but aside from extreme cases they do not invalidate
them.

percent likelihood) of nonincarceration. The certainty in this case
may be anything but a deterrent. And, as will be discussed in a
subsequent chapter, certainty of incarceration for juveniles is
nonexistent, as their incarceration rate in New York City is
infinitesimal.

It is apparent to the police and youth workers in New York that
the target groups of clients, particularly juveniles, perceive accurately the very low certainty of incarceration. It seems reasonable,
under the circumstances, to expect the high and increasing level of
crime.

Preventing the diversion of persons charged with violent crimes
from determination of guilt or innocence and, of greater importance,
mandatory incarceration following conviction could improve the
certainty of incarceration.

Consistency. Sentences of incarceration can be very different for
persons who commit essentially identical violent crimes. The
justification for this includes differences between the persons
sentenced in their likelihood for rehabilitation, prior criminal
history, responsibility to wives and children, employment status,
and danger to society. The goal is to tailor the sentence to the
individual.

Judges, however, vary enormously in how they sentence and
divert, depending on their background, legal experience and philosophy,
and attitude toward rehabilitation. Partridge and Eldridge demonstrated
that a group of 50 judges, when presented with the same presentence
reports, handed down extremely disparate sentences. In 16 of 20
cases there was no unanimity about whether incarceration was
appropriate and, where prison terms were imposed, they differed
widely. For the most severe crime the sentences ranged from 3
years' imprisonment to 20 years and a $65,000 fine. [9] In actuality,
the "tailoring" of sentences, as a response to differences among
defendants, may be more a reflection of differences among judges
than precision of judgment.

The variable lengths of sentences for a specific crime can
provide a chance of a short sentence that may be worth the risk, for
many offenders, if the potential rewards of a crime such as robbery
are high enough. This hampers deterrence.

With consistent sentences the courts would lose the discretion
to "tailor" a sentence to a particular defendant. A typical case
would be a reduced sentence for a contrite, married, employed—
"good risk"—offender convicted of a violent crime but with no
previous arrests. To give such an offender the same sentence for
the same crime as is received by an unrepentant, hostile, unemployed

offender who has many previous arrests (but not for violent crimes) will seem to many an unreasonable proposal.

The broad argument in defense of uniform sentencing is that the sentence is the same for the two cases because the injury to the victim was the same; the deterrent example of the "model" prisoner is just as important as the poor risk; equal sentencing preserves consistency; and there is justice in sentencing equally for the same act.

Nevertheless, if sentences are mandatory could there not be inappropriate sentences in some cases—say, for example, a 90-year-old convicted of robbery? Yes, there could be. However, the possibility also exists in the present system of sentencing. Undoubtedly some offenders are currently given sentences which do not prevent or deter crime or serve the interest of society (false positives). Absolute accuracy of sentencing is no more feasible than any other ideal goal. There may always be some offenders who are sentenced inappropriately in any system of sentencing. The goal is to minimize sentencing errors in a mandatory system.

Perhaps some cases of "false positives" can be screened out by methods similar to those recommended by the Twentieth Century Fund in their system of "presumptive sentencing".[10] In this system, a finding of guilt for committing a crime would predictably result in a fixed sentence unless very specific mitigating or aggravating factors were established—factors specified by legislation.

In any case, mandatory sentences, when compared to the present sentencing system, would decrease greatly the number of offenders who are inappropriately released or given ineffectually brief sentences (false negatives).

Vorenberg opposes mandatory minimum sentencing as a method of increasing the effectiveness of sentencing. He asserts that massive budgetary increases for courts and corrections systems would reduce the pressure on prosecutors and judges to plea bargain to extremely light sentences, and thereby result in sentences more commensurate with the severity of the crime. But money alone would not free the courts to function at the desired level of effectiveness. The extra resources would not control the great disparity in sentencing among judges for similar crimes. This stems in part from the wide range of minimum to maximum sentences which are available, allowing judges enormous discretion.

He urges that legislatures restructure sentencing laws to narrow the range and consequently limit the discretion of judges. (Probably implicit in this recommendation is that differences among judges such as their values, philosophy, and education might determine the punishment—or lack of it—more than the nature of the crime itself if discretion is not limited.) However, Vorenberg opposes mandatory application of these proposed sentencing guidelines.

While the author generally concurs with Vorenberg's analysis, he does not accept the assumption that narrowing the range of sentencing will limit sufficiently the sentencing discretion afforded judges. For example, the effectiveness of sentencing still would be hampered because: first, sentencing by judges for similar crimes still may be inconsistent and inaccurate, although within a narrowed range; and second, a primary cause of ineffective sentencing in preventing and deterring crime—the inappropriate conditional or unconditional release of persons charged with violent crimes—could continue. Since mandatory minimum sentencing should control these two problems (although there may be a cost in terms of some persons who will be punished inappropriately), the author must disagree with Vorenberg's position. [11]

Recommendations

The following recommendations for legislative and procedural changes affecting the criminal justice system are meant as guidelines. The proposal is not a detailed statutory construction, but a schematic outline around which legislation could be built. Where such specific details as years of mandatory sentence are spelled out, they are the evaluation's best judgment and are not meant to be inflexible. Similarly, proposals for procedures are provided more as an illustration of intent than as final models for implementation.

Although the recommendations were conceived as an integrated package of proposals, with all contributing to the achievement of a total intent, there is clearly the possibility that only some of them will be found acceptable or feasible. In that event, the individual proposals, as well as sections within them, can stand independently and can be evaluated in terms of their ability to achieve some beneficial effect for the goal of increasing public safety from violent crime.

Mandatory Sentences

Under the approach proposed here, the overriding factor in the determination of the severity of a sentence would be the seriousness of the injury to the victim. Once the grade of injury (three are proposed) is determined, the following would apply: First, the sentence would be both mandatory and irreducible by probation or parole. Second, the sentence would be the same for all persons guilty of having inflicted that grade of injury in the course of that category of crime. (It would not apply to accomplices who did not inflict that injury.) Third, the mandatory sentences, in almost all cases, would be shorter than the sentences available under present law. Fourth, the sentence would be applied on the basis of the resulting injury, regardless of how inflicted, with a gun, knife, chair, or fists. Finally, the sentences would also be applied to "youthful offenders."

Exceptions would be provided in four cases: (1) sentences for juveniles would be of shorter duration; (2) sentences would be uniformly, but slightly, shorter for those who plead guilty to the crime charged* (although this violates the principle of consistency, it is a practical concession to the reality of the present overload in the courts and correctional institutions); (3) persons with previous records of violent crimes would receive fixed increments of additional sentence time for each prior conviction; and (4) small uniform proportions of time off (about 10 percent) for good behavior would be allowed as a practical aid to the management of corrections facilities. The method of mandatory sentencing summarized above might be more accurately termed "flat" sentencing.

The proposal deals with robbery, rape, aggravated assault, and homicide. Since it is based on grades determined by the seriousness of the injury to a victim, it was necessary to establish new categories of injury. These categories include within them the two basic forms of injury now defined by the New York State penal law, but divide them in a fashion more meaningful for deterrence.

In the current penal law, physical injury means impairment of physical condition or substantial pain. Serious physical injury means physical injury which creates a substantial risk of death, or which causes death or serious and protracted disfigurement, protracted impairment of health, or protracted loss or impairment of the function of any bodily organ. [12]

In place of these two categories, which can be described as "serious physical" and "physical" injury, it is proposed that there be three categories, described as "atrocious injury," "serious physical injury," and "physical injury." The definitions of these terms would be:

Definition	Description
Atrocious injury	The protracted loss or impairment of the function of any bodily organ or limb, or serious disfigurement
Serious physical injury	Injury which necessitates protracted

---

*As opposed to pleading guilty to a lesser charge in customary plea bargaining.

Definition	Description
	treatment in a hospital setting for seven or more days
Physical injury	Injury which requires medical treatment

The proposed changes in the structure of the crime would not alter the substantive definition of the crime. All the types of conduct now defined as crime are included in the new definitions below. The only change would be in the elements of the degrees into which the crime would be divided. *

Robbery. Currently, robbery is punishable within the discretion of the sentencing judge from a term of probation or unconditional discharge to a term in state prison which may be, as a maximum, from 8 1/3 to 25 years. The proposed schedule of sentences provides for periods of incarceration with no release on parole.

Criterion—Degree	Mandatory Sentence	Guilty Plea
1. Atrocious injury	7 years	5 years
2. Serious injury	5 years	3. 5 years
3. Physical injury	3 years	2 years
4. No physical injury†	2 years	20 months

Rape. Existing penal law divides forcible sexual crimes into several categories and degrees. Rape means nonconsensual sexual intercourse between a man and a woman other than his wife, and there are three degrees of the crime. One, punishable by up to 25 years in prison, deals with forcible compulsion; the others are age-related or deal with persons incapable of consent. Sodomy is "deviate sexual intercourse," and the degrees of the crime parallel those for rape. There is also a crime called sexual abuse which involves "sexual contact" less than rape or sodomy, and it is punishable by a maximum of seven years. Although the UCR system includes only forcible or attempted forcible rape as rape, and lists all other sex crimes as sex offenses, the proposal would accord equal seriousness to all forcible sex crimes, with injury to the victim the controlling element. The new scheme for sexual crimes would be:

---

*The descriptions of sentencing practices in New York state for robbery, rape, aggravated assault, and homicide are as of March 1975.

†Some psychological injury is assumed.

Criterion—Degree	Mandatory Sentence	Guilty Plea
1. Atrocious injury	8 years	6 years
2. Serious injury	6 years	4 years
3. Physical injury or rape victim under 11 years of age with no physical injury	4 years	3 years
4. Force, no consent, no physical injury	3 years	2 years

The proposal is addressed solely to the forcible aspects of the crimes as currently defined. Rape and sodomy are treated identically. The rationale in the concept of fourth-degree rape is that any rape victim is injured (psychologically) by the very nature of the crime. The psychological injury is considered greater than that which occurs during third-degree robbery. Similarly, a prepubescent child is considered injured by the crime to the degree shown.

Assault. Existing law defines assault as "physical injury" caused to another person, and judges the severity of the offense according to whether there are aggravating factors. The factors considered are: a weapon, serious physical injury, injury to a police officer, injury as part of another crime, and the mental state of the actor—intentional, reckless, or negligent. The maximum sentence for assault is 15 years, while the intentional infliction of "physical injury" is merely a misdemeanor and punishable by no more than 1 year. Our scheme would encompass all intentional infliction of injury.

Criterion—Degree	Mandatory Sentence	Guilty Plea
1. Atrocious injury	7 years	5 years
2. Serious injury	5 years	3. 5 years
3. Physical injury	3 years	2 years

In this case, the proposed changes cover all conduct currently defined by law as assault, but not all sentences are reduced. What is now simple assault, a misdemeanor, would receive an increased sentence.

Homicide. Homicide under the current law, if it involves the intentional killing of a police or corrections officer or any intentional killing by a person serving a life sentence, must be punished by death. Any other intentional killing or felony murder is punishable by life imprisonment, with parole not possible until a term of 15 to 25 years has been served. Several degrees of nonintentional

homicides—reckless, negligent, or heat of passion—are provided
and punishable by terms of 25 years or less. Negligent homicide is
punishable, for instance, by a maximum term of four years.

The proposed new structure deals with intentional killings and
retains the concept of felony murder. It also retains the notion of
predicate felonies.

Criterion—Degree	Mandatory Sentence	Guilty Plea
1. Intentional, during felony	Death*	No reduction
2. Intentional	15 years	12 years
3. Nonintentional, during felony	10 years	7 years

Youthful Offenders. Youths 16 to 18 are at present tried as adults
but may, at the time of sentencing, be treated as youthful offenders,
limiting any sentence to four years. The proposal would eliminate
this special category.

Recidivists. It is suggested that one-third of the applicable mandatory
sentence be added to that sentence for one prior conviction for any of
the crimes discussed, and two-thirds for two or more prior convictions. Although deterrence of others would be expected, the intent
would be to emphasize the preventive or incapacitating function of the
sentence. This is because the likelihood of recidivism appears to
increase as a function of number of prior arrests for crimes.
Wolfgang, Figlio, and Sellin[13] showed, for example, that the
probabilities of a first, second, and third arrest were .35, .54, and
.65, respectively, among youth in Philadelphia.

Limiting Discretion of Courts and Prosecutors. Certain forms of
dismissal and reduction are reasonable; others are not. On a
substantial plane are the cases where the charge is reduced at the
prearraignment stage by the prosecutor's decision not to charge the
"technical" felony charge, and the charge is reduced or dismissed
in court, with the court's approval. Legislation should be drawn to
limit severely the power of the courts and prosecutors to plea
bargain—to reduce or dismiss charges of the violent crimes of
homicide, rape, robbery, and aggravated assault. Precise, detailed

---

*Since these sentences were proposed, the Supreme Court has
ruled that mandatory application of the death penalty is unconstitutional.
Appropriate modifications are suggested, therefore, to conform to
the ruling of the court so as to apply the death penalty for murder
committed during a felony.

legislation is not proposed here, but it is recommended that the statutes require detailed factual statements on the record, to support any dismissal or reduction of charges for violent crimes. The statement to support a reduction or dismissal of a felony charge would have to contain an allegation of the evidence available and why that evidence does not support the felony charged, and an allegation of how the reduction or dismissal serves the purpose of preventing violent crime by the person charged and of deterring violent criminal behavior by others.

One consequence of plea bargaining, by which individuals are convicted of lesser crimes than they were charged with (and, generally, committed), is that future CJS decisions may be affected to the detriment of the public. For example to relieve alleged prison overcrowding in New York City in 1976 hundreds of convicts were released on parole months earlier than their sentence dictated. Corrections department officials claimed that only those "convicted" of lesser or minor crimes were released. However, many of these convictions may have been bargained down from charges of serious and violent crimes. Further, these convicts may have had histories of similar charges and convictions. Premature release of this kind of convict exposed the public to recidivism to serious crimes which could not have occurred if the full duration of the original sentence had been served.

Selective monitoring of all reduced or dismissed cases, including "343s"* and complaint room reductions, should be done. A selective system by which the administrative judge or a public commission can provide that monitoring would help to ensure that each party to the decision to dismiss or reduce is called to account for his actions. Also, if public light is shed on what is now an unseen, unregulated aspect of the criminal justice system, the responsible officials can be monitored by the electorate.

DIVERSION MAY ADD TO THE INCREASE OF CRIME

Historically, for most arrests, the law required that the defendant who could not provide bail be detained until appropriate court procedures were concluded. Over the years, this practice has been modified in a variety of ways to accommodate the system's inability to house as many people as were being arrested, the courts' inability to process those cases expeditiously, and the burden imposed

---

*The process by which prosecutors refuse to draw up a complaint; "343" is the number of the form used.

on citizens who had to wait for long periods in inadequate facilities until their cases could be heard—and because it was obvious that there was no need for it in many cases.

Accommodations have included release to the supervision of others, such as family members or probation departments, release on one's own recognizance, and lowering of bail or bond requirements. This has resulted in the diversion of a continually increasing number of people from detention.

With diversion firmly established as a court practice, other advantages of the application of the principle came to be recognized. Certain classes of defendants, such as alcoholics or minor first offenders, were a problem to the courts both in terms of numbers and because the resources available to the courts were obviously not suited to a constructive resolution of the problems. To remove such defendants from the system and to provide better service, the courts adopted the practice of diverting them from prosecution to service facilities where, presumably, they could receive more effective help.

As this practice became institutionalized, however, it was seized on and expanded by those who saw criminals as essentially sick people to include persons charged with serious crimes and many with long and severe criminal histories.

Also expanded were the points at which the diversion could take place in the criminal justice process, so that now there can be diversion not only from pretrial detention, but also from prosecution, determination, sentencing, and incarceration.

The courts were inclined to look favorably on the new applications of the diversion principle because they had become inundated with criminal cases. There were insufficient court facilities for processing the cases and insufficient institutions to which the courts could sentence those found guilty. One result was that the courts began to expand their own diversion practices as well as accept those of outside agencies. (Another result was acceptance of an enormous amount of plea bargaining.)

An example is the discretion given prosecutors, at the earliest court contact with a case, to refuse to draw up a complaint and, in effect, dismiss it. This "343" process is, in New York City, theoretically limited to cases of legal insufficiency of evidence, but in practice it is exercised with wider latitude. At later stages the prosecutor can decide not to press a "technical" felony charge and, with the court's permission, to reduce it as a diversion from prosecution. Judges are involved to the extent that they sanction such practices.

----

*To the extent that a "343" type of process is properly used, it is helpful and should be retained, but, like any procedure, it is

This virtual explosion of diversion practices and applications had to be accompanied by an equivalent explosion of programs to which defendants could be diverted, when that was called for. The "diversion projects" included in this evaluation are typical of the effort to provide such programs, although some programmatic models are not represented among them.

Determining Success

Success was measured by whether the diverted individual appeared in court on the date specified. When rated in this fashion, the practices have been considered a success. *

The Pretrial Services Agency, for instance, in an operations report for Brooklyn dated December 1974, reported on 12, 637 releases on recognizance at its recommendation for 30 days at arraignment, and 3, 249 persons released in the same fashion after arraignment. The percentage of those who failed to appear at their next scheduled appearance was 7 percent of the "at-arraignment" cases and 11 percent of the "post-arraignment" cases. These percentages are considered highly acceptable and a demonstration of successful performance by the project.

Benefits from diversion have accrued to the courts, the correctional facilities, the public, and considerable numbers of persons diverted. The great majority of those diverted are not arrested during the period of diversion. The courts and the correctional facilities are relieved of the physical presence and the paper work relating to a substantial number of persons.

---

subject to misuse. Since it already calls for certification by the prosecutor of the impropriety of the charges being dismissed, the problem seems to lie in the area of appropriate policing of those certifications to maintain standards.

A more serious issue is the utilization by prosecutors of their discretionary power to recommend reduction of charges on grounds of legal insufficiency as part of plea bargaining. The power was not granted for that reason, and its misuse tends to undermine the preventive and deterrent impact on the criminal process.

For judges, the principal misuse is the reduction or dismissal of violent crime charges, as a result of plea bargaining, when the evidence supports the felony charged.

*Later, as the policy of diversion was expanded to include diversion to probation or to rehabilitation services as a disposition, success was frequently measured in terms such as adaptation and attitudes as determined by the probation workers.

Adherents publicized these successes widely, and these forms of diversion also became popularly considered as effective criminal justice strategies. It was these reports that may well have contributed to the Congress's decision, in its 1974 amendment of the Safe Streets Act, [14] to include diversion by name as a method to be employed in dealing with juveniles.

In theory, at least, diversion should permit the courts to pay more attention to more serious cases and to dispose of them with more ease. Since this more efficient court system should be focusing on cases involving violent crime, the better administration of the justice system, it is hoped, will contribute to the prevention and control of serious crime. But in reality quite the opposite may happen.

By diverting from detention many persons who are charged with very serious crimes or who have severe histories, the courts have physically freed some individuals to commit crimes that could not have occurred if they were in prison—primarily an anti-prevention effect. Immunizing from prosecution and sentencing similar individuals who would otherwise have been incarcerated has had primarily an antideterrent effect. The latter applies to those others who might have been deterred from crime had the prosecution, sentencing, and incarceration occurred and provided an object lesson.

The question of whether diverted individuals who were or were not appearing for court and probation appointments were also committing additional crimes during time at risk was asked by some investigators. They encountered strong resistance from legally trained staff members of diversion projects, who insisted that the only constitutionally acceptable criterion for success of diversion was appearing in court.

As a result, judges deciding on bail or whether to detain the accused are required to consider arrest charges and criminal histories only in relation to whether the accused will appear in court when they are supposed to. The information cannot be used to determine whether the accused are likely to commit another crime while out on bail, and that likelihood cannot be taken into account in setting the amount of bail or deciding whether detention might be appropriate. This principle applies even when the potential crime could be as extreme as murder.

When judges feel impelled to resort to detention in order to forestall a likely crime by the accused during the period of release on bail, they must violate the constitutional rights of the accused by resorting to spurious grounds for setting bail so high that the accused cannot possibly meet it. In such cases, the judges do not state for the record the actual basis of the decision—that the accused is likely

to commit a crime. In this example, they may only say—falsely—
that the decision results because the arrest charge and arrest
history suggest that the accused will not appear when scheduled if
released on low bail.

Should a judge conform to the criterion of likelihood of court
appearance and release the accused on bail, even though the judge
is virtually certain that the accused will commit a violent crime, that
decision may be supported by such groups as the ACLU. The reasons
advanced for this dubious approach to civil liberties are described
and discussed in a subsequent section of this chapter.

Although criminal behavior during diversion is measurable as
a possible predictor of court appearance, there is still a great
paucity of information about arrests, or other measures of criminal
behavior, during the period of diversion, which has come to be
known as the "time at risk."

We were not successful in measuring some of our diversion
projects during the "at risk" period, but an evaluation by the Vera
Pre-Trial Services Project reported some preliminary results. [15]
One of two groups, released on recognizance (ROR), consists of 138
persons from the Manhattan Criminal Court. The other is of 46 ROR
cases from the State Supreme Court in Manhattan.

Of the criminal court cases, approximately 9 percent were
arrested one or more times during the average of 60 days between
their release through diversion and the final disposition of the case
by the court. Some 75 to 80 percent of the arrests were for felonies.
For the supreme court cases, where the average time between
release and trial was 260 days, 9 of the 46, or 19 percent, were
arrested one or more times. These figures, particularly the latter,
show that diversion in lieu of detention adds to the crime rate to a
meaningful extent. Of greater importance are the violent crimes
committed during time at risk.

Diversion from detention or prosecution of fairly high-risk
recidivist groups of clients is common. In this evaluation, for
example, the juveniles in diversion projects included 33 percent
who had 2 to 4 arrests prior to project entry, 7 percent with 5 to
10 arrests, 1 percent who had 11 or more, and the rest with 1 or
no arrests. Many of these arrests were for serious crimes. One
predictable result, in our judgment, was the extremely high
recidivism rates, number of arrests, and number of violent crimes
in that group.

Among the eight projects* offering diversion services to clients
aged 20 and younger there were 18 client groups at different ages

---

*Projects 1, 2, 3, 4, 5, 6, 7, and 13, Table 3. 1.

(of 20 or less) and levels of severity of prior criminal history. Of the 18, the 8 client groups who had the most severe arrest histories prior to project entry also had the highest recidivism rates, which ranged from 53 percent to 62 percent.

Predicting Recidivism

The evaluation also established that there is a significant relationship between a history of violent crimes before project entry and violent crime after project entry. In this and other studies, however, prior criminal history will predict recidivism significantly only by application to decisions on all individuals who are members of a class (for example, all 13- to 15-year-olds with a past or present charge of a violent crime). A result of not diverting anyone with such a record may be a high false positive rate (detained persons who would not have committed a violent crime during time at risk). Heinz, Wenk, Kozol, and others point out that there is a vast literature on the problem of prediction—lack of accuracy and reliability—and the cost implications of high false positive rates. [16] But there are few rigorous analyses of the cost implications of false negative rates in the sense of victims of recidivism during time at risk. Both points are illustrated by a critic of our final report.

One of his arguments cites the 13- to 15-year-olds to illustrate that if all were detained, 25 percent (1 out of 4) would have been prevented from committing a violent crime (true positives), but 3 out of 4 would have been detained unnecessarily (false positives) (Table 4. 1). * The argument concludes that this high false positive rate reflects a total failure at prediction and justifies release of all 13- to 15-year-olds rather than detention.

However, the analysis is incomplete, which raises a question about the objectivity of the argument. Let us reexamine the analysis.

It is true that detaining all in the example of 13- to 15-year-olds would result in three out of four false positives. On the other hand, if we were to release all of them, this means that three out of four will not be arrested for a violent crime (true negatives) but one out of the four will be arrested for one or more of the violent crimes of homicide, forcible rape, robbery, and aggravated assault (false negative)† (Table 4. 1).

---

*An analysis of actual true and false positive rates is not possible since the group is confined in detention. An analysis of actual true or false negative rates for the clients in this study cannot be done from the data presented in Tables 4. 1 or 4. 3

†It should be noted, however, that about one out of three "true" negatives will be arrested for nonviolent crimes, while the false

Obviously, the decision as to whether to detain all or release all should be based not only on the false positive rate, but also on the extent of false negatives and their respective consequences: A responsible decision is determined primarily by the net utility or cost to society that results from comparing each of these possibilities.

Let us illustrate this with the group of 100 aged 13 to 15 at severity level 2 in Table 4.1. Which is the more desirable decision: to detain all and unnecessarily subject 74 of the 100 to the harsh conditions of detention but save approximately 36 persons the cost of suffering and injury entailed in being the victims of violent crime; or to release all of them, thus saving 74 from the harsh conditions of detention but in effect sacrificing 36 persons to homicide, rape, robbery, or assault as victims of the 26 false negatives. *

Clearly, neither is a palatable or easy decision to make in this hypothetical example, because each choice involves a high cost. But for a behavioral scientist, as opposed to an attorney, it seems inappropriate and biased to take a legal advocacy or adversary role and deliberately present only one choice and not both.

What can be done about the problems relating to prediction with this population? According to the studies discussed above, relatively little. [17] It may be necessary to accept the costs of a high false positive rate because of the greater benefit of fewer victims of violent crime which results from lowering the high false negative rate. †

Deficits from diversion accrue from those perpetrators of serious crimes who are diverted, undermining deterrence for others, and thus adding to the number of serious and violent crimes committed. This increment of crimes brings more defendants to the courts, increases the receptiveness to pleas for diversion, generating an upward spiraling cycle of crime, particularly violent crime. This contradicts the crime reduction intent of the Safe Streets Act by increasing violent crime and reducing prevention and deterrence. Therefore, the funding of this practice by LEAA is not justified in its present form.

Recommendations

Persons charged with a violent crime should not be released prior to determination of guilt or innocence. Decisions about diversion

---

negatives will have additional arrests for nonviolent crimes (Table 4.1).

*And there would be 71 additional arrests for nonviolent crimes (Table 4.1).

†Although the period of detention of false positives can and should be greatly shortened.

from detention should take into account the risk of a repetition of violent crime as well as the risk of the person's failure to appear in court. Legislation establishing a procedure for making this determination in an orderly fashion should be enacted, and it should specify criteria of past arrest history for violent crime for the determination. Also, it should be required that those making the determination state how they have conformed to the criteria, so that decisions can be monitored. Means for monitoring should be established. For this policy to be socially acceptable, the disposition of such cases would have to be greatly accelerated, so that the time in detention would be kept to a minimum. After determination, the innocent would be released; those guilty of violent crime would receive mandatory sentences. Prevention and deterrence would be maximized.

The rationale for the recommendation is that some possible infringement of the interests of some individuals is outweighed by the society's need for protection from the increasing cost in terms of death, injury, and pain of victims of violent crime at this time. * There appears to be no constitutional objection to the quarantining (detention), by force if necessary, of persons suspected as carriers of such socially dangerous diseases as typhoid or plague. The analogy between persons who may commit violent crime while free on bail and carriers of infectious disease is obvious. Can the Constitution be interpreted to detain one and not the other?

Nevertheless, proponents of the current CJS division policy, particularly civil rights groups and legal aid workers, are vehemently opposed to any revisions of the kinds discussed, even though they are generally aware that the revisions would benefit potential victims of violent crimes. Their major argument and concern is that a legal basis for preventive detention (because of risk of recidivism as opposed to court appearance) would weaken basic civil rights concerning presumptions of innocence, due process, and the right to bail. Weakening these rights, in their view, could result in serious abuses and further erosion of basic rights. For example, if the wrong political leadership were to be in power there might be widespread and lengthy detention of persons whose crime consisted

---

*The potential harm to the public safety from releasing high-risk recidivists has become increasingly clear, and preventive detention has been legislatively proposed in some jurisdictions. It has been enacted in one form in the District of Columbia, where hearings required by the due process clause to establish the potential public harm if the defendant is released are part of the procedure. These have proven to be cumbersome and time-consuming.

of opposition to the leadership. This concern surely merits consideration, for such detention has occurred in other countries. Moreover, the revelations concerning the abuse of power during the Watergate scandal are certainly not reassuring. The advocates of diversion argue, therefore, that the obviously important societal benefit of safeguarding the civil rights of persons charged with crime justifies the current means of diversion, although diversion results in the loss of civil rights, injury, and even death to many victims.

This ends-justifies-the-means type of rationale, however, is particularly difficult to accept when one considers the highly questionable and essentially untestable basic assumptions underlying it: that if any civil rights are changed there is a high enough likelihood that they will be misused, as per the example, to make it a reasonably possible occurrence; and that the number of those charged whose civil rights may be weakened, and the "cost" of the violation to them, are greater than the number of potential victims and the cost of them if there are no changes.

In any case, the legal issues should be addressed and resolved. Until then the funding agencies responsible for the creation or supervision of diversion projects should establish an administrative policy that such programs will neither recommend for diversion nor accept from diversion a person with a past or present arrest record of violent crime.

This policy could be implemented with respect to the projects whether or not the recommended court and legal changes are put into effect. It could be imposed by CJCC as a policy for projects in the city, by the New York State Division of Criminal Justice Services as a policy for New York State, or by LEAA and other pertinent CJS agencies as policy across the nation.

The courts could cooperate administratively by withholding recognition from projects that do not meet these criteria. Since the projects have no legal existence, being purely administrative, they might well be controllable by restructuring court utilization of their services. By refusing to approve diversion to nonapproved programs, or the dismissal of charges on the recommendation of nonapproved programs, the courts could assist the reorientation of project objectives.

To the extent that they exercise policies independent of the courts, the orientation toward diversion could also be adopted by or mandated for probation departments and agencies.

JUVENILE CRIME MAY BE
EXACERBATED BY CJS POLICIES

The preceding discussions about deterrence and diversion focused on adult and young men but were also in the main applicable to juveniles. Nevertheless, the extent and severity of crime by juveniles, their special status in the criminal justice system, and the greater difficulty of applying to them the recommendations about deterrence and diversion require a separate discussion.

Juvenile Crime. In 1974, in New York City, 77 juveniles 15 years of age or younger were arrested for murder, 261 for rape, 4,765 for robbery, and 1,312 for felonious assault. When all other felony arrests are added, the number of juvenile felony arrests total 16,764.[18] In 1974, the total number of juveniles incarcerated by the Family Court in state training homes was 150.[19]

The evaluation found that criminal recidivism among juveniles in projects providing diversion and rehabilitation services was highest in magnitude and severity of any of the age groups. Among juveniles aged 13 to 15, arrest recidivism after project entry was 51 percent; there were as many arrests of the recidivists as there were clients in the projects; the proportion of all arrests accounted for by violent crimes was one out of three; and the arrest rate after project entry for violent crimes was 25 percent (Table 4.1). The findings were in keeping with those of other reports nationwide.

Explanations. In the search for an explanation of the extent and seriousness of juvenile crime, correlations have been established between juvenile crime and such environmental factors as broken homes, poverty, minority-group status, and low educational achievement. However, the severity of these factors has generally not increased in the last five years, while juvenile crime has.

Nevertheless, the emphasis in countering it has been on the provision of ever increasing amounts of remedial education and counseling, frequently by paraprofessionals with backgrounds similar to those of the juveniles. It is evident that this approach has neither reduced crime nor prevented it from increasing.

The practices of the criminal justice system in relation to juveniles may provide a better explanation. The system has adopted as a basic premise that juveniles are children, and therefore not legally (or actually) responsible for their acts, and that they should be treated accordingly. The confluence of this and highly permissive theories about maximal conditions for child development and an assumption that a curable pathology underlies serious criminal behavior by juveniles combine to produce a policy in which CJS reactions to juvenile delinquency are inadequate and frequently inappropriate.

Legally, a juvenile whose behavior would be charged as a felony in an adult is not a criminal but a "delinquent." The behavior that legally defines delinquency excludes misdemeanors and runs the full gamut of serious criminal behavior, including homicide. The

reaction of the justice system to delinquency is a totally separate
set of procedures and concepts that replace or modify trial,
prosecution, and public disclosure.

Punishment. For minor offenses, juveniles are not arrested, but are
given YD-1 cards. Jurisdiction is in the Family Court, where most
delinquents are placed on probation or diverted to projects. Detention
is used only in the most extreme cases.

With recidivism high among those juveniles who appear in court,
many of them go through the arrest-and-release process many times.
In the evaluation population of 13- to 15-year-olds, 59 percent had been
arrested not more than once before being diverted to a project. But
34 percent had been arrested two to four times, 6 percent had been
arrested five to nine times, and 1 percent had been arrested ten or
more times. Many of the arrests were for serious crimes.

The incredible fact that there were only 150 incarcerations of
juveniles during an annual period when there were 16,764 felony
arrests shows that juveniles in New York City who are found to commit serious crimes, including murder, are rarely incarcerated. To
assert under the circumstances that this incarceration policy can
either prevent or deter violent crime is itself a serious crime
against common sense.

For the few who are incarcerated, sentences are generally less
than a year in a State Youth Correction Center which, in almost all
cases, has sole discretion over the actual length of the stay. Reported-
ly, dangerous and violent teen-agers have been released in six to
eight months with the explanation that after this length of time a
child "is not motivated to stay."[20]

In 1976, a bitterly fought state legislative amendment was passed
with a goal of "tightening" incarceration practices for certain types
of juveniles.[21] Now, if a 14- or 15-year-old is convicted of first-
or second-degree murder, or first-degree arson or kidnapping, a
Family Court judge has the option of incarcerating the juvenile. If
the juvenile is incarcerated, the first 12 months must be spent in
a State Division for Youth secure facility and the second 12 months
in a residential facility. After completion of the first 12 months and
a dispositional hearing, another 12 months in the secure facility may
be imposed. For the lesser crimes of first-degree assault, man-
slaughter, rape, sodomy, or robbery, and kidnapping or arson in
the second degree (or attempted first- or second-degree murder or
first-degree kidnapping), the following holds: If the option of
incarceration is exercised, 6 months must be spent in a secure
facility, then 6 more in a residential facility. As with delinquents
convicted of more serious crimes, incarceration may be extended
for 12 months in the secure facility under the conditions specified.

One key question is to what extent judges will decide to incarcerate at all for these crimes, since the legislation does not call for mandatory imposition of incarceration. The other question is whether the duration of incarceration specified is adequate. In our view, for the vast bulk of delinquents, the limited time period of incarceration available results in an inability to sentence effectively in relation to severity of charge; there is only a difference of a few months possible between sentences for robbery and for crimes such as shoplifting, particularly for those younger than 14, and the sentences for violent crimes are too short to deter or adequately prevent crime.

The Consequences and More Explanations. Thus, the almost total orientation in the response to delinquency is the welfare of the delinquent. Largely lost in the process has been consideration of the requirements of their victims, or potential victims. In the hope of achieving rehabilitation of delinquents through alternatives to incarceration, the health and welfare of the public have been jeopardized.

The very pervasive assumption among social and educational theorists that mental or emotional pathology underlies most violent crime is applied to children even more than adults. But as discussed earlier, there are problems in identifying or defining, much less treating successfully, the assumed pathology. This study and others have shown that treatment, consisting of the rehabilitative services of remedial education and counseling, does not meaningfully affect the criminal behavior of juveniles.

To the extent that juvenile delinquents can be shown through proper diagnosis to be suffering from a definable mental illness, they should be provided as appropriate and skilled treatment as accredited mental health practitioners can offer. It does not seem likely, however, that a blanket assumption that most juvenile delinquents suffer a form of mental illness susceptible to a cure will be a useful approach to the problem of the high rate of violent crime by juveniles.

Until some other means of controlling delinquent behavior is unequivocally demonstrated to be safer to society, incarceration should be used to prevent and deter violent crime. Because of the unwillingness or inability of the court to punish delinquent violent behavior with appropriate incarceration, prevention of criminal behavior does not occur, and (of possibly greater importance) there can be little, if any, deterrent effect on the criminal behavior of other juveniles.

This state of affairs is not compatible with the LEAA goals of reducing the incidence of crime and safeguarding the welfare of the public. Unfortunately, it would also appear to contradict the express mandate of the Safe Streets Act to increase the diversion of juveniles and decrease incarceration. [22]

Unless appropriate changes are made in law and in the practices of the criminal justice system, there seems to be little prospect of any reduction in the inordinately high rate of violent juvenile crime.

Recommendations

A number of basic steps should be taken within the CJS to provide the conditions under which a coordinated program of effective incarceration for juveniles guilty of violent crimes can be instituted. They are:

Modifications of the mandatory sentences stipulated for adults should
 be made applicable to juveniles aged 13 to 15. The sentences
 for rape, robbery, and aggravated assault should be modified
 according to this schedule:*

Degree	Mandatory Sentence in Secure Facility	Guilty Plea
1. Atrocious injury	5 years	3. 5 years
2. Serious injury	4 years	3 years
3. Physical injury	2 years	1. 5 years
4. No physical injury	1. 5 years	14 months

For homicide, the sentences would be as follows:

Degree	Mandatory Sentence	Guilty Plea
1. Intentional, during felony	Till 21st year of age	no reduction
2. Intentional	Till 21st year of age	no reduction
3. Nonintentional, during felony	Till 21st year of age	no reduction

For recidivists, one-third of the applicable mandatory sentence
 should be added to that sentence for one prior conviction for
 any violent crime and two-thirds for two or more convictions,

---

*Rape would receive one additional year at each degree with approximately 25 percent off for a guilty plea. The fourth-degree sentences would not apply to aggravated assault.

with the total duration of the sentence not to go beyond the
juvenile's twenty-first birthday.

The State Division for Youth, which now has jurisdiction over
incarcerated juveniles, or any other agency with such jurisdiction, should be required to adhere to the full term of the
sentences in a secure facility, and should not be permitted to
exercise any discretionary prior release.

Juveniles with a past or present charge of a violent crime should not
be diverted from detention prior to determination of guilt.

Juvenile records of criminal activity should be treated in the same
fashion as adult records. They should be made available to the
court when the subject of the record comes under the jurisdiction of an adult court, and any current provision for sealing or
destroying records should be revoked.

In the Family Court, judicial or other court decisions dismissing or
reducing charges of violent crime against a juvenile should be
required to state the grounds and conformity to criteria for
prevention and deterrence as stipulated for adult courts, and
should include accountability and monitoring.

The position that mandatory incarceration for periods of several
years is an uncivilized and cruel form of punishment is answerable
by these considerations: The incarceration is not for the sake of
retribution, but to safeguard the welfare and health of other children
and adults, and any "cruelty" (in the sense of the institution in which
the child is incarcerated) depends on the conditions that exist there.
The institution should have every facility that a wealthy society can
provide in terms of general care, education, counseling, and
recreation so that individual development is not impeded. The only
important qualification is secure physical confinement.

If these arguments are not compelling, consider the child who
has contracted a highly communicable and virulent illness (or even
the measles). Upon diagnosis, the child is immediately quarantined,
physically confined, and isolated from any contact with others. Few
if any would advocate release because the child was not responsible
for catching the illness, was undereducated, a member of a minority
group, basically a good child, or a child whose constitutional civil
rights were violated by not following due process before confining
him. Most would agree that what matters is that it is essential to
confine that child until he is no longer in a condition to threaten the
health and welfare of others.

In principle, the health of potential juvenile and adult victims
of crime is as good a criterion for physically confining a delinquent
as the health of potential victims of a communicable disease is a
reason for quarantining a child.

IMPLEMENTATION

The broad guidelines to possible approaches to preventing and controlling violent crime highlighted in the sections on deterrence, diversion, and juvenile crime are not intended as definitive, detailed solutions to the problem. There are none.

There are important issues related to these approaches which are beyond the scope and goals of this study, but which merit careful attention and inquiry. For example, the costs of these approaches under present and future economic conditions were not addressed, nor were the practical problems which might attend implementation. But, we can safely assume, on the one hand, that mandatory sentencing alone implies a reallocation and costly expansion of CJS resources—primarily for courts and corrections departments. On the other hand, the cost of crimes committed by just those criminals who are not incapacitated probably is much higher. * This is based on the potential costs of: medical care; lost earnings; damaged, destroyed, and stolen property; additional use of police and court personnel and facilities; private guards, security devices, and insurance. It also includes the less tangible costs of the effect of fear of crime on the life-style of city dwellers and the deterioration of city services due to loss of taxes from those industries and citizens who move from the city primarily because of crime.

Effective sanctions against violent crime should contribute to general deterrence, and will definitely prevent much violent crime by incapacitation. This should result in a considerably lower cost to the CJS after the initial period of implementation.

In restricting the application of these approaches to violent crime, we have not considered their possible application to such serious crimes as arson and burglary. Also, the possible cost benefits to the CJS of the decriminalization of certain "victimless" crimes are not discussed. Nevertheless, decriminalization should be considered for gambling, prostitution, and possession for personal use of physically nonharmful drugs such as marijuana.

In conclusion, the gravity of the evaluation's findings warrants a reexamination of the existing CJS policies (as discussed in this book) and objective consideration of the alternative approaches to violent crime recommended by the author. These approaches should be addressed—individually or in combination, in whole or in part—by the

---

*An informal test may be made by estimating the cost of the 2,072 arrests charged to the 1,182 clients during a 12-month period, as shown in Table 4.1 by the cost components of crimes outlined above.

academic and criminal justice communities, and by the citizens who are affected by violent crime in large cities nationwide.

NOTES

1. Despite essentially the same statement in the final report, some criticisms have asserted that since the discussions and recommendations about the concepts of deterrence, preventive detention, and CJS policy toward juvenile crime are not derived from the data presented by the evaluation they should not have been included. It may be helpful in responding to put the first two findings and conclusions of the evaluation in perspective.

The final amount and seriousness of the recidivism measured and the lack of criminological differences between "model," well-administered projects and poorly conducted projects were unexpected. It was evident that rehabilitation services failed to respond to the problem of serious crime. Moreover, because of the high cost of violent crime to the many victims of the project clients, the findings have grave implications, not only for CJCC and LEAA, but also for others providing rehabilitation and diversion services in New York and elsewhere. And the evaluation, like most others that assess "action" or "demonstration" projects, had to make recommendations to the funding agency about its findings.

The criteria for judging the discussions and recommendations presented here on the familiar but highly controversial alternative approaches to violent crime should be: (1) their pertinence to the problem of crime in New York and other cities and to the findings reported in the initial two conclusions about rehabilitation and diversion services; (2) the validity of the information and analysis presented about them; and (3) their possible usefulness in lowering the extent of violent crime.

In other words, they should be judged on their merit.

2. Crime Analysis Section, New York City Police Department, 1975.

3. Personal communication with Inspector Michael J. Farrell, Criminal Justice Liaison Division, New York City Policy Department, March 1975.

4. New York Times, February 11, 1975.

5. Ibid. , January 27, 1975.

6. See Charles R. Tittle, "Crime Rates and Legal Sanctions," Social Problems 16 (1969): 409; Isaac Ehrlich, "The Deterrent Effect of Criminal Law Enforcement," Journal of Legal Studies 1 (1972): 259; William C. Bailey, J. Martin, and Louis Gray, "Crime and Deterrence: A Correlation Analysis," Journal of Research in Crime and Delinquency 11 (1974): 124. Studies by economists are reviewed

by Gordon Tullock, "Does Punishment Deter Crime?" The Public Interest 36 (1974): 103; George Antunes and A. Lee Hunt, "The Impact of Certainty and Severity of Punishment on Levels of Crime in American States: An Extended Analysis," Journal of Criminal Law and Criminology 64 (1973): 486; Jack Gibbs, "Crime, Punishment and Deterrence," Social Science Quarterly 48 (1968): 515. For a comprehensive survey of studies, see Charles R. Tittle and Charles H. Logan, "Sanctions and Deviance: Evidence and Remaining Questions," Law and Society Review 7 (1973): 371.

7. For an excellent and comprehensive analysis of punishment and deterrence see generally Ernest van den Haag, Punishing Criminals (New York: Basic Books, 1975). For another excellent but narrower discussion see generally James Q. Wilson, Thinking about Crime (New York: Basic Books, 1975). For additional broad analyses see generally Johannes Andenaes, Punishment and Deterrence (Ann Arbor: University of Michigan Press, 1974); Franklin E. Zimring and Gordon J. Hawkins, Deterrence (Chicago: University of Chicago Press, 1973); Franklin E. Zimring, Perspectives on Deterrence, U. S. Department of Health, Education, and Welfare Publication (ADM) 74-10 (Washington, D. C. : Government Printing Office, 1973).

8. The studies on deterrence and these four attributes of incarceration are few and are frequently not directly applicable to the types of crimes, population, and environment addressed by the evaluation except for a few studies on adequacy and certainty. See generally the works cited in note 7.

9. A. Partridge and W. Eldridge, The Second Circuit Sentencing Study: A Report to the Judges of the Second Circuit, Federal Judicial Center, August 1974.

10. Twentieth Century Fund, Fair and Certain Punishment (New York: McGraw-Hill, 1976).

11. James Vorenberg, "Against Mandatory Minimum Sentences," New York Times, December 22, 1975, p. 29.

12. Penal Law, Section 10. 00 (9) (10).

13. Marvin E. Wolfgang, Robert M. Figlio, and Thorsten Sellin, Delinquency in a Birth-Cohort (Chicago: University of Chicago Press, 1972).

14. Act of September 7, 1974, P. L. 93-415, Title V, §541, 88 Stat. 1142.

15. Personal communication with Jim Thompson, Research Director, Vera Pre-Trial Services Project, March 1975.

16. For a recent discussion see Anne M. Heinz, John P. Heinz, Stephen J. Senderowitz, and Mary Anne Vance, "Sentencing by Parole Board: An Evaluation," Journal of Criminal Law and Criminology 67 (1976): 1; and see Ernest A. Wenk, James O. Robison, and Gerald W. Smith, "Can Violence Be Predicted?" Crime and Delinquency 18

(1972): 396; Harry L. Kozol, Richard J. Bowcher, and Ralph F. Garofalo, "The Diagnosis and Treatment of Dangerousness," Crime and Delinquency 18 (1972): 371; Norval Morris, The Future of Imprisonment (Chicago: University of Chicago Press, 1974), pp. 59, 66.

17. Ibid.

18. Personal communication with Jeremiah B. McKenna, General Counsel, New York State Select Committee on Crime, November 1976.

19. There were also 105 Title II or "voluntary" placements during 1974. Kevin M. Cahill, "Report to the Governor, Governor's Panel on Juvenile Violence," Albany, New York, January 5, 1975, pp. 31, 32.

20. New York Times, February 21, 1975, p. 37.

21. New York 1975 Sessions Laws, Ch. 878, § 3, 16.

22. Act of September 7, 1974, op. cit.

INITIAL EVALUATION METHODS

From 1967 through 1971, CJCC adopted a pattern used by many federal agencies, such as HEW, OEO, and DOL, in an effort to obtain the evaluation data it felt it needed. Some percentage of a project's gross budget was set aside for "evaluation," usually from 5 to 10 percent. The money was generally used to subcontract evaluation or consulting firms. If a project was large enough that the percentage of its budget was a considerable sum of money, it might set up an internal evaluation unit, full- or part-time. In either case, the project director arranged and paid for the evaluation service, and the evaluator was responsible to the director, rather than to CJCC, for whom, presumably, the evaluation was being performed.

Frequently the evaluations, designs, methods, and staff (or agency) would not be selected until after the project had been designed, funded, and implemented. This was generally due to the pressure to meet funding deadlines and a lack of knowledge on the part of the administrators of the importance of including evaluations as integral parts of a project from their inception.

Problems

The problems resulting from this mode of evaluating this sort of service program turned out to be more serious and more varied than even experienced administrators had anticipated. The primary problem was that these evaluators were unable to measure validly the experience with the major objective of all the projects—to reduce criminal behavior. Some evaluators (and/or directors) resisted the very idea that crime reduction was a project's primary goal and insisted that it should be evaluated as the provider of some rehabilitative service, such as remedial education or skills training. Other evaluators accepted the objective of measuring for criminological effectiveness, but underestimated the work, time, and cost, or placed their reliance on undependable measurement devices such as client interviews, project records, and tests of attitude toward criminal behavior.

The net effect of resistance to or confusion about the importance of criminological measurement of program effect, or miscalculation of the tasks involved in obtaining a valid measurement, was that

CJCC found itself with no dependable information about the effect its projects were having on the criminal behavior of their clients.

Because each project had its own evaluation, the outcome was an enormous variety of evaluation goals, designs, methods, resources, and competence of individual evaluators. This made it virtually impossible for CJCC to compare the differential criminological effectiveness of program models in serving similar types of clients. An evaluation that defined recidivism as reincarceration, for instance, could not be compared with evaluations based on such definitions as rearrest, reconviction, or change on an attitude scale. Nor was comparison possible when one project measured recidivism over a three-month period, another over six months, and yet others over two years, or with different times for each client. Some evaluators were given $5,000 to evaluate 50 clients, others had $200,000 to evaluate 5,000 clients.

Some evaluators overestimated the scope and quality of the findings they would be able to produce. There were proposals that promised to measure criminological effectiveness, the outcomes of such rehabilitation methods as employment or education, the importance of such client characteristics as age, sex, or educational attainment, and how all of these had interacted to affect the outcome of the project's effort with the client. Some proposals had an obviously inadequate price for what was promised; some, in addition, promised to deliver results in what was obviously too short a time for the work. Predictably, many of the final products delivered were nothing like what had been contracted for.

Given the funding structure, which made the evaluator responsible to the project director, the objectivity of many of the evaluation efforts was questionable. It was not difficult to suspect that many of the evaluators were biased in favor of the program they were evaluating, and were presenting data in the manner most favorable to the project. It was also evident that some project directors, as the employers, had insisted on their right to review an evaluator's report before it went to CJCC and to modify or delete portions critical of the program.

The fact that many of the evaluation components were added on to a project only after the project had been planned and was operational led to the loss of information about early project participants and greater difficulty and expense in incorporating the evaluation methods and forms into project record-keeping systems. The projects had to collect information about clients for their own programmatic and administrative purposes—information that was identical to that needed by evaluations for retrieval of criminal histories or application of various tests. Examples include correct dates of birth, pertinent street addresses, and education. If the project forms had been designed prior to the evaluation, the format of the items might have made it impossible for an evaluator to use.

Proposed Solution

In 1971, Vera Institute of Justice, under planning grants from CJCC, hired the evaluator (this author) to develop a plan to meet the evaluation requirements of the CJCC. The evaluator developed this plan between January and June 1971. The result was a proposal for an approach to meeting CJCC's evaluation needs, based on a single, independent evaluation program that would produce more valid and comparable data as follows:

It would establish evaluation priorities to ensure adequate measurement of the criminological effectiveness of the "people projects."

It would select the most feasible and accurate measure of criminological impact.

It would standardize the application of this measure in analyses of the various programs so that comparisons between and among them would be possible.

It would attempt to assess the impact of selected client characteristics on criminological outcomes.

It would attempt to assess the relationship between criminological impacts and some of the differences in program models that might have affected those impacts.

It would provide uniform descriptive data about the numbers and types of clients enrolled by the projects, regardless of or prior to the measurement of criminological impact.

The evaluation project would be subcontracted to the City University of New York in an effort to maximize the project's independence. The evaluation results and recommendations would be reported directly to CJCC, rather than to the projects to be evaluated. In addition, the evaluations already in process or still to be performed under contractual obligations, by the individual projects and their own evaluators, would be coordinated by the project.

The formal subcontract with the Research Foundation and Graduate Center of the City University was dated July 1, 1971. There were delays in the funding process, however, and the evaluation project actually became operational during September 1971, terminating on March 31, 1975. The total of LEAA funds awarded to the evaluation over this period was close to $800,000.

COLLECTING PROJECT DATA

The initial implementation objective for the evaluation had to be data collection. The data-collection component of the evaluation was called the management information systems (MIS) unit. Although many of the elements in the implementation of the evaluation design were chronologically concurrent, we shall begin with the MIS data collection.

The initial task was to determine who the project clients were and to collect certain items of information about them. Since it was clear that the evaluation would have to deal with tens of thousands of individuals distributed among nearly fifty separate projects in a large geographical area, it was also clear that evaluation personnel would not be able to perform all the required tasks. The projects themselves would have to help, and some system of standardizing both the work and the data would have to be devised.

Development of the Intake Form

A combination of factors made it essential that a standard intake form be used by all projects and that the MIS unit be deeply involved to assure that the form be properly filled out for each client. In designing a standard intake form, the MIS unit sought to meet the needs of three separate sources through a single instrument. The evaluation required precise identifying information on each client so that criminal records could be retrieved, as well as other items for analytic purposes. CJCC needed, for administrative use, periodic, dependable information on the inflow and servicing of project clients. Since several dozen different projects were under its jurisdiction at any given time, this information had to be standardized. The projects themselves, many of them lacking expertise with record-keeping systems, could benefit from technical assistance and from having a form retrieving the same information about their clients for their own internal requirements. The intake form was intended as a primary standard device for collecting basic information that could meet diverse but overlapping needs.

Data from the uniform intake forms used by each project (for each client) were combined to provide summaries of the standard demographic descriptions of the types of clients served by each project, for example, age, sex, and ethnicity. This summarized statistical information could be used by CJCC in on-going program monitoring, for deciding upon budget reallocation requests, and for decisions that come about during re-funding.

The name, address, date of birth, sex, and police identification (fingerprint) number (if available) of the client from the individual

intake forms allowed the evaluation project to retrieve from the
police department criminal histories of project clients to measure
project criminological effectiveness. These items, plus the date of
project entry, were the most important for retrieval and analysis
of arrest histories and were called "index items." Such information
as the client's age and sex allowed us to compare appropriately the
criminological effectiveness of projects.

Problems in Using the Intake Form

High rates of incomplete or inaccurate items on intake forms
submitted by some projects, delays in receiving forms, and difficulties
in coordinating schedules of MIS implementation were the primary
problems.

A number of projects, particularly those which were community-
based, had a high rate of incomplete or incorrect items. This was
particularly troublesome when the items were required to retrieve
the criminal histories of the clients from the police department, such
as full name and date of birth. Inordinate delays and errors in
submitting data were sometimes found in forms from non-community-
based projects. Projects of city agencies often had independent, over-
ambitious research designs and complex technical requirements which
contributed to these problems.

Another problem was that the intake forms contained some
items that were unclearly defined and others that were not applicable
to every project. A revised version of the form was designed, but
until it was in use each question about each item had to be resolved
as it came up.

The nature of the project staff collecting the data from the
clients in some community-based projects led to another primary
source of error. Many of the staff were not traditionally qualified for
their positions, particularly in keeping records. They were, in the
current terminology, "paraprofessionals." These paraprofessionals
were hired because they may have had skills that qualified them for
other areas of great importance to the project, such as direct
knowledge of the social problems that are the focus of the service of
the project, or ability to establish rapport with the potential clientele.
Nevertheless, the strictly professional aspects of background are
often necessary for the task of record keeping. The data chief is likely
to have paraprofessionals as his staff; he, himself, may have risen
from a similar status. The obligation for training, assistance, and
supervision of the paraprofessionals falls upon the professional sector
of the projects. In this area, the evaluation made clear its desire to
assist.

There was also the constant problem of projects moving in and out of various operational phases. Projects are implemented and funded at intervals, resulting in, at any one time, a variety of early, late, proposed, and closed-out projects. Data-collection plans and schedules had to be coordinated with the phasing of the projects. This was a very difficult problem, and the variable phasing of different projects remained a fact of life. Every effort was made, however, to establish contact with projects early in their cycle, preferably at the stage of application for funds, to reduce the effects of this problem.

Another problem was reluctance on the part of certain projects to provide information about clients. Resistance was sometimes generated by fears for the confidentiality of records or because of differing ideas over what constituted a valid evaluation. These problems were more difficult—although, thankfully, fewer. In time, the last holdout agreed to cooperate with the data-reporting system. Introduction of the data-reporting requirements into projects during early stages usually prevented many of these problems.

The evaluation was afflicted with problems similar to those which plagued most of the projects. We were delayed in funding, had difficulty in recruiting key staff, and had unexpected staff turnover. The resolution of these problems was often difficult and resulted in delays.

Technical Assistance to Projects

To increase the accuracy and punctuality of the information on the intake forms collected from the projects, the evaluation attempted to increase its involvement in the structure of projects' internal record-keeping capacities during their proposal development or refunding, and provided on-site training to permanent staff of the community-based projects. Certain projects clearly required more on-site training services, as reflected by their inadequate data-reporting performance. Early examples of these projects were Manhood and Neighborhood Youth Diversion. A relatively successful case of early intervention in establishing a project's record-keeping capabilities and subsequent training in the major record-keeping role was Youth Counsel Bureau. The director of the evaluation was involved in the initial establishment of a budget line for a "records manager" in this project, developed a job description, and screened applicants for the position.

The importance of early involvement in the design and staffing of a community-based project's record-keeping unit is discussed below. However, we will stress here that outside statistical evaluations of the criminological effectiveness or service outcomes of a project are almost impossible unless a project has adequate internal resources for keeping accurate and timely records of its intake of and work with clients.

If a person's date of birth is not on an intake form, it may not be possible to obtain his criminal history. If, as part of its information program, a project does not follow up clients placed in employment, it is impossible to know whether the employee was fired or quit on the day after placement.

The evaluation offered advice and consultation in the project design stages. In some cases this helped ensure that appropriate staff slots and budget lines were incorporated into proposals so that effective record keeping was possible. We offered advice on job description standards and salaries for budget lines having to do with records, research, and evaluation.

The post of records manager or statistical chief was strongly recommended for projects where it did not yet exist. The evaluation offered technical assistance to the holder of this position. Finally, where feasible, the evaluation helped the records manager directly with his local staff by providing in-service training.

Training

The technical assistance offered by the evaluation's MIS unit in implementing data retrieval and record keeping was largely in the form of on-site training for the senior local project records managers. These managers, in turn, were expected to train and supervise their staffs. The results of their training and of their administrative functions were measured by the degree of timely and accurate data received by the evaluation. Significant problems in data receipts would signal the need for intervention, usually in the form of extra training and advice. In certain instances, this assistance might have to take all staff or large portions of the local staff into the training function. These requests were considered conservatively. The evaluation was not staffed to respond to all requests for in-service training of local project staff.

The MIS unit implemented the standard intake form in 49 projects. During the evaluation 27,733 intake forms were received and processed from these projects.

PROCESSING PROJECT DATA

Checking the Intake Form

Inaccurate identifying information could severely impede the retrieval of criminal records, and incorrect project entry dates might invalidate findings on criminal activity after project entry. Because these index items were crucial to the basic purpose of the evaluation, special procedures were devised to ensure their accuracy.

Scrutinizing. Each intake form received from a project was carefully reviewed by the Central Data Control (CDC) unit. A procedure was used which came to be known as "scrutinizing" and which involved a sequence of specific steps, spelled out in a manual, "Procedures for Scrutiny of CJEP Intake Form." The CDC unit checked each form for legibility, completeness, and internal consistency. Examples of the latter are the consistency between a client's sex and given name,between age and date of birth (the form asked for both), and between a client's sex, age, residence, and so on and his project's requirements with respect to these characteristics.

Correcting Errors. Any intake form that was unclear, incomplete, or inconsistent was returned to the MIS unit for correction. The MIS unit contacted the projects by telephone or in person and attempted to correct the errors. If an intake form could not be corrected for key items, it was filed away and not used. If the corrections were made, the client was assigned a CJEP identification number (ID), * and some of his intake information was keypunched. The information on involvement with the criminal justice system was not punched because of sensitivity by some project personnel and clients and because the item was frequently misinterpreted; most of this information was to be obtained from police records in any case. The drug use information was not punched because of changes in the New York State drug laws, and drug use was therefore dropped as one of the basic variables in the study design. A total of 13,742 intake forms were punched. The balance were uncorrectable or not required for analysis.

The Roster. The computer used the keypunched information to generate a roster for each project listing each client alphabetically, and giving his name, ID number, date of birth, address, date of project entry, and "B" or "NYSIIS" number if available. The police use an identification number for the record of each person 16 years or older who is arrested for any offense for which fingerprinting is

---

*In this nine-digit number the first two identified the project, the next a component in that project, and the fourth the project's year of funding when the client was enrolled. The remaining five digits identified the client.

required; the number is issued the first time the person has such an arrest and is used for any subsequent "printable" arrests he incurs. This is known as the B number, the series that was used by the New York City Police Department, or the NYSIIS number, which is used by the New York State Intelligence and Identification System and is now used throughout New York State. The roster was used for retrieving criminal records, and also for the validation procedure which preceded the retrievals. (Initially validation was done for some clients after the retrieval was attempted.)

Validation. The evaluation became aware that intake information might be wrong even on forms that were "correct" according to scrutiny and on some that were corrected after scrutiny. The awareness grew while working with the projects to correct errors and also while conducting the scrutinizing process itself. A client's name, for example, might be perfectly legible and the given name consistent with the client's sex, but the name could still be incorrect. Certain basic items were interpreted differently by different projects. A project for ex-offenders, for example, recruited its clients while they were still in prison, and some who agreed to join the project but did not subsequently do so were still considered clients. Other projects also counted as clients individuals who applied but never received services because of failure to appear, ineligibility, or other reasons. The date of project entry was often interpreted as the date on which a client applied to a project rather than the date on which he began to receive project services. There was even a problem regarding what constituted a project, or a project "component," since several projects were found to conduct two or more distinct programs which could not legitimately be considered as one in the research design.

Discussions were held with the projects and with CJCC itself to decide how to deal with these problems. The results, together with the awareness that seemingly correct intake forms could be incorrect, led to a decision to undertake what came to be known as "validation." In validation, the MIS unit went to 27 projects, with the roster for each project, and checked the accuracy of each of the six index items (name, sex, date of birth, address, date of project entry, and admission status) for every client on the roster, using documents, records, or other sources of information available at the projects. Corrections were written directly on the roster. The result of the validation procedure was to reduce the number of individuals whose criminal records could not be found by the police, to improve the chances that the criminal records of the remaining clients would be found, and to increase the accuracy of classifying clients for analysis.

Additional Service to CJCC

Through its MIS unit, the evaluation provided a statistical service to CJCC that went beyond evaluation requirements but was important for CJCC administrative purposes. This was the management, collection, and presentation of a monthly summary report that reviewed the current and cumulative case activity of all client-based projects under CJCC funding. This monthly report (see CJEP Form MR-1, Rev. 12-20-73) was designed by the MIS group, which trained project staff in its use, monitored its application, and took responsibility for its timeliness and accuracy. A summary of all reports from the client-based projects was prepared each month for CJCC administration, primarily to signal impending difficulties among the projects in meeting case-load obligations per contract.

The monthly Project Case Activity Report accounted for each project's case load in any given month, beginning with the number of cases carried over from the previous month, adding new cases admitted during the month in question, and subtracting the number of cases terminated during that month to arrive at the net number of cases on the project roll at the end of the month. In addition, the form provided for cumulative admission figures for the current funding period. The information on the form was derived from each project's record-keeping system, which generally, but not always, included the use of the intake form. When the form was completed by a project it was sent to the monitor for that project at CJCC, and a copy was then sent to the evaluation, which made a limited check of the accuracy of the form on the basis of comparisons with intake form records. Since the information given by the project's own form was not subject to the type of scrutiny or validation checks which the evaluation gave to the intake forms used for criminological evaluation, it was probably subject to errors. Some of these errors involved counting as clients individuals who were not truly clients; to that extent, those figures are overstated.

The monthly reports and their summary represented two forms of program accountability. First, each program was committed to a target case load, and this figure was supposed to be included as part of the grant award. The evaluation instituted procedures in early 1971 to include these projected figures in statistical form at the time of grant application through the use of a summary of client characteristics form. In practice, few projects had clear-cut case-load target figures in their grant awards, and even fewer had properly filled out statistical projections at the time of application. The MIS team abstracted these target figures from grant awards and application projections where such figures existed. Where they did not, the MIS team forced a target projection through direct inquiry, either of the project administration or of CJCC monitors. In any event, all programs listed on these summary reports were not committed to a target case-load figure.

Realization of the targeted case-load figures was measured by the monthly reports. The summary of these reports indicated those projects which were likely not to achieve their stated case-load totals. These indications were listed in the monthly cover letter to these reports sent to the CJCC director. Both projected and actual case loads were thus easily observed and compared for all client-based projects using the monthly report system. Comparisons could be made among similar projects. Monthly project case activity reports were received from 48 projects.

COLLECTING DATA FROM THE POLICE

While planning the evaluation, one question was where to obtain the arrest information—from the New York City Police Department or from NYSIIS, which has been developing as the central, statewide source of criminal history information on individuals 16 or older, making extensive use of computer and telecommunications technology. NYSIIS would have been the ideal source of criminal history data, but it was not sufficiently perfected when the evaluation began. The records of the police department were therefore used. (One of the advantages of the NYSIIS records would have been that they show the disposition of arrests, whereas the police department records generally lack this information.)

Negotiations were undertaken between CJCC, as the parent body of the evaluation, and the police department. A formal agreement was signed giving the evaluation permission to use police department records, including taking copies to our premises, and specifying the conditions for such use. One of these conditions was that the evaluation maintain strict confidentiality about the criminal history of any individual, using this history only for statistical purposes. Another condition was that stringent security be observed, including the use of special locked files for the criminal records.

The agreement also stipulated that selected evaluation personnel would be permitted to work at the Bureau of Criminal Identification (BCI) after a check revealed that they did not have criminal records. Generally this involved one individual who was able to perform the retrieval tasks with greater attention to evaluation requirements than might otherwise have been possible. At the time of the latest retrievals, several experienced evaluation staff worked at BCI.

The Retrieval Procedure

The New York City Police Department stores criminal records in various places and under different systems, according to particular needs. The evaluation attempted to develop the simplest possible procedure for retrieving the criminal history data it required. A procedure evolved that was modified with experience. It was based in part on the fact that, in the form in which they are most conveniently available, juvenile records are stored under a different system, in a different place, and in a different format than nonjuvenile records. For criminal justice purposes, an individual is a juvenile in New York State from his seventh birthday until before his sixteenth birthday, and a nonjuvenile is someone 16 or older, although special treatment may be given before the age of 21 under certain circumstances.

Nonjuvenile Records (Yellow Sheets)

The nonjuvenile records used by the evaluation are located at BCI and are known as "yellow sheets" because they are reproduced onto yellow sheets of paper from a master copy of the arrest history of a given individual. The master copy lists every arrest an individual has had beginning with his sixteenth birthday for charges for which fingerprinting is required. * It is kept in a folder containing a variety of forms for the same individual, including fingerprint cards and forms giving details of the arrestee's criminal acts and physical characteristics. The master copy, and hence the yellow sheet, contains spaces for the following information about each arrest:

Date of arrest
Name given by arrestee, sometimes with address at time of arrest
Borough of arrest, or city and state if outside New York City
Arrest number, including precinct number of arrest
Arrest charge:
> Section number of law under which arrest is made, usually the New York State penal law
> Brief description of charge

Name of arresting officer and precinct number where assigned
Court disposition of arrest, including date, disposition, judge, and
> court (usually not filled out)

---

*The department keeps records of nonjuvenile arrests for charges that do not require fingerprinting at its Central Records Bureau.

The arrests listed, except for possible errors, include all those made in New York City. On some records, some arrests made outside the city but within New York State are also listed, as are an even smaller percentage of out-of-state arrests. The reasons are too involved to be dealt with here.

The information identifying the arrestee is noted at the top of the yellow sheet. The current version of the form contains the arrestee's name, alias or nickname, date of birth, sex, height, and address as of first fingerprintable New York City arrest. It also contains a code representing his fingerprint classification, since fingerprints are used as the basic identifying characteristic of the adult arrestee. Another item is the B or NYSIIS number, both of which are noted if the individual has both. This is very important, because the arrest folders are filed according to these numbers rather than by the arrestee's name.

Indexing. CJEP performed a step known as "indexing" because most projects did not have the B or NYSIIS numbers of clients. Indexing involved looking through a huge, multivolume, computer-generated register of every adult arrested for a fingerprintable offense in New York City since 1958. The register is alphabetical and, in addition to the arrestee's name, gives the date of birth, sex, address at first arrest, B number, NYSIIS number, and other information. Any name on the CJEP roster for which the project did not give a B or NYSIIS number was checked against the register.

Match Criteria. If the name and date of birth on the register were exactly the same as those on the roster, it was assumed that the same person was involved. If the names were the same but the birthdates differed slightly (no more than a year apart or a month apart), it was also assumed that the same person was involved. If the names or birthdates on the register were slightly different from those on the roster, the addresses might be checked, although the one on the register was as of the date of first arrest, and the one on the roster was as of project entry, and the individual might certainly have moved in the interim. If they were the same, however, this was considered supporting evidence that the same person was involved. For many individuals the decision as to the match between the register information and the roster information was merely an estimate, for which further verification was sought when the arrest records themselves were examined, sometimes resulting in disconfirmation. The problems of matching were serious and are discussed in various parts of this report.

If the decision was made that the person on the roster was the person on the register, the B or NYSIIS number from the register was copied onto the roster.

Obtaining the Yellow Sheets. The retrieval procedure for adult records began with taking two copies of a roster to BCI, one copy for use in the retrieval, the other to be kept by BCI. The group of clients on a roster was identified by a code number. The project name was deliberately omitted from the roster submitted to the police to protect client and project confidentiality. Indexing was done as needed, and a charge-out card was made for each client for whom a B or NYSIIS number had been found. Since evaluation personnel were not permitted to enter the files, a batch of charge-out cards was given to BCI staff, each card containing the B or NYSIIS number of a client, the date, and the name of the evaluation person who made the request. BCI staff pulled as many folders as they could find, leaving the charge-out cards in place of those pulled.

The first step after receiving a folder was to check that the folder belonged to the client. If so, the master copy of the client's cumulative arrest record was removed from the folder and placed in the duplicating machine to make the yellow sheet copy. If the copy was difficult to read, unclear entries were corrected from the master copy.

The master copy was returned to its folder, on which prescribed entries were made in accordance with BCI rules, and the folder was given to BCI staff for refiling. The yellow sheet was stamped with "Criminal Justice Evaluation Project" and with the date on which it was obtained. On the roster, the outcome of the retrieval for each client was marked near the client's name, and on each page of the roster a summary of retrieval outcomes was entered for all the clients on that page.

Records That Were Not Found. Criminal records were found for most clients, but not for all. Some were in use when retrieval was attempted and were thus out of file; these were usually obtained later. If they continued to be out of file they were reindexed to ascertain that their B or NYSIIS number was correct; if not, they were requested again with their correct identifications and were usually found. There remained 71 out-of-file cases that were not found during the retrieval procedure, and some of these may have been misfiled, missing, or lost.

Many clients could not be found in the register or in a supplemental register of recent arrestees. A second attempt was made to index these clients by evaluation staff, by BCI personnel, or by both. If a client was still not found in the register, other special files were checked by BCI or evaluation staff. If all these efforts proved fruitless the retrieval outcome was labeled "no record," but it was not assumed that this meant the client had never been arrested as an adult.

Some of the no-record clients actually did have sealed records. These were clients whose only arrests were for lesser charges involving possession of marijuana, for which the records were legally entitled to be sealed. Sealed records are kept in a special file accessible only through a court order, which is virtually impossible to obtain, and all evidence of their existence is removed from the index and other sources at the police department, as well as at NYSIIS and the FBI. If an individual with a sealable arrest has been previously arrested for other types of charges, all information on the sealable arrest is removed, but the remainder of the record is unchanged and available. The number of these sealed records is unknown.

There is another group of no-record clients for whom it is theoretically possible to have arrest records, but their number is also unknown. These are clients whose only arrests were for offenses for which fingerprints are not taken. The list of such offenses is changed by law from time to time and was considerably reduced in September 1971, when all misdemeanors were made "printable."

Most no-record cases were probably due to clerical errors. It became obvious, as the evaluation gained experience, how easily the identifying information on a client could be incorrectly transmitted from the client to the project records, to the intake form, to the scrutinizer, to those involved in correcting the intake form after scrutiny, to the keypuncher, and so on. Names were often misread or misspelled; given names were mistaken for surnames, a handwritten "o" was mistaken for an "a," a name might have several spellings (for example, Velasques, Velasquez, Velazquez) or might be so common that the police register listed several individuals with the same surname and given name. A client might have given the project a name different from the one he gave the police upon arrest. The person doing the indexing often had to work with incorrect information or with names that are very common.

Many no-record cases were impossible or suspect because they occurred in projects in which clients had to have an arrest as a condition of project entry, such as ASA Court Referral. Others almost certainly involved arrests, as in projects that were only for ex-offenders. There were so many improbable no-record cases that evaluation staff went directly to the project files to check the identifying information on clients against any sources in the files.

In one type of no-record case the person may actually never have been arrested prior to project entry. This group, to the extent that it existed, was mainly from community-based projects in which clients could enroll simply by walking in off the street. Possibly a few juveniles with only a PINS (Persons in Need of Supervision) record could be included in this category. The number or proportion of these "true" no-record clients among all clients for whom we had a no-record is unknown, but is estimated to be nonsignificant.

Validating the identifying information and the new information that was acquired enabled us to find records for many clients who had formerly been no-record cases. The results of these efforts provided the decisive evidence not only of the necessity to validate for all clients for whom retrievals were ready to be done, but to do the validation before attempting the retrieval, rather than after. The problems encountered in trying to find adult records were even more severe with juvenile records.

Juvenile Records

The juvenile records used by the evaluation were under the jurisdiction of the Youth Records Unit (YRU). There are two types of police department contact with juveniles, each represented by a different kind of record. One type results in arrest and is recorded on an arrest form; it covers essentially the same charges for which adults may be arrested under the penal law and other laws. The other does not result in arrest and is recorded on a form known as YD-1. The YD-1 contacts are usually for behavior such as truancy, running away from home, or being ungovernable by parents, which by definition can apply only to juveniles. The YD-1 contacts are also for certain penal law charges for which a nonjuvenile might be arrested, but the officer apprehending a juvenile for these charges has the discretion either to make an arrest or to file a YD-1. If he chooses the YD-1, the juvenile is released, there is follow-up contact with parents or guardians, but no further action is taken by the police except to record it and its follow-up on the YD-1 form. All YD-1 forms of a given individual are to be destroyed no later than the July 1 following his seventeenth birthday, according to a federal court order. * Unlike YD-1 forms, however, juvenile arrest records are not destroyed.

There may be contacts between juveniles and parts of the criminal justice system other than the police. These involve the Family Court and are initiated by parents, or by institutions such as the school a juvenile attends, when the juvenile's behavior becomes unmanageable. The only time the police become involved in these cases is when they arrest a juvenile on a warrant that is issued because he fails to appear in court as ordered by a judge. This type of arrest is recorded on an arrest form at YRU and was collected and recorded by the evaluation, but it was not counted as an arrest

---

*Known as the Cuevas decision, dated June 28, 1972.

because it did not seem to represent behavior that should be con-
oidorod oriminal. On tho othor hand, somo of tho bohavior reoordod
on YD-1 forms clearly did represent criminal behavior, particularly
the offenses covered by the penal law which the officer had the
discretion to treat as a YD-1 contact. The YD-1 data were collected
by the evaluation, initially in full detail but later only by date of
contact, and the decision was made not to treat YD-1 contacts the
same way as arrests. The decision was based partly on the fact
that much, if not most, YD-1 behavior is essentially "juvenile-
status" activity such as truancy and "ungovernable behavior," and
it does not lend itself to ready classification. Further, most YD-1's
do not represent criminal behavior. The entire undertaking of
collecting, classifying, and analyzing YD-1 activity would have been
infeasible. The CJEP findings on criminal behavior of juveniles
were thus based entirely on arrest records, and therefore understated
the full extent of juvenile criminal behavior to the degree that some
of this behavior was reflected in YD-1 records. (As has been pointed
out previously, the arrest records themselves understate the full
extent of criminal behavior.)

Obtaining the Juvenile Records. Evaluation personnel were not
permitted to work at YRU during most of the period when records
were retrieved. During the last few months of retrievals this policy
was changed somewhat so the evaluation could review certain records
in detail and conduct special studies that required the use of YRU
files. It was at this time that a good deal was learned about juvenile
arrest and YD-1 records. But the retrievals themselves were done
entirely by YRU staff.

    While the adult retrieval procedure consisted of running off a
copy of the yellow sheet containing the client's cumulative arrest
history, such a procedure was not possible with juvenile records
because the latter are not cumulative. Instead, each arrest is
recorded on its own form, as in each YD-1 contact. The forms are
filed alphabetically by name, the YD-1 forms together with the arrest
forms.

    The juvenile arrest forms have been revised from time to time,
and at least five separate versions have been encountered by evaluation
staff. Each version contains certain basic items of identifying information such as name, date of birth, and the date and charges of the
arrest, but many other items are on some versions but not on others,
and the location of each item varies from one version to another.
Obviously a method had to be devised for reducing all this diversity
to a relatively simple, cumulative format for recording the essential
information on all the arrests of any given client. We therefore
designed the "juvenile arrest summary," which itself was revised

several times in consultation with YRU staff as experience was gained
in its use. A comparable form was eventually designed for YD-1
contacts, although initially photocopies were made of the actual
YD-1 forms of each client.

The retrieval procedure began with CJEP delivering two copies
of a roster to YRU, one copy for the retrieval and the other for YRU
files. Also delivered was a supply of the forms designed by the
evaluation for recording the required arrest and YD-1 information
of each client. Our form was filled out for a client only if arrest or
YD-1 information about him was found in the YRU files. On the top
of the form the YRU person entered the client's name, date of birth,
and address; if any of these items was somewhat different on the
YRU record from the corresponding information on the roster, the
YRU version was entered on our form. The assumption was that
the police records are generally more accurate than the project's,
and at least we could check which of the two was correct.

Each YRU arrest form and YD-1 form is on a card or slip of
paper four by six inches in size and is filed alphabetically in a drawer
with several hundred similar forms. There are hundreds of such
drawers, and they are arranged in banks that are moved electrically.
A worker looking for a particular name presses the appropriate
button and the drawers for that part of the alphabet rotate in the bank
until they become accessible.

For each name on the roster the YRU worker searched the
appropriate drawer for any arrest or YD-1 forms that seemed in his
judgment to be those of the client. The principal criteria for
determining whether a form in the file belonged to the client on the
roster were similarities in name and date of birth, and sometimes
in address. These are the same criteria used when indexing adult
records, but there is an important difference. With adult records
there are only two determinations of whether the identifying
information in the police files matches that on the evaluation roster
for a given client: first, at the time of indexing, and second, when
the arrest folder is received for duplicating the master copy of the
cumulative arrest record. After this determination is made there is
little question that every arrest on the cumulative record belongs to
the same person (even though it is still possible that the person
might not be the project client). This is because the identification
of the adult arrestee is established to a great level of certainty by
means of fingerprinting, even if the arrestee gave the police different
names and dates of birth each time he was arrested. No fingerprinting
is allowed with juveniles, however, and their identification is therefore less certain than that of adults, which may be one reason why
the police department does not keep cumulative records for juveniles.
This means that the YRU worker must make the judgment, for every

arrest and YD-1 form he looks at, as to whether the identifying
information on the form matches that on the roster closely enough
for the same person to be involved. Many juveniles have numerous
arrest and YD-1 forms on file, often with discrepancies in names,
dates of birth, and other identifying information, in spite of police
efforts to verify such information at the time of each arrest and YD-1
contact. The problem of matching the information in the file with
that on the roster can therefore be very complex, and in many cases
the best that can be made is an educated guess, taking account of the
various kinds of information on the forms, such as mother's maiden
name, schools attended, the chronological sequence of addresses,
in addition to name, birthdate, and address. To ease this difficulty
YRU staff have made a practice of wrapping in a rubber band all
arrest and YD-1 forms that they judge to belong to a particular
juvenile whose records they have occasion to look up, even if some
of the identifying information differs from one form to another. An
example of the uncertainties of matching occurred when, in the course
of working with juvenile arrest histories after the retrieval had been
completed, one client's record with several arrests was judged by
evaluation staff, after very painstaking review, to be that of three
different people. As a result of this disquieting finding, evaluation
staff conducted a special "match check study," described shortly.

For each arrest form that the YRU worker judged to belong to
a particular client, he entered certain items of information on the
evaluation's arrest summary form. On the original version of the
form these items included the date of arrest; the arrest number,
precinct number, and borough of the arrest; and the arrest charge
expressed as a description of the offense and/or the section number
of the law under which the arrest was made (usually the penal law).
On a subsequent version of the form only the date and charges of the
arrest were entered. The final version of the form was the most
complete of all and required for each arrest not only the arrest items
as in the original version but also the client identifying information
as it appeared on the YRU arrest form for that arrest. The latter
items were age, birthdate, address, borough, last and first name,
mother's maiden name, and a "comments" column for any other
information that might assist in clarifying the identification. The
purpose of having all these items for each arrest was to enable
evaluation staff to judge more accurately whether an arrest was that
of the client, since the arrest summary had been completed by YRU
personnel.

After completing its search for records and filling out the
summary forms for arrests and for YD-1 contacts, the YRU staff
entered the result of the search on the roster next to the name of each
client. This was usually done by means of a stamp saying "Record

Retrieved" or "No Record Retrieved. " We were notified when a
retrieval was completed, and the roster and the retrieval records
were picked up. Subsequently, our personnel entered the retrieval
outcome for each client near his name on the roster according to our
procedures. This included whether or not an arrest record had been
retrieved and whether or not a YD-1 had been retrieved. A special
retrieval was made for juveniles who, even though they were under
16 at the time of project entry, would reach their sixteenth birthdays
during the period measured for arrest recidivism. For these clients
(in addition to retrieval of their juvenile records) a retrieval was
attempted at BCI for any arrests they may have had beginning at
age 16. For these retrievals, a separate roster was used, which
indicated the juvenile clients whose adult records were to be retrieved.
This procedure was exactly the same as was used for adult records
generally, except that the retrieval outcome, in addition to being
entered on the roster used for retrieving the adult record, was also
entered on to the regular roster which contained the outcome in
terms of retrieval of juvenile arrest and YD-1 records.

Arrest Record Sources by Age Group

The initial design of the evaluation took into account expected
differences in criminal behavior of four different age groups: 7 to 15
(juveniles), 16 to 18, 19 to 20, and 21 and older. The retrieval
procedures differed for most of these age groups.

7 to 15. For juveniles, as previously noted, retrievals were made at
YRU of arrests and YD-1 contacts. An additional retrieval was made
at BCI for juveniles who would reach their sixteenth birthdays during
the period after project entry (six or twelve months) for which a
retrieval was being made for an arrest recidivism analysis. This
procedure gave the entire criminal history of a juvenile.

16 to 18. The BCI does not have the arrest history prior to the
sixteenth year of age. For this reason, both the juvenile and adult
arrest histories were obtained for this group. One set of rosters
was submitted to YRU for arrest history during the years 7 to 15 and
another set to BCI for arrests in the years 16 to 18. At YRU no YD-1
information was requested for this group.
    In the earliest retrievals for this group, nonjuvenile records
were retrieved at the Central Records Bureau of the police department
rather than at BCI, because at that time both juvenile and nonjuvenile
records were kept at Central Records and it seemed more convenient
to retrieve the nonjuvenile arrests of the 16 to 18 group there than
at BCI. At Central Records the nonjuvenile records are filed in the

same way as juvenile records, that is, a separate record for each arrest rather than a cumulative record of all arrests for an individual.

To test whether this was indeed the better alternative, yellow sheets were also obtained for this group from BCI, and comparisons were made between the yellow sheets and the adult records obtained at Central Records. In some cases arrests were found at BCI that were not on the yellow sheets, and in some cases the reverse was found. For some arrests there were differences in detail for the same arrest. Eventually it was decided that only the yellow sheets would be used, because they are simpler to obtain and do not have some of the problems of matching and transcription as juvenile records, which were also part of working with Central Records files. The adult arrest data obtained from Central Records was used by the evaluation, but all subsequent retrievals of adult arrest histories for the 16 to 18 age group were made at BCI. The Central Records files, incidentally, include nonprintable arrests along with those for which fingerprints are taken, and any of the former that were retrieved were used, although they were not obtained for other 16- to 18-year-old clients for whom the yellow sheet from the BCI was the only source of nonjuvenile arrest history.

19 to 20 and 21 and older. Only the yellow sheets were retrieved for these age groups. Any arrests before age 16 are, therefore, not included as part of this evaluation.

An important result of the different retrieval procedures for each age group is that complete arrest histories are available for clients who were 7 through 18 years of age at the time of project entry, but only nonjuvenile histories are available for analysis for clients who were 19 or older. These considerations must be kept in mind when the findings of the evaluation are considered, particularly those having to do with criminal history prior to project entry. On the other hand, restricting comparison between clients to those within these age groups controls for this factor in pertinent analysis.

Six-Month and One-Year Retrievals

We attempted to have findings ready as early as was feasible. Since the projects were being evaluated in terms of client arrest rates after project entry, a minimum and uniform period after entry had to have passed for each client during which arrests could have taken place. Although the preferred time span was one year after project entry, we collected such data at six months after entry in an attempt to make findings available to CJCC as soon as we could.

Draft preliminary findings were submitted with the six-month data, but the final report contains only one-year findings.

New clients were continuously admitted to the projects, and retrievals were undertaken as soon as a large enough number of clients had accumulated. The criterion used was that at least 50 clients were necessary to do the final statistical analysis for any combination of client types by age, project component, or level of criminal severity. * Thus, for projects which had a large number of components and different ages of clients, we might, of course, need several hundred for whom at least six months after their admission date had elapsed and who were eligible for retrieval. When the evaluation became operational, several projects had been in existence for some time and had accumulated more than enough clients by the time our first retrieval was to be done.

As a matter of fact, seven projects supplied enough clients at the time of first retrieval that additional retrievals for those projects were judged unnecessary. The seven projects were ARC, BYCEP, Independence House, Manhood, Morrisania Legal Assistance, Second Chance, and Youth Counsel Bureau. One of the seven, Youth Counsel Bureau had so many clients with six months or more since project entry that a random sample was taken of the total number of clients available. More than 1,300 intake forms had been received from this project, of which we processed over 400. By means of a table of random numbers, a simple random sample of approximately 150 clients was selected as being sufficient for retrieval and analysis.

For the remaining 11 projects in which the initial retrieval resulted in low numbers, another retrieval was done as soon as a reasonable number of additional clients had passed six months since project entry.

The first wave of retrievals consisted of all clients who entered the project no later than July 31, 1972, and whose intake forms had been scrutinized and corrected. The decision had been made to exclude females from the analysis, so they were not included in the retrievals. A separate roster was generated by computer for each age group within each project, but the retrieval itself was not undertaken until March 1973, which allowed at least six months to have passed since the client's entry into the projects.

The first retrievals actually allowed an extra two months over the six months, so that there would be time for all arrests that took place during the six months to be entered onto police department records. By then, clients in some of the projects had entered more than a year earlier, and for these clients the initial retrieval

_____

*Reduced to 20 for the final analysis.

included arrest histories for more than the first year after project entry (as well as the first six months, of course).

For the one-year retrievals, rosters were made with all names that had been on the six-month retrieval rosters, except for some clients who were found to have died and some who, according to police records, were found to belong in an older or younger age group than the one they were in at the time of the six-month retrieval. As a general practice, we accepted the date of birth from the police record, particularly that of the yellow sheet, if it differed from that of the intake form. The greater accuracy attributed to police records was based on the finding that the police take pains to verify the identifying information of a client, using driver's licenses and other sources of information, whereas most projects did not engage in verification to this extent, if at all.

The same procedure was followed with the one-year retrieval, except that revised versions of the juvenile arrest summary and YD-1 summary forms were used. In general, the juvenile and adult records were retrieved as before, but some of the latter, particularly the last groups that were submitted for retrieval, were retrieved entirely by evaluation personnel. Previously, BCI staff pulled the folders from the files, but after BCI moved into a new building, our personnel were permitted to perform this function. These latest retrievals of adult records were done with thoroughness that would not have been possible before, because several evaluation staff persons performed the retrieval rather than only one person, and everyone by then had acquired considerable familiarity with the records from having processed and coded the six-month retrievals.

The one-year retrievals presented a different kind of problem than the six-month retrievals, because the former had to be matched with the latter. In the case of nonjuvenile records, a complete yellow sheet was run at the time of the one-year retrievals, and subsequently this was compared with the yellow sheet of the same client that had been retrieved for a six-month period. In addition to comparisons of the identifying information, each arrest was compared for date and charges. The entire system was developed to ensure that when the one-year records were coded and keypunched, these operations would not be repeated on arrests for which they had already been done in the six-month retrieval. A by-product of the one-year retrieval was that records were found for many clients for whom no records had been found previously. This supported the hypothesis that lack of a record (a "no record" stamp) did not necessarily mean that a client had not been arrested, but rather that some clerical error had probably taken place.

Matching the records retrieved at one year with those retrieved at six months was especially troublesome with juvenile records, since

YRU personnel copied by hand the arrest information from each card or slip in the file onto the evaluation summary form. A procedure was designed which would save YRU personnel the work of having to recopy arrests for the one-year retrieval that had already been copied for the six-month retrieval. The procedure deliberately included some duplication, partly as a check on the accuracy of the six-month retrieval, and involved an overlapping period of two years plus any new arrests occurring since the six-month retrieval. For juveniles for whom no record at all had been retrieved at six months, YRU was requested to copy any arrests that were found in the files, no matter how far back they occurred.

When the one-year juvenile retrievals were brought back to the evaluation office, they were compared with the six-month retrieval for each client for the period of overlap. This was a painstaking task, and many discrepancies were found involving dates or charges of arrests on the six-month retrieval that were not on the one-year retrieval, and vice versa. Permission was received for an evaluation staff member to check these discrepancies in the YRU files, and this was the first time our staff had ever been permitted in the files. The discrepancies were resolved, and many of them fell into certain patterns. Perhaps the most common explanation for discrepancies in dates was that the date on which a crime occurred had been entered instead of the date on which the arrest was made, and in many cases these two dates are different. This type of discrepancy could have serious consequences in the computation of project arrest rates, which use the date of arrest in determining whether or not a client was arrested after project entry. In fact, a separate study was done of this problem and of the impact of such discrepancies on arrests if the date of occurrence of a crime were used instead of the date of arrest. (This study is described on page 205.) Another consequence of this type of discrepancy, had it not been resolved, would have been to count a client as having more arrests than he actually had.

Another type of problem was that a particular arrest might have more or fewer charges on the one-year retrieval than on the six-months retrieval, or that an arrest might have been included on either of the retrievals for someone other than the client, despite similarity of name and other identifying information. All juvenile records were reviewed at least twice for discrepancies between the six-month and one-year retrievals during overlapping periods. A great deal of effort went into resolving these discrepancies, including examination of YRU files, consultations with YRU personnel, and discussions among all levels of our staff.

The Match Check Study for Juvenile Records

The match check is called a study even though the work did not begin as a study and most of it was not conducted as a study. It was essentially the checking or verification of matching undertaken to maximize the likelihood that each arrest ascribed to a juvenile was truly that of the client and not someone else. Considerable effort was expended on the match check, and a great deal was learned about the nature and difficulties of matching with juvenile records. Much of what was learned undoubtedly applies to the interpretation of juvenile arrest data elsewhere as well as in New York City and, to a lesser extent, to nonjuvenile records, also. All corrections made as result of the match check were incorporated into the evaluation data base.

Purpose and Background. The match check study originated while we were resolving discrepancies between many of the juvenile records retrieved 12 months after project entry with those retrieved for the same clients 6 months after entry. * In resolving these discrepancies we found two cases for which the discrepancy occurred because the arrest history contained arrest charges from persons other than the person represented by the arrest history. For one of these clients we concluded that all his arrests after project entry were those of another person; if we had counted them, the arrest rate for the client's project would have been slightly overstated (but not at a statistically significant level). The other client had one mismatch arrest but, although it occurred during the year after project entry, it would not have affected the one-year arrest recidivism rate because the client had another arrest during this period.

These cases caused concern that "overcounts" (that is, counting the arrests of more than one person as belonging to the one person) might be sufficiently widespread among juvenile clients to result in inflated arrest rates. In addition, we felt that further search might yield arrest or YD-1 records for some clients for whom no record at all had been found before. Finally we decided to search for arrest records for clients for whom only YD-1 records had been found by the YRU. We therefore decided to check the records of several hundred juvenile clients to determine whether the identifying information on

---

*The 6- and 12-month retrievals for all records are designated, respectively, as F1 and F2.

each arrest record correctly matched that of the project intake
form.

The match check study unfolded in three stages. The first took
place after the problem was discovered, when the F1-F2 discrepancies
were being resolved. Nearly 50 cases were selected for match
checking, most because they were thought the likeliest to have match
problems (for example, clients with numerous arrests or common
names). The result was that a few cases were found in which arrests
for more than one person had been counted for one person (also, a
few arrests had not been counted that should have been counted for
particular clients, and a record was found for a client for whom
none had been found before).

The second stage arose because of the stage-one findings and
the F1-F2 discrepancies, all of which led to concern about the
accuracy of findings for juvenile projects in a forthcoming report.
It was decided that there would be time for only one out of four such
projects to be included in the report, but that the retrieval for that
one project (Neighborhood Youth Diversion, NYD) would be entirely
redone by evaluation staff, using a special procedure designed to
minimize match problems. The result was a retrieval that was
believed to have been done with sufficient accuracy to allow inclusion
of the project in that report.

The third phase was done with the other three juvenile projects
and was focused on three kinds of cases: those with the greatest
likelihood of two or more persons being counted as the same person
(for which clients with three or more arrests on their F1 and F2
records were used); those for whom no record had been found in the
F1 and F2 retrievals; and those for whom only YD-1 forms had been
found in the F1 and F2 retrievals. The same procedure was used as
in stage two, with an improved version of the form. The principal
result of stage three was the finding of records for clients for whom
none had been found before.

Criteria for Determining a Match. Criteria for matching nonjuvenile
names and records had been satisfactorily worked out as described
elsewhere. This experience, in addition to what was learned in the
exploratory first stage of the match check study, led to the establishment of special criteria for the study. The following items were
recorded for each juvenile arrest that could be considered a possible
match:*

---

*Some items were not always available, for example, mother's
maiden name.

Name (last, first)   Arrest charges
Address, borough   Arrest number
Date of birth   Precinct number of arrest
Age   Mother's maiden name
Date of arrest   Comments

The sources for this information were the YD-1 and other arrest
cards. At the top of the form we entered the client's name, address,
date of birth, and so on as those items appeared on the roster prepared
from information obtained by the projects. The juxtaposition facilitated
a judgment by our staff or that of the YRU concerning the correctness
of the match in a way that had not been possible with the forms used
previously.

Procedure. Until the match check study, the determination of a
match for a juvenile record had been made exclusively by YRU
personnel, who also did the actual retrieval. Special permission was
obtained for evaluation staff to work directly in the files of the YRU;
one during stage one, three during stage two.

In retrieving the records of a client, the file drawer containing
the records for that name was placed on a table and the client's name
was searched for, with another CJEP staff member observing. Sometimes the client's records could be found easily, but at other times it
was necessary to look through dozens of records to find those which
might belong to him. After records were found that were judged to
be those of the client, the file was reviewed by a second staff person.
Then, taking each record in turn, one person read the available
information to the other, who copied it on the special arrest summary
form. This was checked by having the second person read from the
file record while the first checked that the correct entries had been
made on the arrest summary form. After a form was completed, the
information on it was reviewed by both. The form was reviewed again
by the third person, who in some instances checked further in the
files, sometimes finding records that had not been found before.
Problems were discussed among the three staff members and, if
necessary, with YRU personnel until they were resolved. If any
problems remained, all information was written on the arrest
summary form and the problems were discussed by senior evaluation
staff until the issues were finally cleared. Subsequently, the new
information on the special arrest summary form for each client was
compared with that of a computer printout of the same information
that had previously been entered into the computer memory from the
F1 and F2 retrievals, and any discrepancies were resolved.

The same procedure, together with the improved version of
the form, was used in stage three with clients from three projects:

Alternatives to Detention—Probation (ATD-PROB); Alternatives to Detention—Human Resources Administration (ATD-HRA); and Protestant Board of Guardians (PBG).

The match check was done on 350 juvenile records in the "A" groups* of four projects, after the F2 retrieval was completed. For NYD it was done on every case submitted for retrieval. For ATD-HRA, ATD-PROB, and PBG, we decided not to use all cases but, as previously noted, only those we believed were most likely to have matching problems. These included clients with three or more arrests from their first arrest through one year after project entry. Also included were clients for whom no record had been found on the F1 and F2 retrievals, and clients for whom the only type of record found was the YD-1.

Among the 350 cases checked, 233 were cases for which we were looking for overcounts (records in which more than one person had been counted as the same person), 48 were "YD-1 only" cases for which we tried to find arrest records, and 69 were no-record cases, for which we sought arrest or YD-1 records.

Results. The match check study investigated two types of problem cases. The results could potentially have affected at least three of the evaluation's measures.

The first type of problem cases included:

1. Arrests for more than one individual on a single individual's arrest record, resulting in overcount of arrests;
2. Valid arrests not recorded on an individual's arrest record, resulting in undercount of arrests;
3. A showing of YD-1 contacts only, when arrests should also have been recorded, resulting in undercount of arrests.

Three of the measures that could have been affected were arrest recidivism rates; number of arrests after project entry for a given client, and seriousness score of arrest history prior to project entry of a given client.

A second type of problem cases showed up as "no-record" cases. It included two possibilities: persons who really had not been arrested, and arrested persons whose records could not be found.

The match check was done only for clients in the "A" groups.

_____

*"A" groups were the first group from any project for which a police records retrieval was done. "B" groups, retrieved second, were groups of entirely different individuals.

<u>More Than One Person on One Record</u>. An overcount occurs when
two or more individuals with arrests are counted as one project
client. Both the number and the seriousness of the client's arrests
will be overstated; the project's arrest rate will be affected if there
are enough such cases during the year after project entry.

The three cases of overcount were all at ATD-PROB and would
have resulted in a 1 percent overstatement of the project's arrest
rate, which is not statistically significant. There would also have been
an overstatement of the number of arrests for the project, but again
not significant. The possible effect of this error rate for the unchecked
population of the project was estimated to be not significant.

For all four projects, the three cases were less than 1 percent
of the 233 persons checked in the "A" groups. Thus, even if the
overcount cases had not been discovered and removed from the data
base, they could not have overstated the arrest recidivism rates
significantly. This also suggests that if the "B" groups had been
match checked, the results would have been similar to those of the
"A" groups.

<u>Arrests Not Recorded</u>. Arrests not recorded would have caused us
to undercount arrests. A search for the same name, similar names,
given names that could be mistaken for a surname, nicknames, and
so on could easily entail reviewing hundreds of records for each
case, or even checking the entire file for misfiled cards. Obviously,
such a search would not be feasible for each name. A reasonable
effort was made, however, by checking a small number of cases
intensively. NYD was the project for which possible undercount
findings were analyzed systematically.

Among 123 "A" group cases in NYD, a total of six undercount
cases was found (not including the no-record or "YD-1 only" clients
for whom arrests were found by the match check). All six had
undercounts for the period before project entry; for four of these the
check found one more arrest than had been found previously; for each
of the other two cases, two more were found. One of the six cases
also had an undercount after project entry—by one arrest.

For the other 117 clients—95 percent of the total—there were no
undercounts. Had they not been corrected in the match check, the
undercount of these 5 percent of clients in NYD would have understated
the number of arrests, and the seriousness scores, but probably not
at a significant level. The arrest recidivism rate would not have
been affected at all. These findings indicated it was not necessary
to continue checking for the other three projects and the "B" groups.

<u>YD-1 Only</u>. Checks were done for every case for which the YD-1 was
the only type of record found in the F1 or F2 retrieval. The total of

48 "YD-1 only" cases was checked in the four projects to determine whether any of the clients involved had been arrested. The effect of such arrests, provided they occurred before the end of one year after project entry and were "countable" (for example, excluding warrants), could only increase the number of arrests after project entry of a client, his seriousness score, and perhaps the project's arrest recidivism rate.

Ten of the 48 "YD-1 only" cases were found to have had arrests. An analysis was made of the 6 in NYD. Of these, one was found to have been arrested both before project entry and during the year after entry. When added to the 66 recidivists among the 112 clients in the NYD "A" group analysis, this case would not cause any change in the project's 60 percent arrest recidivism rate. Although the client would show arrests and seriousness scores where none had been shown before, when averaged in with the other project clients, he would probably have little or no effect on the mean number of arrests or the mean seriousness scores for the project.

As for the other nine cases for which arrests were found, it seems likely that, had they not been found, the arrest recidivism rates of the "A" groups of the other three projects would be slightly but not significantly understated, and there would be virtually no effect on the mean number of arrests and mean seriousness scores per project. There seems to be no reason why the "B" groups would be affected differently.

"No Record". There were 69 juvenile clients, from the "A" groups, for whom no record of any arrest or YD-1 contact had been found in the regular retrieval. As with the "YD-1 only" cases, every one of the no-record cases was match checked to find arrest records or YD-1 records. Records were found in the match check for 16 of the 69 clients. A few of the records found were for arrests or YD-1 contacts that had not occurred until after the F2 retrieval had been completed, but most were for earlier arrests or YD-1 contacts.

It is possible for a client not to have a record if he never had an arrest or YD-1 contact (the "true" no-record) or if he did have arrests or YD-1 contacts but their records could not be found (the "false" no-record). The 16 for whom records were found in the match check were obviously "false" cases, and they composed approximately one-fourth of the no-record cases. The other 53 cannot all be "true" cases because such cases generally can only stem from two of the projects, NYD and PBG, which had only 33 no-record cases between them. To qualify for the other two projects, Alternatives to Detention—HRA and Alternatives to Detention—PROB, almost all applicants were required to have been arrested because

of the nature of the projects; it is therefore extremely unlikely that
any of the "true" no-record cases were in these projects.

In NYD, records were found for five cases that had formerly
been no-record, and one of these cases had an arrest during the year
after project entry. If these cases had been excluded from the 112
"A" group cases for whom the arrest recidivism rate was computed,
the rate would have been 61 percent. It was 60 percent with these
cases included, a nonsignificant difference.

It would seem that the addition of the no-record cases for whom
records were found in the match check would have a minimal effect,
if any, on the arrest recidivism rates of the other three projects,
and that a similar effect would be likely with the "B" group as well.

These cases would, however, change the number of arrests
and seriousness scores for the clients involved, for which both
figures would otherwise have been zero, but there would probably
be little or no effect on the project as a whole when these individual
clients were averaged in with the others. While the addition of "false"
no-record clients probably does not affect the arrest recidivism
rates, the omission of the "true" no-record clients causes the rates
to be somewhat overstated, but not to a very great degree.

Interactions. The various types of errors, when corrected, can affect
the arrest recidivism rates in various ways, in some cases increasing
these rates and in some cases decreasing them. Their interaction
may to some extent be one of mutual cancellation. Their overall
effect seems likely to be minimal, although probably in the direction
of a net understatement. It should be remembered that all corrections
made as a result of the match check were incorporated into the
data base.

Summary of Retrieval Outcomes

In the first wave of retrievals no records were found for
approximately 20 to 25 percent of the clients in some projects, such
as Manhood, for whom retrievals had been attempted. These proportions seemed high, and efforts were made both to lower and to
explain them.

To reduce the number of no-record cases, the MIS unit stepped
up its program of training project staffs in filling out the intake form,
particularly the index items that were essential for retrieval purposes.
Another means was to resubmit all no-record cases to the police
department.

A small study was undertaken comparing retrieval outcomes
for the same clients in the 16 to 18 age group whose records were

TABLE A. 1

Arrest Record Retrieval Outcomes
for the 18 Projects

Age Group	Total Clients submitted for retrieval	Arrest records not retrieved				Arrest records retrieved	Per cent retrieved
		Sealed	No record	File out	Total		
7–15	991	0	186	0	186	805	81
16–18	756	4	49	27	80	676	89
19–71	2183	1	225	44	270	1913	88
Total	3930	5	460	71	536	3394	86

Source: Compiled by the evaluation project.

retrieved both from the Central Records Bureau and from the BCI, but the results were inconclusive.

A fair number of records were retrieved at the time of the one-year retrieval for clients for whom no records had been retrieved at the six-month retrieval.

The net result of our various efforts was that by the time the final analysis was to be done, the overall retrieval rate was 86 percent.

The final retrieval outcomes by age groups are presented in Table A. 1.

PROCESSING POLICE DATA

Processing of the retrieved police data started with the coding of the arrests.

Coding Arrest Histories

Although the primary purpose in coding is to permit electronic data processing, a second purpose was to facilitate analyses by type of offense. We were interested not only in whether an offense had been committed after project entry, but also in what kind of offense it was.

Preliminary Exploration. Prior to establishing a definitive coding
system and procedure, it was necessary to examine a sample of
criminal records, both adult and juvenile, to determine how offenses
were recorded. In carrying out this preliminary exploration, we
learned a great deal about the complexity of the laws under which
individuals may be arrested or have CJS contacts that are noted on
the police records used by CJEP. The problem was already complex
because of the variety of laws and charges in New York City and in
New York State, but some arrests had taken place outside New York
State, including a small number in foreign countries. Throughout the
period of approximately one year during which coding was done, new
information was continually obtained which had to be incorporated
into the system.

    The principal law under which clients were arrested was the
New York State penal law, one version of which was enacted in 1909,
a later version in 1965. Most arrests of project clients came under
the 1965 version, which is referred to as the "new penal law," or
NPL (the 1909 version is referred to as the "old penal law," or
OPL). There are other New York State laws under which client
arrests took place, such as the vehicle and traffic law (VTL), the
public health law (PHL), the alcoholic beverage control law (ABC),
and the agriculture and markets law (AM). Other arrests took place
under the New York City administrative code (AC), and federal arrests
took place under the U. S. criminal code (USCC) and under military
laws. Each law has its own numbering system under which each
section number of the law pertains to a different type of offense. The
correspondence between section number and type of offense led to the
basic device—the use of the section numbers—for determining what
each of our codes should be. The general practice in our coding was
to use the exact section number of the law, preceded by a digit
representing whichever type of law was involved in the arrest charge.
The code numbers each had a total of six digits, and modifications had
to be made in the basic system if the section numbers for a particular
law did not fit the six-digit format.

    Many arrests contained more than one charge, and sometimes
the charges came under more than one law. The procedure consisted
of coding each charge in an arrest regardless of how many charges
there were.

Mechanics of Coding. The details of the coding procedure, including
the mechanics, are specified in the evaluation coding manual. In
general, the procedure consisted of placing a red dot to the left of
the date of each arrest and a red dot to the left of the code number of
each charge in an arrest (to facilitate punching). If the arrest was
made under a law other than the 1965 revision of the New York State

penal law, the coder wrote, in addition to the number of the other
law, the digit representing the particular law under which the arrest
took place. If the charge had to be modified because it did not fit the
six-digit format, the coder crossed out the code on the record and
entered the modified code. If the charge was given as a description
without a section number, the coder entered the code appropriate to
that offense. The coder checked that the red dot had been entered
next to each charge and each date of arrest. If an arrest had more
than one charge, the various charges were bracketed to indicate that
they were all part of the same arrest. Each arrest was given a number
beginning with 21, continuing in the order in which the arrests were
listed on the record until all the arrests were numbered.

    Although the general practice was to code every entry on the
arrest sheet and to program the computer to determine exactly whether
and how that entry would be used, there were a small number of
charges that coders were instructed to cross out. Examples of these
were entries stating that an individual was paroled, or that he was
wanted by the police, or that he had simply registered with the police
in a community which required such registration by ex-offenders.
These entries do not represent arrests.

    Another check was made for arrests that took place outside
New York State. Because of tremendous variation in arrest practices
and possible differences of interpretation of the meanings of various
charges throughout the country, it was felt that the meaning of a
given charge in an arrest outside New York State was uncertain in
comparison to the meaning of the same charge in New York State.
Many of the out-of-state charges were also for offenses that had no
apparent New York State counterpart and would have required considerable research and wide knowledge of the law to classify properly.
For these reasons, all out-of-state arrests were given the same
code number—800,000. On the other hand, arrests that took place
within New York State, but outside New York City, were considered
to be comparable with those within New York City but were
distinguished by having 7 as either the first or second digit of their
code, depending upon the law involved.

    The records were also checked to be sure that no arrest was
coded more than once. On the yellow sheets this check for duplication
consisted of examining not only the dates and the charges for each
arrest, but also the police department arrest number; the arrest
number was checked because it is possible for more than one arrest
to take place on the same day, and for each arrest to have the same
charges. With clients for whom both juvenile records and yellow
sheets were obtained, each type of record was checked to be sure
that it did not contain an arrest that was listed on the other. With
juvenile records, considerably more attention was given to checking

for duplications than was done with adult arrests. This was especially the case when the six-month and one-year retrievals were compared for overlapping periods.

Attempted Crimes and Auto Thefts. There were special problems in coding attempted crimes and auto theft, both of which occurred frequently on the records. Attempted crimes are indicated under the new penal law by 110, followed by the code number of the type of offense involved. With one exception, the police department disregards the fact that a crime was attempted when it transmits statistics on types of crimes to the FBI, and an attempted crime is thus treated as a crime that was actually executed. We also followed this practice, and coders were instructed to cross out the number 110 whenever it appeared. The one exception was attempted murder, which the police count as aggravated assault. It was therefore given a special code devised to retain the identity of the offense as attempted murder, but it was classified as aggravated assault.

Although it is a common offense, there is no section of the penal law for auto theft as such. Instead, arrests for auto theft offenses are recorded with the section numbers for grand larceny or petit larceny, along with many other types of offenses that fall under these categories. Because auto theft is an important offense in its own right and is on the FBI's list of index crimes (the seven crimes considered to be the most serious), a way was sought to determine which arrests were for auto theft and to recode them accordingly. Fortunately, most arrests are listed with a brief description of the offense along with the section number of the law that pertains to a particular charge. The brief descriptions often noted that auto theft was involved (for example, grand larceny—auto, or GLA). A pattern of particular charges in a multiple-charge arrest also suggested auto theft. For example, there might be a larceny charge without indication of auto theft, plus a charge such as unauthorized use of vehicle. This was interpreted as auto theft and given the special code for it, as were similar patterns of charges and arrests where the description suggested auto theft.

It is likely that some larceny arrests that were for auto theft were recorded in ways that made it impossible for coders to determine that auto theft was involved. This means that some arrests coded as larceny were really for auto theft. To the extent that this occurred, our findings on larceny arrests are overstated and those for auto theft arrests are understated.

Preparation of Arrest Records for Coding. Before coding was begun, certain steps were taken to ensure that each record was properly identified. The client's identification number was noted on each page, and the arrest record was stamped to indicate whether it was a six-month or one-year retrieval. Since many records consisted of two or more pages, particularly those of older clients (some with several dozen arrests), each page was numbered with the page number itself and the total number of pages in the record. If a one-year retrieval contained no additional arrests since the six-month retrieval for a client, the arrest record for each retrieval was marked to indicate that it was the same as the other, thus avoiding additional and unnecessary keypunching. Where six-month and one-year retrievals were different, an indication to that effect was marked on each record so that it was readily apparent that additional keypunching needed to be done. The one-year retrieval was also marked so that the arrests already keypunched from the six-month retrieval were easily distinguished from all additional arrests, the latter being the only ones that required further keypunching (the six-month retrievals had been keypunched before the one-year retrievals had been done).

An idea of the complexity of some of these preparations can be obtained by considering that with juvenile clients the records included the arrest summary, the YD-1 summary (or copies of the YD-1 forms themselves), and yellow sheets for those clients who had reached their sixteenth birthdays at the time of retrieval and been arrested; any or all of these records might have been obtained in the six-month as well as in the one-year retrieval. Similarly for clients who were 16 to 18 at the time of project entry, any juvenile arrest summary or yellow sheets, for the six-month or one-year retrievals, had to be assembled and properly marked. For clients in this age group whose records were among the earliest to be retrieved, the fact that the adult records of these clients for the six-month retrieval were on handwritten summary forms rather than on yellow sheets complicated matters even further.

Considerable thought and effort went into developing the procedures used in preparing records for coding, building into these procedures a system of thorough checking. Staff were trained and supervised in the procedure that had been agreed upon. Every step was checked by whatever system was considered most effective for that particular step, primarily double checking.

Materials Used. Each coder was equipped with the coding manual and a copy of a booklet, Crime Code Number System, of the New York City Police Department. This booklet contains information on all offense categories used by the police department. It includes the description of the charge; the section number of the 1965 version of the New York State penal law that pertains to the charge; the classification of the charge into felony, misdemeanor, or violation; and the police department's own code number (known as PD number) for that charge. The PD numbers are especially important even though we did not use them, because they are the basis on which the police department converts each of the hundreds of different PL charges into the 26 offense categories of the FBI's Uniform Crime Reporting (UCR) system. This, however, was not the concern of the coder, who used the booklet only to establish the section number of the penal law or other law under which an arrest was made, and the description of the charge.

One step in the coding consisted of verifying that the section number of the law was appropriate to the description of the offense, since the usual practice is to record both, and sometimes a section number is not appropriate to the yellow sheet description given for it. In these cases the section number was changed to agree with the yellow sheet description. This practice was followed on the advice of the police department. The booklet was also used for arrests that had descriptions only, without section numbers. The booklet listed the charges, both alphabetically by description and in numerical order of the penal law and various other laws.

Certain other materials were used in the development of the coding system and as reference works during the coding itself. These included the penal law itself, in an edition covering changes that were enacted in the 1973 session of the state legislature. [1] Some of the changes involved new section numbers, especially for drug offenses, that were not in the booklet. Other reference works were the old penal law in a two-volume edition of a comparatively recent revision, [2] the Family Court act pertaining to juveniles, the vehicle and traffic law, the criminal procedures law, and other documents.

In addition, special information relative to coding was obtained in discussions with police department personnel and CJCC attorneys, and by library research.

Another resource was sometimes used for arrest records with such problems as a missing date of arrest or missing charges. For these problems, the client's arrest folder itself was reviewed, since some of the detailed records it contained clarified these problems. These records were also used in a few cases of conflicting dates of birth. For similar problems on juvenile records, the YRU staff, on behalf of CJEP, contacted another section of the police department where detailed records were kept, and the problem was usually resolved in that way.

Uncertain Arrest Charges. Many charges were found while coding which did not seem to resemble the arrests covered by the penal law. At the time of coding, it could not be decided exactly how these charges would be treated in the analysis. A special category of codes was created for these charges, with 99 as the first two digits.

The principal type of charge in the 99 series was found on juvenile records and was for warrants. Usually these were designated by descriptions with the sections of the law, although sometimes a section number was given, or sometimes a notation such as "Family Court warrant." These warrants are issued because the juvenile does not appear in Family Court on a date specified by a judge and is subsequently arrested through a warrant to ensure appearance. As previously noted, this did not seem to fit the concept of criminal behavior in which the evaluation was interested and, consequently, the decision was made not to count these warrants as arrests.

Similarly, 99 codes were given for offenses such as absconding from a training school or for violations of parole or probation. These types of charges were for offenses committed while the individual was still under sentence for prior arrest, so they, too, were not counted as arrests.

A few 99 codes were counted as arrests if it was known that their charges were for the types of offenses usually covered by the penal law. One such charge was for a sealed arrest on a record on which other arrests were not sealed and where there seemed to be reasonable evidence that the sealing had taken place. A similar charge occurred when the record indicated that youthful offender treatment had been given to an individual but the charge was not on the record. Youthful offender treatment is given under certain circumstances to individuals between 16 and 18 years of age and involves a less severe sentence than would ordinarily be given for the type of offense committed. Thus, the sealed arrests and youthful offender arrests were considered as regular arrests, despite the 99 codes. They were counted in the computation of arrest rates and in the analyses involving seriousness of offenses, using estimated scores for the latter. They were not counted, however, in analyses by type of offense, because the arrest record gave no indication of the specific offense for which the arrest had been made.

YD-1 contacts were not coded as arrest charges.

Table XII of the coding manual lists all arrests in the 99 series. Subsequent to the decision to code these as 99, other decisions were made as to whether or not each of these items should be considered as an arrest and, if so, how it should be classified in terms of type of offense and seriousness score.

Arrests After One Year. The basic evaluation design called for the study of arrests during the first year after the client entered the project. For many clients the records were retrieved some time after the first year had expired. All information was retrieved that was on the record as of the date of retrieval, and all such information was coded. Although some of this arrest history extended until 18 to

24 or more months after project entry, the analysis was confined
to arrests during the first 12 months after entry, and the subsequent
arrests that were coded and punched were not included in the one-
year analysis.

Checking for Accuracy. Every step in coding was checked by a person
other than the initial coder. The person who checked generally had
more experience with coding than the first coder of an arrest record,
and was also particularly sensitive to such special problems as auto
theft arrests, out-of-state arrests, charges that required codes
other than the section numbers of a particular law, and descriptions
without section numbers. The records were completely checked to
see that red dots were appropriately placed and that each arrest was
properly numbered. Instructions were given and stressed that any
problems should be discussed with supervisory staff, who reviewed
samples of the arrest records after they had been checked.

Special care was given the one-year retrieval against the six-
month retrieval for each client. Even in preparing these forms for
coding, a rigorous procedure was used in which coders worked in
pairs. One would read the ID number and other identification
information while the other would write these items down; immediately
after, the first would read the same information from the original
source and the second would check that it had been correctly entered.
In comparing the six-month and one-year yellow sheets, a coder
would align them and check for similarities and differences; then the
second coder would repeat the procedure.

A number of special codes, or codes that were ambiguous,
were reviewed again by having the computer print out the identification
of each client who had such a code. All murder codes were reviewed
to be sure they did not really represent attempted murder, and in the
checking a number of instances of the latter, plus a few other errors,
were found and corrected.

Special cases with sealed records, youthful offender arrests,
a group called unclassifiable, and a few other codes were all checked.
In many cases the checking involved reviewing the detailed information
of the arrest files at the police department. It sometimes happened
that while reviewing the records which contained these codes, other
corrections were made, such as the discovery of a larceny arrest
which in fact represented auto theft.

Keypunching. After the records were coded they were submitted for
keypunching. The coding procedure, apart from the determination of
the codes for each charge, had been developed in conjunction with the
Central Data Control Unit and in particular with the keypunching staff
of that unit. Apart from the identification information for each client,

a separate card was punched for each arrest, giving its date and the code of each of its charges. Each card was punched twice. The second punching was for machine verification of all first cards, and any discrepancies were resolved. Subsequently, every corrected punch card was checked manually by comparing it with the actual criminal record form from which it had been punched. The machine verification and the manual verification were each done on a 100 percent basis for the arrest-charge coding. This was done for the arrest records of 3,742 clients.

In resolving discrepancies between the six-month and one-year retrievals, particularly with juveniles, corrections were promptly submitted for keypunching under special procedures developed between the Criminology Unit and the Central Data Control Unit. In a subsequent operation, all of the keypunching information on the criminal record was transferred to a magnetic tape. The taping itself was checked by generating computer printouts of some of the taped information and checking these printouts against the original sources.

Date of Occurrence versus Date of Arrest—A Study

The evaluation was concerned with criminal behavior after project entry and used the arrest as the measure of such behavior. One of the limitations of this measure is that some arrests are not made until some time after the crime is committed. For example, a victim may make a complaint to the police about being robbed, and the alleged perpetrator of this crime might not be apprehended for weeks or months. Although most arrests take place on the same day as the crimes for which they are made, the lag between date of occurrence and date of arrest is common enough that it could conceivably have affected evaluation arrest rates.

Arrests which took place during the year after project entry could have been for crimes committed before project entry. If we counted the arrest date as the date of occurrence, the arrest recidivism rate would overstate the criminal behavior for the project involved. At the other extreme, arrests that took place more than a year after project entry could have been for crimes committed during the year after entry. If we counted these arrests as though they were occurrences, the project's arrest recidivism rate would understate the criminal behavior.

We conducted an exploratory study to obtain some idea of the effect on arrest rates of this lag. Two groups of clients were selected. Each was to test one of the ways in which the arrest rates might be affected. The first group was believed most likely to have had arrests after project entry for crimes committed before project entry. In an attempt to isolate those most likely to affect the arrest rate, a client was selected for this group if he had only one arrest during the year after project entry and if that arrest took place during the first three months after entry. The second group was selected to emphasize clients who might counterbalance the first group. It consisted of all clients who had no arrests during the year after project entry, but had one or more arrests during the subsequent three months.

A computer printout for each group was generated. Police files were examined which contained the date of occurrence and a description of the complaint for which an arrest was made. This information does not appear on the yellow sheets or on juvenile arrest summaries. For adult clients it was necessary to look through the arrest folder at forms containing detailed information on each arrest. For juvenile clients, the date of occurrence appeared on certain versions of the YRU arrest form but not on others. When the date of occurrence could not be found at the YRU, it was necessary to go to the Central Records Unit and to examine microfilm files, for which special permission was required.

Results. The first group consisted of 238 clients; dates of occurrence were found for 229. The second group consisted of 136 clients, dates of occurrence were found for 131. In the first group, of the 229, nine clients had committed crimes before project entry but were not arrested for these crimes until the first three months after project entry. These clients were in six projects.

In the second group, of the 131, five clients allegedly committed crimes during the year after project entry but were not arrested for these crimes until the thirteenth, fourteenth, or fifteenth month after entry. These clients were in three projects.

If arrest rates were based on the date of occurrence instead of the date of arrest, the effect of the nine clients in the first group would be to reduce the arrest rates. The effect of the five clients in the second group would be to increase the arrest rates in their projects. There was some cancellation effect in two projects, each of which had two clients in each sample, and the net effect was no change.

The net effect on the arrest rates of the seven projects in which the cases in both groups occurred was not significant.

The results of the study are not considered definitive since it was merely exploratory. The groups were deliberately selected to maximize the chances of affecting the arrest recidivism rates. The study was intended to provide relatively prompt feedback; whether it should be done in greater depth was to depend upon its findings. Since the findings showed only a very slight and nonsignificant effect, even though the clients were selected to maximize the effect, it was decided that the results of a more definitive study would not be different and that the effort was unwarranted.

Classification of Offenses

The evaluation was concerned not only with whether a client was arrested after project entry, but also with the type of offense for which he was arrested. Approximately 400 separate charges were coded from client criminal records. These offenses ranged from murder to loitering and begging. Whether a client's arrests after project entry were for serious or minor charges was important, because the evaluation was to determine whether the pattern of criminal behavior prior to project entry is predictive of such behavior after entry. Another aspect of the evaluation involved the use of an actual score for the seriousness of the client's criminal behavior before and after project entry, and the method of computing this score was based upon the types of offenses committed, with a different score assigned to each class of offense. In addition, a good deal of conventional thinking, as well as thinking in the criminal justice system and among criminologists, is in terms of offense type.

Use of UCR Scheme. The basic framework for the offense classification system used by the evaluation was that of the 26 categories of the FBI's Uniform Criminal Reporting system. This system is used by all of the thousands of local police departments that contribute crime statistics to the FBI. It is not only descriptive, but provides a rule-of-thumb judgment of the seriousness of an offense. The categories are numbered 1 to 26, and these numbers are considered to be a rough ranking by seriousness, particularly the first seven, known as serious or index crimes. The first four, involving homicide, forcible rape, robbery, and aggravated assault, are commonly referred to as violent crimes, or crimes against persons. The next three, burglary, larceny, and auto theft, are commonly referred to as serious property crimes. The other nineteen are called nonindex crimes, examples of which are arson, stolen property, weapons, narcotics offenses, and disorderly conduct.

Conversion of Arrest Charges to UCR Categories. With a small number of exceptions, nearly all of the 400 arrest charges on clients' records were converted into the 26 UCR categories.

Each state has its own penal law and other laws under which arrests are made, and its own system for classifying offenses under these laws for purposes of UCR statistics. In addition, many municipalities, including New York City, have special laws of their

own among which some offenses are reported in UCR statistics.
New York City also has its own system for converting penal law and
other charges into UCR categories. For the most part, we used the
conversions of the New York City Police Department.

Every offense for which an arrest is made by the New York
City Police Department, including arrests under laws other than the
New York State penal law, is classified under the police department's
own system of PD numbers. The PD numbering system runs to
nearly 1,000, each number for a separate offense, although not all
numbers between 1 and 1,000 are currently used. Each PD number
has been classified by the Crime Analysis Unit of the police department into one of the 26 UCR codes or into no UCR code at all (most
vehicle and traffic offenses). The evaluation obtained the police
department booklet of conversions from PD number to UCR category.

The problem, however, was that the arrest charges on the
yellow sheets and juvenile records are not given in the PD codes.
Instead, they are given by the section number of the law under which
the arrest was made—in most cases, the 1965 penal law. It was
therefore necessary to build into the system a way of converting from
the section number (or recoded section number) on the arrest record
into UCR categories. For this, another booklet of the police department was used, the Crime Code Number System, which gave the
description of the offense, the corresponding section number of the
law for each charge that was listed, and also the PD number for that
charge. The UCR categories for each PD number were transcribed
from the police department list onto the Crime Code Number System
booklet, next to each charge listed there. Subsequently, the UCR
category, if any, of each of the approximately 400 arrest charge
codes was placed in the computer memory.

Although the police department material gave the conversions—
not only for penal law charges, but also for charges in other laws for
which the New York City police make arrests—these conversions were
essentially for laws currently in use and did not cover the old penal
law, which expired in 1965. It was not difficult, however, to determine
the UCR categories of most OPL offenses, because extracts from the
new penal law were obtained which gave, for each OPL section
number, the section number(s) of the NPL or of any other law to
which it converted. For most OPL section numbers, it was simple
to determine UCR categories by way of the NPL section numbers to
which they were converted.

Problem Categories. One problem occurred because several section
numbers from the NPL each converted to more than one UCR category.
Each of these section numbers encompasses what the police department considers to be several different offenses, each of which is

given a different PD number. For example, larceny is considered
to cover 23 separate offenses, each with its own PD number, and
these 23 offenses are classified into five separate UCR categories.
Since the only number that was keypunched from the arrest record
for a petit larceny arrest was 155. 25 (prefixed by 0), it would be
impossible to know from that number itself how to classify such an
arrest into a UCR category.

This problem occurred with six NPL numbers. It was resolved
by examining the 1970-72 arrest statistics of New York City as
categorized by PD number. For each NPL number in question, the
number of New York City arrests for the three-year period was noted
for each of the PD numbers to which that NPL number converted.
The figures were then added together for all PD categories which
converted to a particular UCR category. The UCR category which
included the majority of arrests was then used to represent the UCR
category of all arrests with that particular NPL number. With minor
modification for one NPL number, this was the procedure used for
the NPL numbers that convert to more than one UCR category.

Another problem occurred with arrests under the US criminal
code (USCC). Although some material on hand gave a limited amount
of guidance in determining the UCR categories of these offenses,
there was not enough to be confident about any decisions reached with
this material. At the very least, however, it was decided that the
types of crimes involved were similar enough to the criminal activity
represented in the New York State offenses, and that federal arrest
practices were probably sufficiently standardized, so that the
description of a particular offense could be used as a reasonable
basis for its classification into a UCR category. Despite library
research, there was still some ambiguity. Accordingly, the USCC
offenses found on client records were discussed with a CJCC attorney
and, on the basis of his recommendations, each of these offenses
was classified into a UCR category. A USCC arrest was classified
into a UCR category only if it occurred in New York State. If it
occurred outside New York State, it was given the blanket 800,000
code that was applied to all out-of-state arrests and which superseded
all other classifications.

As for the out-of-state arrests themselves, although they were
all counted as arrests for purposes of computing arrest rates, they
were not classified into a UCR category because of uncertainty as to
their precise meaning. It was felt that the diversity of practices in
making and classifying arrests throughout the country was too great
to permit any reasonable certainty that such arrests were necessarily
comparable to those in New York State by type of charge, and the
blanket 800,000 code was therefore used. Any tabulations and analyses
by type of offense, therefore, do not include out-of-state arrests.

Two other charges were counted as arrests in the computation of arrest rates, but were excluded from tabulations by type of offense because there was no way to know the exact type of offense involved even though there was no doubt about the fact that arrests had taken place. These are sealed arrests and youthful offender arrests, in each of which the charges are unknown.

The Most Serious of Multiple Charges. Many arrests contained more than one charge. A burglary charge, for example, was frequently accompanied by a stolen property charge. Although each was classified into a UCR category, there was a problem about how to classify the arrest as a whole. It was decided that each arrest with more than one charge would be classified into only one charge, the UCR category of the most serious charge. For this purpose the 26 UCR category numbers were considered as ranked according to seriousness, with category 1 (homicide) as the most serious and category 26 ("all other" offenses) as the least serious. Thus, an arrest with burglary (UCR 5) and stolen property (UCR 13) was classified as burglary.

The UCR rank was our basis for classifying multicharge arrests by seriousness for the purpose of analyses by type of offense. Analyses by a mean seriousness score were another basis for classification of multiple-charge arrests.

SEVERITY OF PRIOR ARREST HISTORY

Our basic purpose was to evaluate the projects in terms of the criminal behavior of clients after admission. A fundamental premise was that if two or more projects were compared in this way, the comparison would be reasonable only if the clients were similar. The initial design called for client similarity to be measured in terms of age, sex, heroin addiction, and seriousness of criminal history prior to project entry. Heroin addiction was dropped because reliable information on it was almost impossible to obtain.

Despite some problems, age at project entry has been a relatively simple measure to obtain. Severity of prior criminal history, however, has presented major conceptual and methodological problems, some of which were discussed earlier in this report.

Sellin-Wolfgang Index of Severity

An index based on the criminal event as opposed to a legal classification of the event was developed by Sellin and Wolfgang to rectify some of the weaknesses of the present crime classification. [3] Approximately 800 policemen, university students, and juvenile court judges in Philadelphia assigned ratings (magnitude ratios) to 141 different offense events. The analysis of the ratings resulted in numerical weights that could be assigned to objective "elements" of a criminal event. These elements essentially represented the dollar amount or the amount of physical harm caused by the criminal event. For example, a person robbed of $125 is pistol-whipped, suffers a broken nose, and requires hospitalization. The objective elements of dollars and the physical injury would be assigned a total score which represents the degree or ratio by which the event was rated more or less severe than an alternative criminal event (rated by the same judges). Thus, each criminal event (arrest) in a person's history could be assigned a numerical score by using the scale. The arithmetic sum of the scores would be a measure of the total criminal history.

The scale was developed to construct an index of severity that could be used for adults as well as juveniles if there were accurate and complete arrest histories available. The index would describe the severity of criminal behavior of a given age class or type of individual, and also measure change over time as, for example, changes in seriousness rates based on units of 100,000 members of a population.

The main advantage of the scale was that it provided a statistically and logically justified reconciliation of the problem of combining the frequency of crimes with the types of crimes committed in a single mathematical value.

Our evaluation proposed to use the Sellin-Wolfgang scale for two purposes other than those of an index. We proposed to use it to measure the criminal histories of clients prior to project entry so that we would not compare groups of clients with criminal histories of different severity. Next, we thought we might use it to measure change in the severity of criminal behavior after project entry of a group of clients. In the last case we would be using the measure as a dependent variable.

The Sellin-Wolfgang scale was found to be not useful for the evaluation because the required information was not conveniently available from the central arrest records of the police department, because of the amount of work involved in scoring the arrests and the degree of training and skill the scorers would need, and because the sheer volume of arrests in the study would have entailed work exceeding the resources of the evaluation.

An alternative approach was suggested by Marvin E. Wolfgang and Robert M. Figlio, of the University of Pennsylvania. The approach had never been used before and, unlike the original scoring system, was to receive its first test in this evaluation.

The Cohort Study

The proposal was to develop mean seriousness scores for each of the 26 UCR categories, with separate sets of mean seriousness scores for each of the age groups used by the evaluation, using data Wolfgang and Figlio had collected in their Philadelphia "cohort" study. [4]

The initial development of each Sellin-Wolfgang score was empirical and was based on 16,586 arrests. The cohort study used as its population all boys born in 1945 who lived in Philadelphia from their tenth to their eighteenth birthdays. Nearly 10,000 boys were involved, one-third of whom had at least one contact with the police before their eighteenth birthdays. The records of the Philadelphia Police Department contain sufficient detail about the criminal event for which an arrest or other police contact was made to permit a computation of the Sellin-Wolfgang seriousness score. This score was computed for every police contact among these boys prior to age 18. Subsequently, it was computed for every arrest from age 18 to 25, but this was done only for a 10 percent sample of the cohort population. The figure of 16,586 arrests is thus weighted to account for the fact that the 10 percent sample was used for offenses at age 18 through 25, whereas 100 percent of the arrests prior to age 18 were used; the unweighted number was 10,853 arrests.

Mean Seriousness Score
Derived for the Evaluation

The derivation by Wolfgang and Figlio consisted of taking all the arrests in a given UCR category and computing its seriousness score. Each arrest had been scored on the basis of descriptive information in the record. The scores of all of the arrests in a given UCR category were then added together and divided by the number of arrests in that category, and the mean seriousness score was the result. The same procedure was repeated for each of the 26 categories (and for others in the Philadelphia system that are not among the 26 UCR categories) except for categories in which no arrests had taken place.

A series of separate scores was computed for each of several age groups, depending upon the age at which the arrest was made, as shown in Table A. 2. The scores were computed for each offense category for each age from 6 through 25, and for the age groups of under 16, 16 to 18, 19 to 20, 21 and older, and all ages combined. From these and other possible combinations, we could select the age groups deemed most suitable for our analytic purposes. The

Mean Sellin Score (MSS) Values Assigned to Arrest Charges by UCR Offense Categories

U C R Offense Category	UCR No.	A G E G R O U P			
		7 -15	16-18	19-20	21+
Homicide	1	2,633	2,776	2,800	3,282
Forcible rape	2	996	971	2,351	1,377
Robbery	3	308	438	816	740
Aggravated assault	4	540	759	961	830
Burglary	5	247	319	420	359
Larceny-theft	6	151	185	294	342
Auto-theft	7	261	294	343	299
Other assault	8	190	213	213	214
Arson	9	300	300	300	300
Forgery & counterfeiting	10	240	182	477	477
Fraud	11	51	317	349	349
Embezzlement	12	151	185	294	342
Stolen property	13	92	87	204	204
Vandalism	14	121	148	235	274
Weapons	15	185	199	332	420
Prostitution	16	148	724	113	113
Sex offenses	17	261	143	326	702
Narcotics	18	127	141	453	402
Gambling	19	71	61	78	76
Families & children	20	76	85	85	86
Driving under influence	21	72	73	80	80
Liquor laws	22	40	48	56	152
Drunkenness	23	65	66	73	73
Disorderly conduct	24	34	50	44	22
Vagrancy	25	38	49	58	1
All other offenses	26	32	40	44	44
Harassment, PL240.25[a]	8	143	135	135	133
Out of state, foreign	32	107	142	302	372
Sealed, charge known	33	(b)	(b)	(b)	(b)
Sealed, charges unknown	33	1	1	1	1
Youthful offender, charge unknown	34	(c)	136	(c)	(c)

Notes: (a) This is the only New York State penal law assigned a separate MSS from that of its UCR category (8).

(b) Assigned the MSS specific to the charge.

(c) Not applicable for these age groups.

Source: Most of the data was provided by Marvin E. Wolfgang and Robert M. Figlio from the Philadelphia Birth Control Study. Some of the data is from the evaluation described in the text.

plan called for assigning to a given arrest the MSS of the UCR category into which the arrest is classified, with consideration for the age group involved. After discussion with Wolfgang and Figlio, it was decided that the age groups we would use for MSS purposes were 15 and under, 16 to 18, 19 to 20, and 21 and older. These age groups corresponded to those used by the evaluation.

Problems with the MSS. A review of the MSS material by the evaluation staff revealed several problems. Some were resolved by the staff itself, some were resolved after discussions with Wolfgang and Figlio, and for some, no solutions could be found.

One problem was that there were no MSSs at all for five UCR categories because no one in the Philadelphia cohort group had been arrested for charges in those categories. The categories were arson, embezzlement, vandalism, offenses against families and children, and driving under the influence of alcohol.

The absence of arrests for some of these charges was to some extent an artifact of the classification scheme in use in Philadelphia at the time. For example, arson was a subcategory of "all other offenses" (UCR 26) in the version of Directive 110 that was in effect prior to the 1964 revision. Since the boys in the cohort study were all born in 1945, they reached their eighteenth birthdays by 1963, and most of the arrests on which the MSSs were based took place prior to age 18. An arrest for arson at that time would thus have been classified by the arresting officer into the Philadelphia crime code for "all other offenses" and thus would not have been identified as arson. Apparently there were no arson arrests from 1964 onward because they would have appeared as an independent category (UCR 9) in the version of Directive 110 in effect at the time.

We decided to estimate MSSs for each of the five categories, in accordance with the character of the particular offense involved. Hence, embezzlement was considered to be equivalent to larceny, since it is classified as larceny under the New York State penal law. The estimated MSSs used for embezzlement were therefore the same as those used for larceny (UCR 6), with variations according to age group. The MSSs for arson and vandalism were estimated after discussions with specialists in the police and fire departments and insurance companies on the nature and cost of these offenses, and the collection of any available figures that could somehow be used, in accordance with the principles of the Sellin-Wolfgang scoring system, for estimating the MSSs. The MSSs for the five can be seen in Table A. 2.

A similar problem occurred for certain offenses in categories for which MSSs were available for some age groups, but not for others. For the 19 to 20 age group, for example, in addition to the five offenses for which no MSSs were available for any age group, another five were not available for this age group, so that a total of ten MSSs had to be estimated.

The general assumption was that there is some constant relationship between the seriousness scores of different age groups for the same offense. In the case of stolen property (UCR 13) the MSS of the 19 to 20 age group was estimated to be the same as that of the age group 21 and older, for which an MSS was available. In the case of narcotics offenses (UCR 18) the MSS for the 7 to 15 age group was estimated at 10 percent less than that of the 16 to 18 age group, for which an MSS was available.

There was also a problem in determining the MSS for out-of-state, sealed-record, and youthful offender arrests that were obviously countable in the arrest rates, but for which the nature of the offense was unknown or could not be determined with sufficient accuracy. The principal charge of this type was the out-of-state arrest, and the decision was made to assign to it the average MSS of all charges in a given age group. For example, an out-of-state arrest in the 19 to 20 age group was given the average of the MSSs for all 26 categories of offenses for that age group.

An MSS was required for each of the 26 UCR categories for each of the four age groups, for a total of 104 MSSs. Of these 104, the number that had to be estimated was 28, or more than one in four. Another 27 of the 104 were based on fewer than 10 cases, including 11 that were based on one or two cases each. Thus, more than half of the MSSs were either estimated or were based upon a relatively small number of cases.

The problem of MSSs based on zero or few cases was not as acute for the seven index crimes. Of the 28 MSSs for the four age groups for these seven crimes, none had to be estimated (all were based on at least two cases), and 19 were based on 10 or more cases, including 16 based on 20 or more cases. This is especially important because more than half (56 percent) of the arrests of the CJEP population before project entry were for index crimes.

There seemed to be no solution to the problem of offense categories with no MSSs except to make estimates, and no better solution for the problem of MSSs based on a small number of cases than to use them as they were.

Another troubling problem was that the MSSs for "all other offenses" seemed inordinately high for the 19 to 20 and 21 and older age groups in relation to the MSSs for the same category for the 7 to 15 and 16 to 18 age groups and in relation to other MSSs of the 19 to 20 and 21 and older age groups. We decided to try two alternatives and to use the one yielding the best predictions in MSS analyses. One alternative consisted of the actual MSSs and the other, estimates that were considerably lower than the actual MSSs. The prediction equations were then run using each alternative, but there was very little difference in the results. The actual MSSs were therefore used. In addition to the "all other" MSSs, there was at least one other MSS that seemed inordinate, but it too was used "as is. "

A different problem with the "all other" category was that the Philadelphia data for this category include approximately 500 contacts for "incorrigible" and "runaway" cases which are juvenile-status offenses and not counted in the "all other" category (UCR 26) in New York. This problem—the degree to which the UCR category differed from Philadelphia to New York—probably applied to most or all of the 26 UCR categories, but may have been most pronounced with the "all other" category because it is by nature heterogeneous. Nevertheless, the outcomes of our validation study were to determine final use of the scale.

Another factor was that there appeared to be a lot of variance for some of the offenses as measured by the standard deviation in relation to the MSSs. These offenses were: sex crimes (other than forcible rape), narcotics, disorderly conduct, and "all other" offenses. It is possible that the actual criminal events or the sub-categories of offenses in each of these categories were themselves very heterogeneous.

A question which naturally arose for offense categories for which no arrests had been made among the Philadelphia cohort group was why no arrests had been made. The explanation in the case of arson was given above. For narcotics offenses, however, it did not seem reasonable that no one under the age of 16 should have been arrested for this type of charge. The answer that emerged was that the cohort boys, having been born in 1945, spent most of their lives before their sixteenth birthdays during the 1950s, when the use of narcotics was fairly uncommon among juveniles, not only in Philadelphia, but elsewhere as well. Widespread use of narcotics, particularly among younger people, did not occur until later. This explanation places all the MSS data of the cohort group into the perspective of time and place. The arrests and other police contacts upon which the MSSs are based took place approximately between 1952 and 1970 and in the City of Philadelphia, rather than in New York. They also reflect the arrest and classification practices as well as the laws under which the Philadelphia police operate.

The proposed use of the MSS by the evaluation was based on several assumptions. The first was that the Sellin-Wolfgang scores, originally derived from a Philadelphia population, would be applicable in measuring the criminal history of a New York City population. The second assumption was that the "derived" mean (the MSS) that

we proposed to use would reasonably reflect the severity of the
behavioral "event" represented by a New York City arrest charge.
A third assumption was that the many serious methodological problems
in applying the scale to the New York population could be overcome.

However, it was also true that the Sellin-Wolfgang scale is the
best standardized instrument available for measuring the severity of
criminal behavior and the only one that could reconcile the problem
of frequency and type of arrest. Furthermore, we had neither the
intent nor the resources to develop a new measure of severity or to
restandardize the Sellin-Wolfgang scale on a New York City population.

Taking all of these considerations into account, we decided to
invest the time and effort involved in testing the predictive and
concurrent validity of the scale for our New York City population,
and for our intended use. Further, we proposed to compare the
effectiveness of the scale with that of other measures of severity,
such as number of arrests. If the Sellin-Wolfgang scale were demonstrated, in our use of it, to be lacking in validity, we could make the
decision later not to use it. If it worked according to the criteria of
validation, its use would be justified despite possible "weaknesses."

The Use of the MSS. Each arrest on a client's criminal record was
assigned a MSS unless that arrest was not counted in the computation
of the arrest rate. This included the very first arrest on the record
and every subsequent countable arrest through the end of the first
year after the client entered a project. The MSS used for a particular
arrest was based on the age at which the arrest took place rather than
on the age at which the client entered the project. Thus, if a client
was arrested at age 14, the MSS used was the one for his particular
offense for the 7 to 15 age group and, if the same client was arrested
again at age 17, the MSS for that arrest was the one for the client's
particular offense for the age group 16 to 18. If both of these arrests
were for exactly the same offense, each would be given a different
MSS.

If an arrest had only one charge, it was simply assigned the
MSS of the UCR offense category containing that charge. If an arrest
had more than one charge, it was assigned the MSS of the most
serious of the charges in the arrest. The most serious charge was
determined by the magnitude of the MSS of each of the charges in
the arrest; the charge with the highest MSS was considered the most
serious. For example, a 26-year-old had an arrest for robbery,
weapons, and stolen property. The MSSs for these offenses for the
21 and older age group were, respectively 583, 264, and 155. The
arrest would be given the MSS of 583, that of robbery, because it is
the highest of the three and hence the most serious.

This procedure for determining the most serious charge in a multiple-charge arrest is different from the procedure used in classifying arrests by type of offense. The latter procedure involved using the 26 UCR category numbers for the ranking of seriousness, with the lowest category number as the most serious and the highest number as the least serious. Thus, the very same multiple-charge arrest might be treated one way for classification by type of offense and a different way for assigning an MSS. For example, if a client was arrested at different ages but each time for the same multiple-charge arrest, it is possible that the most serious charge in one of the arrests would be different from that of the other arrests if the rank of each charge was different in each age group. The MSS for each of these arrests would still be that of the most serious charge even though the charge considered most serious might differ in each of the two arrests.

Once an MSS was assigned to an arrest, it could then be added to the MSSs for all the client's other arrests prior to project entry, thus yielding a measure of the total seriousness of that individual's criminal history.

For clients who were 19 or older at the time of project entry, the criminal histories that were collected began at age 16. For those 18 or younger the entire criminal history was collected.

Validation of a Measure of Severity

Our testing of the predictive and concurrent validity of the MSS had to be guided by the use we intended to make of that instrument. The basic objective was to make sure that in our comparisons of projects we did not fall into the error of comparing the arrest rates of groups of clients whose criminal histories had markedly different severity.

For example, YCB's 16- to 18-year-old clients were almost entirely first offenders for nonserious offenses. Project BYCEP, on the other hand, provided services to 16- to 18-year-olds after release from the Rikers Correctional Facility. Generally, these ex-convicts had lengthy and severe criminal histories. It would have been inappropriate to compare the arrest rates of the two projects.

Given this intended use, the predictive validity of the scale should have been testable by ascertaining the extent to which the prior criminal history of individuals predicted their arrest recidivism after project entry. The higher the severity of criminal history prior to project entry, the more likely recidivism should be. Next, the higher the severity of criminal history prior to project entry, the more severe the recidivism should be (that is, the higher the MSS after project entry). The latter would be a more refined measure of predictive validity than the former. If either or both predictions occurred, there would be support for the validity of the MSS as a measure of severity for the New York City project clients.

The concurrent validity of the MSS would be ascertainable by the extent to which there was a high correlation between the MSS and other measures of severity when both were applied to the same task, such as the predictive tasks described above, but not too high a correlation. Two other measures of severity were the numbers of arrests prior to project entry and the type of arrest charge prior to project entry, such as violent crimes. Note that the MSS is the synthesis of the two measures and thus contains more information than either. The results of the test of concurrent validity should also be usable in selecting for the evaluation the most valid or useful of the three competing measures of severity.

In reading the account of our validation study which follows, the reader is urged to bear two definitions in mind for the sake of clarity. First, MSS stands for the Philadelphia-derived "Mean Sellin Score" value. The term does not represent the (arithmetic) mean Sellin-Wolfgang score of project clients in the evaluation. When we refer to "arithmetic means" in some of our validation efforts, the reference is to means of MSSs. Second, the term "recidivism" in this report refers to one or more arrests during the twelve months after project entry. This is also the meaning of the term "arrest recidivism." Other types of recidivism will be specified by modifiers.

Method

The various analyses of validation are grouped by type; the sequence is fairly chronological.

Clients. For all of the validation tests to follow, 2,900 male, 7- to 71-year-old clients were used from the 18 projects in the evaluation.

Regression Analyses. The relationship between prior criminal history and recidivism was tested by a stepwise linear regression analysis. The dependent variable was recidivism. The independent variables were total MSS before project entry, the year of age at project entry, and the interaction between the total MSS and the age. This was done across the 18 projects. Table A.3 shows that the F-value is highly significant for both the independent variables and their interaction. However, this is probably due to the large number of degrees of freedom (2,896) for the residual sum of squares.

TABLE A. 3

Stepwise Linear Regression Analysis of
Recidivism on Total MSS before Project Entry
and Year of Age at Project Entry, Across Projects

Statistics	Dependent Variable: Recidivism Independent Variables		
	Total MSS Before Project Entry	Year of Age at Project Entry	Total MSS X Age Interaction
1. F	90.368*	33.270*	7.263*
2. Simple r	0.028	−0.124*	−0.002.
3. Variance accounted	2.49%	1.53%	0.20%
4. Regression coef.	0.000	−0.016	−0.000
5. Total multiple r	0.206		
6. Total multiple r^2	0.042		

Note: Clients, 2,900; Degrees of Freedom for F and Simple r,
2,896.
* P is less than . 05, two-tailed test for r and one-tailed for F.
Source: Compiled by the evaluation project.

The simple correlations between total MSS before project entry
and recidivism, and between the interaction and recidivism, were
not significant at the 5 percent level. However, the simple correlation
between the age at project entry and recidivism was negative and
significant at the 5 percent level.
The total variance accounted for by these variables was 4. 2
percent, of which 2. 5 percent and 1. 5 percent were accounted for
respectively by the total MSS before project entry and the age at
project entry. Interaction accounted for 0. 2 percent. The very low
amount of variance accounted for by these variables led us to
question the utility of a linear model for defining a relationship
between them. But that was not an entirely satisfactory explanation.
The findings were absolutely unexpected. That age and prior criminal

history accounted for less than 5 percent of the total variance in their relationship to recidivism seemed incongruent with a great many empirical findings in criminology. As a result, there followed the lengthy and detailed series of statistical analyses described below. They were our effort to clarify the outcomes of the first regression analysis.

Similar negative results were obtained when the analysis above was done using as the dependent variable total MSS within twelve months after project entry, instead of recidivism. This tended to refute the hypothesis that the more severe the criminal history prior to project entry, the more severe the recidivism would be.

The significant negative correlation between age (by year) and recidivism suggested that it might be useful to explore differences among age groups. In other words, we decided that we would use nine age groups where the differences between the groups were assumed to represent possible qualitative differences, for example, 13- to 15-year-olds qualitatively as well as quantitatively different from 35- to 39-year-olds in the way that their individual year within their age group might relate to recidivism.

Therefore, the stepwise linear regression analysis was done using the nine age subgroups* $(7-12)^f$, $(13-15)^{f, r}$, $(16-18)^{f, r}$, $(19-20)$, $(21-24)^{f, r}$, $(25-29)^{f, r}$, $(30-34)^r$, $(35-39)^{f, r}$, and $(40-71)^{f, r}$. The F values and the correlations between MSS and recidivism were generally significant for each age group. For the F values this may have been due to the large numbers of degrees of freedom, which ranged in the age groups from 111 to 614. There was no appreciable improvement in the total variance accounted for by the independent variables, which ranged from 1.6 percent for the age subgroup 21 to 24 to 15.7 percent for the age subgroup 35 to 39.

Since the data suggested logarithmic or square root transformation, the regression analyses were also done using these transformations. However, the results were generally not different from the preceding.

At this point we added a measure of concurrent validity, the number of arrests before project entry, as an independent variable. We repeated the stepwise regression analysis by the nine age subgroups and also used year of age at project entry as an independent variable. The significance of the F values and correlations were similar to those in the preceding analysis. (There was one additional age group with a significant F and one with a significant r.) The total variance accounted for by these variables for the nine age subgroups

---

*f = P less than .05 for the F value. r = P less than .05 for the correlation value r.

ranged from 1. 8 percent for the age subgroup 30 to 34 to 12. 6 percent for the age subgroup 40 to 71.

The results of both preceding analyses showed no substantial difference in their outcomes. The variable, total number of arrests before project entry, was similar to the variable, total MSS before project entry.

The types of arrests before project entry were tested as the third possible measure of validity. This concurrent validation of the MSS introduced violent crimes (homicide, forcible rape, robbery, and aggravated assault) as the type of crime. The number of arrests for violent crimes prior to project entry was the independent variable.

Stepwise linear regression was used with arrest recidivism as the dependent variable for the same nine age groups. The year of age at project entry was another independent variable. The overall F values were generally significant for younger but not older (19 and older) age groups. The simple correlations were significant for four of the nine age groups. The variances accounted for by the independent variables were once again very low, 6 percent being the most for any of the age groups.

The analysis was repeated with the dependent variable of violent crime recidivism. Again the results were more or less similar, with the total variance accounting for less than 8 percent for any age group. The results of the two preceding analyses were somewhat less adequate than those for the measures of MSS and number of arrests.

Further analysis of the violent crimes was performed using recidivism of robbery as the dependent variable. In this case the independent variables used were the number of arrests for robbery before project entry, the total MSS before project entry, age at project entry, and all the resulting interactions. The age subgroups used here were 7 to 15, 16 to 18, 19 to 20, and 21 and older. Except for the variable year of age at project entry, all correlations were significant (P less than . 05) for the three age groups 7 to 15, 16 to 18, and 21 and older. The overall (all independent variables and inter-actions together) F-value was significant for these three age groups. However, the F-values for each independent variable within each age group turned out to be not significant for almost all the variables and their interactions. Finally, the variance accounted for by the regression ranged from 2 percent, for the age group 21 and older, to 10 percent for 16 to 18—all unsatisfactorily low.

The results of the preceding analyses led us to drop type of arrest, that is, violent crimes, as a possible useful measure of severity for our comparisons of projects. This left the MSS before project entry and the number of arrests before project entry as the remaining alternatives.

TABLE A. 4

Outcomes of Three Analyses of Variance of
Recidivism on Three Measures of Severity

ANALYSIS OF VARIANCE	MEASURE OF SEVERITY Before Project Entry	F-VALUE	RECIDIVISM Total Variance Accounted for by Recidivism
I	Total MSS	91.065*	1.5%
II	Total number of arrests	106.622*	2.1%
III	Average MSS per arrest	2.448	0.06%

Note: Clients, 2900; Degrees of Freedom, 2882.
* P is less than . 05, one-tailed test.
Source: Compiled by the evaluation project.

We then tried using three ascending levels of seriousness for
the independent variables total MSS before project entry, and total
number of arrests before project entry. * We ran the regression by
each of the nine age subgroups for each of the independent variables.
The three levels of seriousness for each age subgroup were determined by using the method of Dalenius. [5] The results of these analyses
were generally similar to the earlier ones. There was no improvement.

Analysis of Variance. We decided to assess the relationship among
MSS before project entry, recidivism, and year of age at project entry
by the nine age subgroups with an analysis of variance.
    Table A. 4 shows that, although the F-value was highly significant
because of the large number of degrees of freedom for the residual
sum of squares—2, 882—the total variance accounted for by recidivism
was only 1. 5 percent.

---

*It should be noted that the decision to classify the dependent
variables by levels stemmed from the results of nonregression tests
described below.

The client's MSS prior to project entry was expected to increase with age. In an effort to control for this possibility within the nine age groups, we decided to use the average arrest MSS prior to project entry (per client) instead of the total MSS per client. For the independent variable average MSS per arrest before project entry, the F-value was not significant and the variance was 6 percent. The number of arrests before project entry was also assessed by the analysis of variance.

The F-value in the analysis of variance was highly significant, but the degrees of freedom were high. Only 2.1 percent of the variance was accounted for by recidivism.

Table A. 4 gives the F-values and the variance accounted for by recidivism in each analysis. These results indicated that a linear model was not appropriate for the evaluation of our data.

t-Tests. Because the outcomes of the analyses of variance and the regression models strongly suggested that if a relationship existed between severity and recidivism it was not linear, our next effort was to see whether there was a relationship. In other words, did arrest recidivists have significantly more severe criminal histories prior to project entry than nonrecidivists?

Severity of criminal history was measured by both the total MSS and the number of arrests prior to project entry. The F-ratio test was used to determine whether the population variances were the same for the recidivists and nonrecidivists for each of the two severity measures. If the variances were significantly different, then the table t-value was computed using Cochran's approximation.

The relationship was tested for the nine age groups shown in Table A. 5, which gives the t-values of the comparisons. Most of the comparisons were significant. This lends support for a nonlinear relationship between severity of criminal history and recidivism. The MSS and number of arrests do not appear to be very different in outcomes.

As discussed above, the severity of criminal history as measured by the total MSS and the total number of arrests was expected to increase with age. If it was also the case that older clients were arrested more than younger ones after project entry (for any reason), the significant t-values in most of the nine age groups above might have been accounted for by those two effects, rather than the relationship tested. Therefore, we decided to do a separate t for each year of age using the same method of analysis. There were 28 individual years containing 2,733 clients for this analysis. Individual years which contained fewer than 20 clients were not used. There were 23 of these years, containing 167 clients. The individual years not used are shown in Table A. 6. For each of the 28 remaining years we did

TABLE A. 5

t-Values for Recidivists versus Nonrecidivists
by Severity of Criminal History

Measure of Severity Before Project Entry	AGE GROUP								
	7 –12	13–15	16–18	19–20	21–24	25–29	30–34	35–39	40–71
MSS	1.64	5.44*	6.39*	1.69	2.87*	3.88*	2.01*	3.99*	2.64*
Number of Arrests	2.20*	5.65*	7.42	2.16*	3.15*	4.23*	1.82	3.43*	2.64*
Degrees of Freedom	145	567	615	245	545	366	168	119	112

Note: Clients, 2900.
* P is less than . 05, one-tailed test
Source: Compiled by the evaluation project.

the t-test on differences between recidivists and nonrecidivists for
total MSS before project entry, and on the total number of arrests
before project entry.

The results in Table A. 6 show that all of the t-values for each
of the years within the groups 13 to 15 and 16 to 18 were significant
for both measures. It was also the case that the number of arrests
and the MSS did increase with age for both the 13- to 15- and 16-
to 18-year-olds. However, the arrest rates within the two age groups
remained relatively constant, that is, they did not appear different.
These findings suggested (for at least these two age groups) that the
significant results of the t-test by nine age groups did not result from
MSSs and number of arrests increasing with age and interacting with
the possibility that older people are arrested more than younger
people.

Table A. 6 shows that for each of 19 years over 18 there were
only 8 that were significant for one or both measures. However,
although not all the years were significant, 17 of the 19 were in the
predicted direction, while 26 of 28 were in the predicted direction
for those measured.

Our conclusion at this point was that a relationship between
severity of criminal history and recidivism seemed to hold strongly
for the 13- to 18-year-olds, and to some extent for those 19 and
over.

TABLE A. 6

Significance of t-Test Outcomes of the Differences
between Recidivists and Non-recidivists by MSS and
by Number of Arrests Prior to Project Entry

	MSS		Number of Arrests	
Age	All Years Retrieved	3 Years Only	All Years Retrieved	3 Years Only
10	0	0	0	0
11	0	0	0	0
12	0	0	+	+
13	+	+	+	+
14	+	+	+	+
15	+	+	+	+
16	+	+	+	+
17	+	+	+	+
18	+	+	+	+
19	0	0	0	+
20	0	0	0	+
21	0	+	0	+
22	+	0	+	0
23	+	+	0	0
24	0	0	0	0
25	0	0	0	0
26	0	0	0	0
27	+	0	+	+
28	+	+	+	+
29	0	+	+	+
30	+	+	0	+
31	0	+	0	+
32	0	0	0	0
33	0	+	0	+
34	0	0	0	0
35	+	+	+	+
36	0	0	0	0
38	+	+	+	+

Note: Clients, 2733.
+ Outcome is significant; P is equal to or less than . 05.
0 Outcome is not significant; P is more than . 05.

The above hypothesis was also assessed by the t-test using only three years' criminal history prior to project entry. The rationale for using a partial criminal history was that, for the older clients, arrests occurring in the immediate past may have related to recidivism more than arrests which took place many years in the past. For example, it was possible that for the 21 and older group the lack of significant t-values stemmed from a "wash-out" effect from older ex-convicts with long, severe, past criminal histories but no recent history.

For most juveniles our criminal histories generally did not exceed three or four years. Also, for the years 19 and 20 our criminal records did not exceed four years because we did not retrieve juvenile records for clients belonging to the age group 19 to 20. Thus, to a great extent the three-year criminal history was most applicable for clients aged 25 and above, who generally have longer criminal records.

On Table A. 6, inspection of the MSS outcomes for each of 13 years, 25 and above, shows one year (27) in which the change went from a significant relationship to a nonsignificant one, and three years (29, 31, 33) when the change went from nonsignificant to significant. The net change was 2 out of 13 in the direction of significance. For number of arrests, three (30, 31, 33) out of 13 changed in the direction of significance, and there were no reversals. These results suggested that there is some tendency for older clients with only long early records to "wash out" the effects of severity on recidivism when included among those with more recent criminal histories.

Kolmogorov-Smirnov Test. Here the hypothesis was that there is a significant difference between the distribution of recidivists and the distribution of nonrecidivists over levels of number of prior arrests. The nine age groups were used.

The distributions were obtained by using six levels of number of arrests before project entry for each age group. Table A. 7 shows that for five age groups the distributions differed significantly. For the MSS distributions were obtained by using ten levels of total MSS before project entry, for each age group. These distributions showed a significant difference for all age groups except 7 to 12 and 19 to 20. These results indicated that the distributions or recidivists and nonrecidivists differ over levels of number of prior arrests.

X^2-Test for Linear Trend. The X^2-test was done to determine whether the proportion of recidivists increases with increasing levels of severity. The number of arrests had six levels for each age group and the MSS had ten levels.

TABLE A. 7

X^2 Values for the Nine Age Subgroups in Kolmogorov-Smirnov Test and X^2-Tests for Linear Trends

Age Group	Clients	Number of Arrests Before Project Entry at 6 Levels for Each Age Group		Total MSS Before Project Entry at 10 Levels for Each Age Group	
		X^2 Linear Trend Test	X^2 Kolmogorov-Smirnov Test	X^2 Linearity Test	X^2 Kolmogorov-Smirnov Test
7–12	147	5.29*	5.06	1.69	2.45
13–15	569	24.29*	30.07*	29.86*	22.74*
16–18	617	57.03*	62.64*	37.72*	38.23*
19–20	247	1.55	14.23*	2.21	2.00
21–24	547	9.80*	8.75*	12.14*	8.75*
25–29	368	9.24*	8.45*	14.66*	9.54*
30–34	170	5.43*	5.10	3.07	8.13*
35–39	121	2.99	1.79	20.48*	10.16*
40–71	114	0.36	0.07	13.52*	10.10*
Total	2,900	–	–	–	–
Degrees of Freedom		1	2	1	2

Note: Clients, 2,900.
* P is less than .05
Source: Compiled by the evaluation project.

In Table A. 7 there is a significant linear trend between increasing levels of the number of arrests and the proportions of recidivists in each level for all age groups except 19 to 20, 35 to 39, and 40 to 71. When the variable used for level of severity is the total MSS before project entry, a significant linear trend was observed for all the age groups except 7 to 12 and 19 to 20. It may be concluded that, in

general, the proportion of recidivists increases as the level of
severity increases.

Conclusions about Validity

The results of the regression analyses and the analysis of variance strongly suggested that the relationship between severity of criminal history and recidivism was not linear. Further, we are unable to explain satisfactorily why the proportions of variance accounted for by severity of prior criminal history and age were as low as they are in these two analyses. However, it was decided that for the purpose of our evaluation analysis, the MSS and the number of arrests were sufficiently valid to use as measures of severity of criminal history prior to project entry. The decision was based on two considerations.

First, the results of the t-tests, the Kolmogorov-Smirnov tests, and the chi-square trend analyses supported a significant relationship between measures of severity and recidivism, particularly for the 13- through 18-year-old groups. Although the relationship might not be linear, it appeared to exist.

Second, a nonstatistical reality was that our knowledge of the projects' entrance criteria gave us some insight into the severity of the clients' prior criminal history. For example, when we looked at project arrest rates for the 16- to 18-year-old age group (without controlling for severity), the lowest arrest rate (24 percent) of the nine projects belonged to the Youth Counsel Bureau. This project, with few exceptions, accepted only first offenders with misdemeanors. The other projects with 16- to 18-year-olds, such as Project BYCEP with a 59 percent arrest rate and Independence House with a 61 percent arrest rate, accepted almost entirely ex-convicts from Rikers Island with long and severe criminal histories. The assumption that one could compare YCB's recidivism rates to the other two and conclude that it was the most effective seemed absurd. Although we did not have as compelling a contrast among projects with clients who were over 19 years of age, there was some similar evidence among those projects as well. These empirical realities made more pervasive the assumption that the test results demonstrated adequate validity for the measures.

The Selection of a Measure of Severity

The next decision that had to be made was whether to use the MSS or the number of arrests as our measure of severity. The results of the preceding tests seemed to indicate that the two measures were generally equally valid (with the number of arrests perhaps slightly better). Therefore, we decided to use both in doing our final comparative analysis, but to select the number of arrests as our final measure of severity unless the outcomes between the two were very different. The outcomes were similar.

We therefore selected the number of arrests as our measure of severity because it is easier and cheaper to compute than the MSS, and more easily understood by readers.

A Caution. Some discussion is necessary of the possible implications of our decision to choose the number of arrests over the MSS as our measure of severity, and of the various judgments we have made about the "validity" of the MSS. The reader is reminded that the MSS is not a Sellin-Wolfgang score. The MSS is a mean derived from Sellin scores solely for potential use by this evaluation. Our tests of the predictive and concurrent validity of the MSS did not constitute a direct test of the Sellin scale. The outcomes of our analysis of the validity of the MSS should not be generalized to Sellin-Wolfgang scores at this point. The Sellin scale, to the best of our knowledge, is still the best standardized measure of severity of criminal history. Further, its ability to reconcile mathematically the number of arrests with the types of charges is in principle advantageous. We are not able to explain satisfactorily why our findings showed the number of arrests to be at least as effective as the MSS in terms of the various tests of validity we have reported.

The original Sellin-Wolfgang scale was employed to derive an index to be used as a descriptive measure of severity. We used the MSS to control for individual differences between clients and as a possible dependent variable. In our judgment it would be fruitful to validate these two uses for the actual Sellin-Wolfgang scale, but to do this by applying the scale to measuring descriptions of actual criminal "events," as it was constructed to do. Then, predictive and concurrent validation of the Sellin-Wolfgang scale would be a more direct and accurate assessment of its validity and utility.

Levels of Severity

Three approaches were considered in determining the levels of severity to use in classifying criminal history prior to project entry.

First, the evaluation attempted to determine whether there were clusters that could be identified in a distribution of severity scores for each age group across projects wherein each cluster represented a level of severity for that age group. If successful, the method would allow comparisons between projects of clients at each level. Preliminary inspection of the distributions of MSSs and numbers of arrests by age groups did not show enough positive findings to continue the effort.

It was suggested that determination of levels of severity be done by identifying "qualitative" breaking points that might be related to severity. [6] For the MSS, for example, inspection of the original Sellin-Wolfgang scale showed that a score from 0 to 1 indicated a level where there could have been nothing more than minor physical injuries for an event. This would have been the preferred way of determining levels and would have made possible the same type of comparisions as above. We ran out of time, unfortunately, and could not attempt the method.

We wound up with a less preferred method that we had initially developed and used as part of the validation procedure. This method of determining the levels of severity used the Duncan Multiple Range Test, as corrected by the method of Dalenius. [7]

One purpose of using the Duncan test and the Dalenius method of forming homogeneous groups was to identify mutually exclusive and exhaustive levels of severity of criminal history prior to project entry for each age group to be used in the analysis.

This was a two-step process. First, the Duncan test was used to determine within each age group how many different clusters of projects there were where each cluster contained projects whose average MSS (or average number of arrests) before project entry would be such that the project with the lowest average MSS in that cluster would not be significantly different from the project with the highest average MSS in that cluster. Further, the Duncan test determined for each age group the clusters of projects which were significantly different from each other to the extent that there was at least one project with an average MSS in one cluster significantly different from the average MSS of at least one project in a different cluster in that age group.

Given the criteria above, when the Duncan test was applied to the projects within an age group, the clusters which resulted might not be mutually exclusive. In other words, some projects might have been in more than one cluster. This overlap could have created problems in interpreting the outcomes.

Therefore, as a second step, the method of Dalenius was applied to the clusters of projects in each age group in order to make them mutually exclusive. The mutually exclusive clusters of projects which resulted were then defined as levels of severity for that age group.

Table A. 8 shows the outcomes of the Duncan sort of the projects by the seven age groups for mean MSS and mean number of arrests prior to project entry, and the subsequent determination of mutually exclusive levels by the method of Dalenius is shown by Table A. 9.

TABLE A.8

Clients Grouped by Duncan Test:
By Age and Severity of Mean MSS and
Mean Number of Arrests Prior to Project Entry

AGE	SEVERITY GROUP	MEAN MSS — Project and Component
7-12	1	ATD-PROB(pcis), PBG, ATD-HRA(fbh), NYD 225 244 276 292
13-15	1	PBG, ATD-HRA(fbh), ATD-PROB(pcis), MLA 257 290 391 404
13-15	2	ATD-HRA(fbh), ATD-PROB(pcis), MLA, NYD 290 391 404 461
13-15	3	ATD-PROB(pcis), MLA, NYD, ATD-HRA(gh) 391 404 461 628
13-15	4	ATD-HRA(gh), ATD-PROB(sdr/dc) 628 642
16-18	1	YCB, LPQ, ARC 361 562 603
16-18	2	LPQ, ARC, MLA, INDH 562 603 621 760
16-18	3	ARC, MLA, INDH, PUL 603 621 760 883
16-18	4	INDH, PUL, BCC, BYCEP, ASA 760 883 933 981 1009
19-20	1	ARC, BCC, MLA, PUL 857 895 959 1095
19-20	2	PUL, INDH 1095 1428
19-20	3	INDH, ASA 1428 1476
21-29	1	BCC 1366
21-29	2	ARC, NAACP(i/n), MANHD, VERA(c), 2211, 2226 2300 2302 VERA(w), SHARE, ASA, SCH 2318 2475 2486 2521
30-39	1	BCC, MANHD, ARC, SCH, VERA(w), ASA, 2942 3524 3723 3918 4318 4639 NAACP(i/n) 4686
30-39	2	MANHD, ARC, SCH, VERA(w), ASA, 3524 3723 3918 4318 4639 NAACP(i/n), VERA(c) 4686 4801
40-71	1	ARC 4734
40-71	2	NAACP(i/n) 7459

AGE	SEVERITY GROUP	MEAN NO. OF ARRESTS — Project and Component
7-12	1	PBG, ATD-PROB(pcis), NYD, ATD-HRA(fbh) 0.81 1.00 1.09 1.21
13-15	1	PBG, ATD-HRA(fbh), ATD-PROB(pcis), MLA 1.01 1.24 1.42 1.53
13-15	2	ATD-HRA(fbh), ATD-PROB(pcis), MLA, NYD 1.24 1.42 1.53 1.75
13-15	3	ATD-PROB(sdr/dc), ATD-HRA(gh) 2.39 2.87
16-18	1	YCB, LPQ, MLA 1.61 2.07 2.14
16-18	2	LPQ, MLA, ARC, INDH 2.07 2.14 2.81 2.87
16-18	3	ARC, INDH, PUL, BCC, BYCEP 2.81 2.87 3.06 3.35 3.59
16-18	4	ASA 4.60
19-20	1	BCC, MLA, PUL, ARC, INDH 2.69 2.73 2.80 3.00 3.80
19-20	2	INDH, ASA 3.80 4.26
21-29	1	BCC, NAACP(i) 3.31 4.26
21-29	2	NAACP(i), MANHD, SCH, ARC, 4.26 4.67 4.80 5.24 VERA(c), VERA(w), NAACP(n), SHARE, 5.53 5.57 5.59 5.74
21-29	3	VERA(c), VERA(w), NAACP(n), SHARE, 5.53 5.57 5.59 5.74 ASA 6.16
30-39	1	BCC, MANHD, SCH, ARC, VERA(w), NAACP(i/n), 6.55 7.73 7.73 9.90 10.55 10.64
30-39	2	ARC, VERA(w), NAACP(i/n), ASA 9.90 10.55 10.60 11.43 VERA(c) 11.84
40-71	1	ARC, NAACP(i/n) 12.85 18.69

Source: Compiled by the evaluation project.

TABLE A. 9

Clients Grouped by Duncan Test and Dalenius Method: By Age and Mutually Exclusive Levels of Severity of Mean MSS and Mean Number of Arrests Prior to Project Entry

AGE	SEVERITY LEVEL	MEAN MSS Project and Component
7-12	1	ATD-PROB(pcis), PBG, ATD-HRA(fbh), 225 244 276 NYD 292
13-15	1	PBG 257
	2	ATD-HRA(fbh), ATD-PROB(pcis) 290 391
	3	MLA, NYD 404 461
	4	ATD-HRA(gh), ATD-PROB(sdr/dc) 628 642
16-18	1	YCB 361
	2	LPQ, ARC, MLA 562 603 621
	3	INDH, PUL 760 883
	4	BCC, BYCEP, ASA 933 981 1009
19-20	1	ARC 857
	2	BCC, MLA 895 959
	3	PUL, INDH, ASA 1095 1428 1476
21-29	1.	BCC, ARC, NAACP(i/n), MANHD 1366 2211 2226 2300
	2	VERA(c), VERA(w), SHARE, ASA, SCH 2302 2318 2475 2486 2521
30-39	1	BCC, MANHD, ARC, SCH 2942 3524 3723 3918
	2	VERA(w), ASA, NAACP(i/n), VERA(c) 4318 4639 4686 4801
40-71	1	ARC 4734
	2	NAACP(i/n) 7459

AGE	SEVERITY LEVEL	MEAN NO. OF ARRESTS Project and Component
7-12	1	PBG, ATD-PROB(pcis), NYD, ATD-HRA(fbh) 0.81 1.00 1.09 1.21
13-15	1	PBG, ATD-HRA(fbh) 1.01 1.24
	2	ATD-PROB (pcis), MLA, 1.42 1.53
	3	NYD, ATD-PROB(sdr/dc), ATD-HRA(gh) 1.75 2.39 2.87
16-18	1	YCB 1.61
	2	LPQ, MLA, ARC 2.07 2.14 2.81
	3	INDH, PUL 2.87 3.06
	4	BCC, BYCEP, ASA 3.35 3.59 4.60
19-20	1	BCC, MLA, PUL 2.69 2.73 2.80
	2	ARC, INDH, ASA 3.00 3.80 4.26
21-29	1	BCC, NAACP(i), MANHD 3.31 4.26 4.67
	2	SCH, ARC, VERA(c) 4.80 5.24 5.53
	3	VERA(w), NAACP(n), SHARE, ASA 5.57 5.59 5.74 6.16
30-39	1	BCC, MANHD SCH, ARC 6.55 7.73 7.73 9.90
	2	VERA(w), NAACP(i/n), ASA, VERA(c) 10.55 10.64 11.43 11.84
40-71	1	ARC, NAACP(i/n) 12.85 18.69

Source: Compiled by the evaluation project.

Implications for Validation from the Analysis

In the final analysis for the first evaluation task, the Duncan test was applied to the arrest recidivism rates of the projects to determine whether there were subgroups within each level of severity for each age group—to determine whether there were differences among the projects. This was done for the severity levels that had been established by average MSS, and it was also done by average number of arrests prior to project entry.

The outcomes showed that the average number of arrests provided clearer results. Consequently, average number of arrests, rather than MSS, was chosen as the measure of severity to be presented in the evaluation report. Table A. 10 shows that the Duncan results, when using average number of arrests, were two mutually exclusive subgroups of projects within each of two levels of severity. When the MSS was used, the results were two subgroups of projects in each of two levels of severity, but the project subgroups were overlapping rather than mutually exclusive.

As noted above, this application of the Duncan test was being employed as part of the final analysis to answer questions about whether differences between projects affected the arrest recidivism of similar clients. In the analysis section devoted to those evaluation questions, the method is also described briefly. However, because those results had important implications for questions relating to the validation of a severity measure, and the final choice of competing measures, they are also mentioned here.

The validation effort assumed a relationship between the severity of client criminal history prior to project entry and recidivism after project entry. As discussed earlier, the overall results of our validations provided fairly strong support for that relationship for clients 20 years old and younger, and marginal support for that relationship for clients 21 and older.

The results of the Duncan test with arrest rates (Table A. 10) appeared to correspond with the earlier findings. The four age groups 20 and younger reflected a relationship between severity of criminal history and recidivism. As the levels of severity increased within an age group, the recidivism rates appeared to increase at those levels. *

---

*The apparent exception (the reversal of high and low arrest rates for the projects in levels 3 and 4 for the age group 16 to 18) was not statistically significant when the arrest rates of the five projects were compared by a X^2 test. The P was less than . 01 for the X^2 value of 789 (Table A. 10).

On the other hand, the results for the three age groups 21 and older did not appear to show any correlation between levels of severity and arrest recidivism rates.

This finding might have been interpreted as meaning that levels of severity for those 21 and over were not valid. Therefore, it could have been that the levels simply prevented comparisons between projects with the same arrest rates within the age group. For example, for ages 30 to 39, Manhood in level one, and NAACP in level two did not have significantly different arrest rates when compared by a t-test (P = . 296).

However, the main issue was whether the imposition of levels of severity affected the answer to the basic questions: Do differences between projects affect the arrest recidivism rates of similar clients? Are some projects "better" than others? Overall results from an analysis within levels of severity had provided an initial answer of no to that question. It was now necessary to test that answer in the new light of whether the severity levels were valid for clients over 21.

To test that issue, the answer provided by the test of project arrest rates within levels of severity for an age group was compared with the answer from analysis of the project arrest rates pooled across levels of severity within the same age group. The test was done for the age groups 21 to 29 and 30 to 39.

The analysis consisted of a X^2 test applied to arrest recidivism rates across levels of severity. It resulted in no significant differences between any of the eight projects for the age group 30 to 39.

The initial answer of no did not change. Analyzing across levels of severity had allowed the answer to be applied to all of the projects rather than just those within each level. Hence, the net result was more confidence in the generalizability of the initial answer of no.

For the age group 21 to 29, the test consisted of the application of the Duncan test to the arrest recidivism rates of the ten projects and components across levels of severity in this age group. * The

---

*Before examining the results, it should be remembered that the application of the Duncan test to a group of projects may result in subgroups that are not mutually exclusive. One or more projects may be a member of more than one subgroup. This overlap allows some comparisons between subgroups of project comparisons. The criteria the Duncan test uses to sort into subgroups is that there has to be at least one project in a subgroup which is significantly different from at least one project in the other subgroup. These overlapping subgroups are converted into mutually exclusive levels of severity by the Dalenius method to clarify interpretation of results.

TABLE A. 10

Projects Grouped by Statistically Equivalent or Different Arrest Recidivism Rates within Each Level of Severity by Mean MSS and Mean Number of Arrests Prior to Project Entry

AGE of Client	LEVEL OF SEVERITY By Mean MSS Prior to Project Entry	PROJECT AND COMPONENT	ARREST RECIDIVISM Rates By Per Cent	PROJECTS GROUPED BY ARREST RECIDIVISM RATES Within the Level of Severity
7-12	1	PROTESTANT BOARD OF GUARDIANS	19	Same
		ALTERNATIVES TO DETENTION - HRA Family Boarding Home	29	
		ALTERNATIVES TO DETENTION - PROBATION Pre-court Intensive Service	40	
		NEIGHBORHOOD YOUTH DIVERSION	41	
13-15	1	PROTESTANT BOARD OF GUARDIANS	40	Same
	2	ALTERNATIVES TO DETENTION - HRA Family Boarding Home	29	1
		ALTERNATIVES TO DETENTION - PROBATION Pre-court Intensive Service	62	2
	3	MORRISANIA YOUTH SERVICE CENTER Legal Services	47	Same
		NEIGHBORHOOD YOUTH DIVERSION	62	
	4	ALTERNATIVES TO DETENTION - HRA Group Home	55	Same
		ALTERNATIVES TO DETENTION - PROBATION Supvd Deten Release & Day/Eve Ctr	59	
16-18	1	YOUTH COUNSEL BUREAU Long-term Parole	24	Same
	2	ADDICTS REHABILITATION CENTER	34	
		MORRISANIA YOUTH SERVICE CENTER Legal Services	41	Same
		LEGAL PROPINQUITY	42	
	3	PROBATION - URBAN LEAGUE	60	Same
		INDEPENDENCE HOUSE	61	
	4	ASA - ADDICTS DIVERSION PROGRAM	53	
		VOI - BRONX COMMUNITY COUNSELING	56	Same
		PROJECT BYCEP	59	
19-20	1	ADDICTS REHABILITATION CENTER	50	Same
	2	VOI - BRONX COMMUNITY COUNSELING	44	
		MORRISANIA YOUTH SERVICE CENTER Legal Services	46	Same
	3	PROBATION - URBAN LEAGUE	47	
		ASA - ADDICTS DIVERSION PROGRAM	49	Same
		INDEPENDENCE HOUSE	72	
21-29	1	VOI - BRONX COMMUNITY COUNSELING	33	
		PROJECT MANHOOD	36	1
		ADDICTS REHABILITATION CENTER	44	
		ADDICTS REHABILITATION CENTER	44	
		NAACP PROJECT REBOUND Intensive and Non-Intensive	49	2
	2	PROJECT SECOND CHANCE	28	
		PROJECT SHARE	29	
		VERA SUPPORTIVE WORK PROGRAM Wildcat	33	Same
		ASA - ADDICTS DIVERSION PROGRAM	36	
		VERA SUPPORTIVE WORK PROGRAM Control Group	44	
30-39	1	VOI - BRONX COMMUNITY COUNSELING	10	
		PROJECT SHARE	32	
		ADDICTS REHABILITATION CENTER	34	Same
		PROJECT MANHOOD	36	
	2	VERA SUPPORTIVE WORK PROGRAM Wildcat	21	
		VERA SUPPORTIVE WORK PROGRAM Control Group	26	Same
		ASA - ADDICTS DIVERSION PROGRAM	31	
		NAACP PROJECT REBOUND Intensive and Non-Intensive	33	
40-71	1	ADDICTS REHABILITATION CENTER	15	Same
	2	NAACP PROJECT REBOUND Intensive and Non-Intensive	29	Same

(continued)

AGE of Client	LEVEL OF SEVERITY By Mean Number of ARRESTS Prior to Project Entry	PROJECT AND COMPONENT	ARREST RECIDIVISM Rates By Per Cent	PROJECTS GROUPED BY ARREST RECIDIVISM RATES Within the Level of Severity

7-12	1	PROTESTANT BOARD OF GUARDIANS
		ALTERNATIVES TO DETENTION - HRA
		  Family Boarding Home
		ALTERNATIVES TO DETENTION - PROBATION
		  Pre-court Intensive Service
		NEIGHBORHOOD YOUTH DIVERSION
			19
			29
			
			40
			
			41
				Same

13-15	1	ALTERNATIVES TO DETENTION - HRA Family Boarding Home PROTESTANT BOARD OF GUARDIANS	29 40	Same

	2	MORRISANIA YOUTH SERVICE CENTER
		  Legal Services
		ALTERNATIVES TO DETENTION - PROBATION
		  Pre-court Intensive Service
			47
			
			62
				Same

	3	ALTERNATIVES TO DETENTION - HRA
		  Group Home
		ALTERNATIVES TO DETENTION - PROBATION
		  Supvd Deten Release & Day/Eve Ctr
		NEIGHBORHOOD YOUTH DIVERSION
			55
			
			59
			
			62
				Same

16-18	1	YOUTH COUNSEL BUREAU Long-term Parole	24	Same
	2	ADDICTS REHABILITATION CENTER MORRISANIA YOUTH SERVICE CENTER Legal Services LEGAL PROPINQUITY	34 41 42	Same
	3	PROBATION - URBAN LEAGUE INDEPENDENCE HOUSE	60 61	Same
	4	ASA - ADDICTS DIVERSION PROGRAM VOI - BRONX COMMUNITY COUNSELING PROJECT BYCEP	53 56 59	Same
19-20	1	VOI - BRONX COMMUNITY COUNSELING MORRISANIA YOUTH SERVICE CENTER Legal Services PROBATION - URBAN LEAGUE	44 46 47	Same
	2	ASA - ADDICTS DIVERSION PROGRAM ADDICTS REHABILITATION CENTER INDEPENDENCE HOUSE	49 50 72	Same
21-29	1	VOI - BRONX COMMUNITY COUNSELING PROJECT MANHOOD NAACP PROJECT REBOUND Intensive	33 36 36	Same
	2	PROJECT SECOND CHANCE	28	1
		VERA SUPPORTIVE WORK PROGRAM Control Group ADDICTS REHABILITATION CENTER	44 44	2
	3	PROJECT SHARE VERA SUPPORTIVE WORK PROGRAM Wildcat ASA - ADDICTS DIVERSION PROGRAM	29 33 36	1
		NAACP PROJECT REBOUND Non-Intensive	59	2
30-39	1	VOI - BRONX COMMUNITY COUNSELING PROJECT SECOND CHANCE ADDICTS REHABILITATION CENTER PROJECT MANHOOD	10 32 34 36	Same

	2	VERA SUPPORTIVE WORK PROGRAM
		  Wildcat
		VERA SUPPORTIVE WORK PROGRAM
		  Control
		ASA - ADDICTS DIVERSION PROGRAM
		NAACP PROJECT REBOUND
		  Intensive and Non-Intensive
			21
			
			26
			
			31
			33
				Same

40-71	1	ADDICTS REHABILITATION CENTER NAACP PROJECT REBOUND Intensive and Non-Intensive	15 29	Same

Source: Compiled by the evaluation project.

TABLE A. 11

For the Client Age Group 21-29, Projects
Grouped by Statistically Equivalent or Different
Arrest Recidivism Rates within Levels of Severity

Level of Severity	Project and Component	Projects Grouped By Arrest Recidivism Rates
1	BCC, MANHD, NAACP(i) 23 36 36	Same
2	SCH 28	1
	VERA(c), ARC 44 44	2
3	SHARE, VERA(w), ASA 29 33 36	1
	NAACP(n) 59	2

Source: Compiled by the evaluation project.

outcomes of this test were compared to the outcomes of the Duncan
test applied to the ten projects within the levels of severity for this
age group (Table A. 10). (Since the comparisons are between the
results of two Duncan tests, the term "test" will be used for the
first in an effort to minimize confusion.)

The following results are shown in Tables A. 11 and A. 12:

- Both approaches result in allowing comparisons between BCC,
  MANHD, and NAACP(i).
- The test adds Second Chance as comparable to the projects above.
- The test adds SHARE, VERA(w), ASA, and VERA(c) as compar-
  able to the four projects above.
- Both approaches allow comparison between VERA(c) and ARC.
- The test adds VERA(c) and ARC as comparable to NAACP(i).
- Both approaches prohibit comparison of SCH with ARC because of
  significantly different arrest rates.
- Both approaches prohibit comparison of Second Chance with
  NAACP(ni) because of significantly different arrest rates.
- Both approaches prohibit comparison between NAACP(ni) and the
  projects BCC, NAACP(i), MANHD, SCH, and VERA(w).

The implications were:

1. In no case did the test prevent comparisons between projects that the Duncan test by levels of severity allowed.
2. The test allowed comparisons between projects that the Duncan test by levels prevented.
3. The test, by allowing additional comparisons between projects, did not change the answer (of no) provided by the Duncan test by levels of severity, but allowed more confidence in the generalizability of that answer just as in the case of the 30 to 39 age group.
4. The fact that the test prevented exactly the same comparisons that the Duncan test by severity levels did also resulted in no change of the "no" answer to the question.
5. If the test prevented comparisons that the Duncan sort allowed, the answer to the question might have changed. This did not occur.

Conclusion

Therefore, the major conclusion from the results of this comparison for the 20- to 29-year-olds was the same as that for the 30- to 39-year-old group.

TABLE A. 12

For the Client Age Group 21-29, Projects
Grouped by Statistically Equivalent or Different
Arrest Recidivism Rates across Levels of Severity
(Severity of Mean Number of
Arrests Prior to Project Entry)

Project and Component	Projects Grouped By Arrest Recidivism Rates
SCH, SHARE, VERA(w), BCC, MANHD, ASA, NAACP(i), VERA(c) 28 29 33 33 36 36 36 44	1
SHARE, VERA(w), BCC, MANHD, ASA, NAACP(i), VERA(c), ARC 29 33 33 36 36 36 44 44	2
VERA(c), ARC, NAACP(n) 44 44 59	3

Source: Compiled by the evaluation project.

If levels of severity were invalid because the assumed relationship between the severity of prior criminal history and arrest
recidivism was false, and if an answer of no is generated by applying
the Duncan test within the invalid levels of severity of an age group,
then the answer of no is still valid. It is simply less generalizable
to other projects than it would be if the Duncan had been applied to
the projects within the age group across the levels of severity. *
     The next question was whether the mutually exclusive levels
of severity resulting from the use of the method of Dalenius affected
the answer of no. †
     The method of Dalenius was used to convert clusters of over-
lapping projects into mutually exclusive levels of severity by forcing
each project into one and only one level of severity within an age
group. However, in cases of overlap this means that two or more
projects cannot be compared across levels, despite the fact that their
mean number of arrests prior to project entry were statistically no
different. Therefore, the method of Dalenius may be preventing comparisons of the arrest recidivism of some projects because of an
artificial separation into exclusive levels.
     It is difficult to see how this attribute of the Dalenius method
may affect the answer to the question, given the preceding results
of the comparison of a Duncan sort across levels of severity with one
within levels of severity for the age groups 21 through 29 and 30
through 39. The results of the tests for the two age groups clearly
indicated no difference in the answer to the question but simply
increased confidence in it if the levels of severity were collapsed.
     In any case, the comparison above was not a direct test of the
question raised about the Dalenius. In order to test this it might be
required that the Duncan sort of the arrest rates of projects within
the pre-Dalenius clusters of projects in an age group be compared
with the same sort across the clusters (that is, levels) of projects
for that age group.

CRITERIA FOR ANALYSIS

     Basic ground rules of the analysis and how they were arrived
at and applied were described in detail in the preceding description

---

*It would have been interesting to have done the test and com-
parisons on the age groups where the relationship between severity of
prior criminal history and recidivism was significant.
     †The method of Dalenius is not questioned here in terms of
internal mathematical validity or the appropriateness of its application
to the Duncan in order to clarify interpretation of outcomes.

of methods, but they are summarized below. * Considerations are also presented relating to the analysis of differences between arrest rates before and after project entry and the effects of certain characteristics of clients on recidivism.

Clients Included in the Final Analysis. There had to be at least a one-year period for each client after the date of project entry over which arrest recidivism could be measured on a police record. †

A client was included for analysis if any kind of a police record was found for him. The record could contain no arrests but some other police contact, such as a YD-1 contact or warrant. The police contact on a record might have been before project entry, during the year after entry, or subsequently.

For the 3,930 names submitted, 370 records were retrieved but excluded from the analysis because there were fewer than 12 months available for recidivism. Clients for whom no police records of any kind were retrieved were excluded from the analysis. There were 460 of these names reported as "no records" (NR) by the police (Table A. 1).

When record retrieval was terminated, there were, in addition to the 460 NRs, 76 "file-outs" and sealed records remaining which were also classified as NRs. There remained a total of 3,024 names of clients with police records.

For one small subgroup of the NR clients, it could be hypothesized that the reason no police records were found was that these clients had, in fact, never been arrested. The effect of omitting these clients from the arrest recidivism rates would be to overstate the rates†† (but probably not by much).

For most cases for which no records were retrieved (the second subtype), it is probable that such records actually existed but were not found because of reasons which include: project or evaluation error with client-identifying information, records misfiled by the police or missing, "sealed" records, CJEP not retrieving juvenile records for clients 19 or older (because some of these clients might have such records), and, clearly, the 76 "file-outs" and sealed

----

*See text for additional details.

†An additional month was allowed so that the police had adequate time to post all arrests for the one-year period.

††It should be noted that a proportion of these 536 NRs belong to clients who would not have met the 12-month criterion of the evaluation. Therefore, the proportion of the subgroup of these types of NR clients would have to be estimated on the basis of a number less than 536.

Page 85, before Subhead: Add the paragraph As discussed earlier, the diversion of those with only nonserious present or past criminal charges appears to benefit the CJS. Careful diversion of these types of persons should be continued.

Page 118, line 30: For 205 read 134.

Page 158, line 34: For pervasive read persuasive.

Page 171, lines 21-22: Read as part of list below Arrests recorded for the period after the 12 months during which recidivism was measured

line 23: Delete consisted of:.

Page 174, line 21: For 30 read 39.

Page 188, line 22: For John Vorenberg read James Vorenberg.

ERRATA

Page x, line 8: For Severity read Seriousness.

Page xvii, line 20: Insert and after staff.

Page 25, line 27: Insert In the literature, before For example.

Page 26, note: For pp. 139-68 read pp. 139-40.

Page 33, Table Source: For project evaluation read evaluation project.

Page 34, line 4: For (see Chapter 2, note 8) read (see p. 12, note†).

Page 35, note 3: For 85 read 88.

note 5: For John Vorenberg read James Vorenberg.

Page 36, Head: For SEVERITY read SERIOUSNESS.

Page 37, Subhead: For Severity read Seriousness.

Page 39, Table Source: For project evaluation read evaluation project.

Page 41, Table Source: For project evaluation read evaluation project.

Page 46, below Table: Insert *P ≤ 0.05.
Table Source: For project evaluation read evaluation project.

Page 47, Table Source: For project evaluation read evaluation project.

Page 48, below Table title: Insert Clients with No Arrest for Violent Crimes Before Project Entry vs. Clients with One or More Arrests for Violent Crimes Before Project Entry.

Table Source: For project evaluation read evaluation project.

Page 55, note: For (see Chapter 3, note 4) read (see p. 25, lines 17-26).

Page 56, line 16: Delete only.

Page 64, note 5: Add He also stated that for a few of these categories of studies positive results are reported in "The Effectiveness of Correctional Treatment" (summarized in "What Works?"). This is so. But Martinson does not describe or recommend these few and isolated exceptions as being effective treatment (rehabilitative) approaches. Instead he raises questions about their validity and feasibility. Thus, neither these nor any other considerations in Martinson's "California Research . . ." article appear to contradict or significantly modify the frequently quoted assertion from p. 25 of "What Works?".

Robert Fishman, Criminal Recidivism in New York City: An Evaluation of the Impact of Rehabilitation and Diversion Services (New York: Praeger Publishers, 1977).

continued

records which we classified as NRs after final retrieval. It is estimated that the omission of this second subtype of clients had little effect on the arrest recidivism rate of any group because the best estimate of the arrest recidivism rate among the omitted cases is that of the group from which they are omitted.

The initial pool of clients with police records totaled 3,024, of which 2,900 were from the 18 projects and 129 from the control group.

The number of these clients who had been in more than one project was determined. This comparatively simple question turned out to be a very difficult programming task and was not completed till after the major analysis presented here had been completed.

A computer check of the B numbers and NYSIIS numbers of these clients showed that 39, or about 1.3 percent, had been in more than one of the 18 projects or the control group. Thus, the actual number of different clients in the pool was 2,985. For the evaluation purposes of comparing criminological outcomes of different projects and the magnitude and severity of those outcomes, however, the slightly double-counted pool of 3,024 does not seem to be an inaccurate unit of analysis.

Some Police Contacts Not Counted As Arrests. Arrests recorded for the period after the 12 months during which recidivism was measured consisted of:

YD-1 cards for juveniles

All types of warrants

Arrests contingent upon prior arrests (such as those for bail jumping, escape, absconding from temporary release) that might be considered double counts of criminal behavior

Charges which the New York City Police Department does not classify into any of the 26 Uniform Crime Reporting offense categories by which arrest statistics are submitted to the FBI (mainly under the vehicle and traffic law)

A few charges under the old penal law which were transferred to laws other than the new penal law and do not appear to represent criminal activity

Military arrests in New York State, many of which are for charges such as insubordination and absence without leave, which are unique to military service, and for many of which the charge could not be determined from the police records*

---

*It should be noted, however, that due to an error in a coding decision, military arrests outside of New York State were treated as

Arrests we did not know about, which occurred outside New York
City or New York State and were not on the New York City
police record, or arrests mistakenly not recorded on the
arrest records by the police, particularly in the case of
juveniles

The net result of all these exclusions would be to understate
the magnitude of the criminological outcomes, for example, recidivism
rates and numbers of arrests.

Ages. The evaluation selected seven age groups on the basis of
differences between them that were qualitative (prepubescent 7- to
12-year-olds versus mature 40- to 77-year-olds), or legal (13- to
15-year-old "juveniles" and 21- to 29-year-old "adults"), or which
provided flexibility in analysis or reporting. The seven age groups
were: 7 to 12, 13 to 15, 16 to 18, 19 to 20, 21 to 29, 30 to 39, and
40 to 71.

Project Components

There were initially 3, 025 clients in the seven age groups. We
collapsed all within projects' second retrieval groups with those
groups initially retrieved (A plus B). Differences, if any, between
project effects or between clients taken in during the first six-month
period and those in the subsequent six-month period were unanalyz-
able and not high among our final evaluation priorities.

Within projects, we combined all components where we had
reason to believe that clients in one component had also received
services from another. This overlap would have resulted in an over-
count. The projects and their combined components were Addicts
Rehabilitation Center, residence and nonresident day care;
Independence House, long-term and short-term service; VOI Bronx
Community Counsel, daytime, evening, and teen-age; Project
Share, residential and nonresidential; Alternatives to Detention—
Probation, supervised detention release and day/evening center.

We dropped from the analysis any subgroup within a project
where the number of clients within the age group and project (or
component) was fewer than 20. There were 19 of these subgroups

---

regular out-of-state arrests. This mistake may not be significant.
There were 1, 273, or 8 percent, of the 16, 187 arrests that were out
of state. Of these it is estimated that the proportion of military arrests
was negligible. This estimate was based on the fact that within New
York State there were 22 military arrests which accounted for less
than 0. 1 percent of the 14, 914 New York State and City arrests.

containing 115 clients. We mistakenly dropped 14 "unserviced clients" from Neighborhood Youth Diversion and 35 "service unverified" clients from ASA.* As a result of dropping the 164 clients above, we were left with 2,860 clients for this analysis. (We were unable to determine how many of the 39 clients who had been in more than one project had been among either the group dropped or those remaining. The best estimate may be that about 1.3 percent of each group were in more than one project. Therefore, about 98.7 percent of the 2,860 are estimated to be different individuals.)

For the remaining project components t-tests were used to see if there were differences between components by average number of arrests prior to project entry. We did this by age levels. For those age levels in which there were differences, we kept the component separate, for example, NAACP Intensive, 21 to 29. If there were no differences, we combined them—NAACP Intensive and Non-intensive, age 30 to 39, and Manhood Counseling Sessions and Job Referral.

Arrest Rates Before and After Project Entry

Are client arrest rates during the 12 months after project entry lower than in a 12-month period before? A principal problem was the identification of a valid 12-month period before project entry for the comparison.

Several evaluations of drug addiction treatment programs had used the period immediately preceding project entry for comparison purposes. They reported highly significant decreases in criminal behavior. It has been argued that these positive results may have been due to a regression (mathematical) effect, rather than project impact. We felt that the positive outcomes, measured in this way, were additionally questionable because of design characteristics of the drug projects that were shared by the projects we were to evaluate.

The nature of the projects we were to evaluate was such that arrest just prior to project entry was in a number of cases explicitly necessary for admission, and in many other cases implicitly necessary. In some diversion projects, whether related to addiction or not, each client had to be arrested before a court could order diversion to the project. Other projects found that priorities, theirs or the

---

*The drops were a mistake because both were diversion projects where clients were referred to the project only because of the intervention of the project. It would have been valid and important to address the question of the effects of the project on all those diverted to it, even if they never showed up or did not receive services.

clients', had the effect of linking project entry to arrest, even if not as a formal requirement. This made the 12 months prior to project entry invalid for a comparison of arrest rates to the 12 months after project entry, because the pool of clients virtually had to have a high arrest rate in the prior period. (It must be noted that the identification of explicit or implicit arrest requirement is in no way intended as a criticism of project design. The error being discussed is in the measurement of project impact.)

Comparison would be invalid because arrest was not similarly guaranteed during the 12 months after project entry. Clients, in principle, had more "opportunity" to be arrested or not arrested. Furthermore, some clients might commit crimes and not be apprehended (arrested). Therefore, compared to the artificially high arrest rate before project entry, the rate for the period after project entry had to be lower, even if the project had no impact. In a mathematical sense, the comparison would be of two arrest rates with different bases.

Method. To verify this possibility, arrest rates for 12 months before and after project entry were compared by X^2 tests across and by projects for six age groups—7 to 12, 13 to 15, 16 to 18, 19 to 20, 21 to 30, and 40 to 71.

As expected, the analysis across projects showed arrest rates in the 12 months after project entry significantly lower than the rates for the 12 months before project entry for each of the age groups. Inspection of the results of individual projects, however, confirmed that the significance of the decreases in arrest rates across projects was attributable to an artificially high arrest rate for the 12-month period before project entry.

For example, ASA Court Diversion had arrest rates of 100 percent, 98 percent, and 95 percent for the age groups 16 to 18, 19 to 20, and 21 to 39, respectively. Morrisania had a 96 percent rate for 16- to 18-year-olds. For most of the other projects the rates ranged from 50 percent to 93 percent. The lowest rates, for six of the projects, ranged from 27 percent to 48 percent for the 21 to 39 age group. *

For most projects it was clear that some clients had to be arrested to be eligible for project entry, and the existence of those

---

*These were primarily rehabilitation projects for ex-convicts who for the most part were in jail during the year before project entry and could not have been arrested. This leads to an error in the opposite direction when making comparisons of the years before and after project entry.

arrests would artificially inflate the projects' arrest rates for the 12-month period preceding project entry.

Conclusion. This left open the question of which 12 months prior to project entry to compare with the 12 months after project entry. We narrowed the choice to two possibilities. One was to take the period from the twenty-fourth to the twelfth month (the second year) prior to project entry. The other was to take the 12 months preceding the last arrest, and to exclude that arrest from the computation of arrest rates.

The second year prior to project entry had the advantage, in principle, of having provided the client an opportunity of arrest equal to his opportunity during the 12 months after project entry. It also allowed all persons of equal age at project entry to be compared during an equal age prior to project entry.

The drawback was with juveniles, particularly very young ones. For example, the difference in criminal behavior between the age periods of 12 to 14 and 13 to 14 may be quantitative and qualitative. The effect of this might well have been an artificial reduction of the arrest rate in the period prior to project entry.

The advantage of the second alternative—the 12 months prior to the last arrest—was that it, in principle, also afforded a client an opportunity to have been arrested or not in the 12-month period prior to project entry equal to the opportunity for arrest or nonarrest during the 12-month period after project entry.

Its weakness would be that of the introduction of variability, particularly in measurement of juvenile behavior. Clients entering a project at the same age with more than one arrest would have their last arrest excluded, but their next arrests would probably be at different dates. For example, two juveniles of the same age at project entry, say, 13 years and 3 months, might be measured for arrest rates prior to project entry during different ages—the first might be measured during the age period 12 years and 2 months to 13 years and 2 months; the second might be measured from the age 11 years and 4 months to 12 years and 4 months. The effect would be that of counting a less criminally active age for one juvenile, while counting a somewhat more criminally active age for the other. Thus, the comparison period would actually suffer from the same type of weakness as the first alternative: qualitative and quantitative differences in criminal behavior at very early ages and at late ages, a maturation effect.

Weighing these strengths and weaknesses in both alternatives, we selected the second year prior to project entry on the ground that it would introduce no variability into the comparison of before-and-after behavior for clients of the same ages. We had already identified one variability-connected drawback in the "before last arrest" measure, and there might be others. We did not have the opportunity of testing both and determining which worked better.

Heroin Charge, Race/Ethnicity, and Recidivism

Heroin Charge. There had been an initial intention to control for clients with a record of heroin addiction in making comparisons between projects. However, we were not able to determine types of drugs or addiction from arrest charges or other sources. Later, funding of drug addiction treatment projects by the CJCC was ended. As a result, controlling the evaluation for heroin addiction was not feasible.

Nevertheless, an attempt was made to obtain at least some information about the drug addiction status of clients on the basis of available information—arrest charges and some knowledge about the projects and their clients. Two disconnected methods were used.

First, the proportion of clients who had any drug charge on their arrest record prior to project entry was computed for each of the 18 projects (but not for Vera Control Group). The reader should recall that if there was more than one charge in an arrest, we would have recorded only the most serious.* Since drug charges are number 18 in the UCR ranking of severity, our method of determining charges would not pick up most drug charges. Therefore, arrest charges were reanalyzed. If there was any drug charge for an arrest, that arrest was assigned the drug charge. The analysis was done for the initial pool of 2,900 clients by the age groups 16 to 18, 19 to 20, and 21 and over.

The results show that some of the non-drug addiction treatment projects for clients 21 and older had very high drug charge rates. The four projects were: NAACP, 64 percent of clients; Manhood, 58 percent; Second Chance, 57 percent, and SHARE, 60 percent. These rates were not much lower than those in two projects which dealt only with heroin addicts: ASA Court Referral, with 83 percent; and ARC, with 78 percent. Since the clients of the four non-drug treatment projects were almost entirely black or Puerto Rican, it was assumed that most of the drug charges represented heroin. This assumption is based on evidence which suggests that poor, adult blacks and Puerto Ricans at that time were rarely users of cocaine or "soft" drugs.

There was a pilot study to determine whether there were recidivism rate differences between the clients of two drug projects

---

*By UCR ranking, or by MSS during the validation of that measure.

ASA and ARC, and the clients of eight selected nondrug projects. However, the ambiguity of the New York City drug arrest charge and the proportion of clients in all the projects who did not have any drug charge arrest led to uninterpretable results, and the effort was not continued.

There was probably a goodly proportion of heroin addicts in projects for those 21 and older, but it is not possible to conclude anything about the effects of this on recidivism.

Race and Ethnicity. There was no significant relationship between race and ethnicity and arrest recidivism, or violent crime arrest rates, for six of the seven age groups when tested by the X^2. The relationship was significant for the 16- to 18-year-olds on both measures. The white clients had lower arrest rates than black or Spanish-surnamed clients. * However, approximately 75 percent of the white clients were from a project (YCB) which accepted many socioeconomically middle-class whites who had to be first offenders with nonserious arrest charges. The vast bulk of the black and Spanish-surnamed clients, on the other hand, were probably in the lowest socioeconomic class and definitely had more severe criminal histories. Therefore, the finding is inconclusive.

"Completers" versus "Dropouts". The evaluation intended to compare the recidivism rates of those who completed projects and those who dropped out. This was not done. First, there was too much variability between and within project definitions of services and client status to permit any comparisons. Second, project records generally were too incomplete or inaccurate to allow this type of assessment, particularly in community-based projects. Finally, we were unable to implement a standardized system of identifying "completers" and "dropouts" across projects, although we did preliminary work on the instruments that would be necessary, such as a standard change of status form to be used by all the projects.

"Self-Report" Study. A "self-report" study for the clients was intended. The task would allow a measure of unreported crimes and unapprehended crimes and a cross-check of police records of apprehended crimes. Our problem here centered on the issue of confidentiality. At that time, under New York State law, we were liable to a subpoena if certain information about a client was required

---

*For arrest recidivism the X^2 value was 21.8537 with 3 df. P is equal to or less than .0001. For the violent crime arrest rate after project entry X^2 was 18.4829 with 3 df. P is equal to or less than .0004.

by the criminal justice system. Next, several projects expressed
serious resistance to the study on the basis of confidentiality. We
decided not to do the study because of the policy implications.

REFLECTIONS

On looking back over the four years of work discussed in this
appendix, it becomes apparent that we invested an enormous amount
of resources and time in attempting to maximize the accuracy of our
data. Generally, the effort proved unnecessary. For example, our
"match check" study of juveniles and the investigation of discrepancies
between date of arrest and date of occurrence of the crime were
expensive, time-consuming efforts and showed that the errors had
negligible effects. The results of these efforts indicated that most
of the errors we were checking for would not have been significant.

Although it may sound like a rationalization, we feel that these
expensive efforts at maximizing accuracy were absolutely necessary.
In any evaluation of "demonstration projects" where there is a new
evaluation design or method to be used, unexpected problems arise.
At the time the problems emerge, the only criterion for deciding
whether or not to invest time examining them is that of the problem's
possible effect on the goals of the evaluation. Clearly, discrepancies
of identity of project clients and the arrest records assigned to them
could have seriously impaired the accuracy of our evaluation and the
conclusions we arrived at. Therefore, at the jarring moment when
the possibility of serious error arises, it is necessary to invest as
much as may be called for to see whether the error is significant
or not.

We have prepared this lengthy, perhaps compulsively detailed
description of our methods, because we feel that the information in
this appendix may be of use to other evaluations which may have to
deal with arrest records in police departments or with project records
on clients.

We were impressed during the course of the evaluation by the
number of times that related evaluation projects had to rediscover the
wheel of how to retrieve, process, or code police arrest records,
a job which we experienced as very expensive and time-consuming.
Therefore, this appendix is a legacy to evaluation projects that may
need this type of information now or in the future.

NOTES

1. Penal Law of the State of New York, 1973-1974 (Binghamton,
N. Y. : Gould Publications).

2. The Consolidated Laws of New York—Annotated, vol. 39—Penal Law, pts. 1 and 2 (Brooklyn, N. Y. : Edward Thompson, 1944).

3. Thorsten Sellin and Marvin E. Wolfgang, The Measurement of Delinquency (New York: Wiley, 1964).

4. Marvin E. Wolfgang, Robert M. Figlio, and Thorsten Sellin, Delinquency in a Birth Cohort (Chicago: University of Chicago Press, 1972).

5. T. Dalenius and J. L. Hodges, Jr. , "Minimum Variance Stratification," Journal of the American Statistical Association 54 (1959): 88-101.

6. Personal communication with Robert M. Figlio, January 1975.

7. Dalenius and Hodges, op. cit.

APPENDIX B:
PROJECT DESCRIPTIONS

The 18 projects for which reports are included in this evaluation are described below. The individual descriptions are excerpts from the project descriptions reported by CJCC in its annual 1973 Criminal Justice Plan.

ADDICT DIVERSION PROGRAM—ASA

The project operates in the Brooklyn and Manhattan Criminal Courts, which established a voluntary placement and referral service for arrested drug abusers with the objective of providing treatment as an alternative to the standard criminal process. The Addiction Service Agency interviews, screens and places in treatment programs inmates going through the detoxification program of the Department of Correction. The Criminal Court judges before whom their cases are pending are asked to release them in the custody of the programs involved, either as a pre-trial release condition or on probation after conviction. The courts receive progress reports prepared by ASA.

ADDICTS REHABILITATION CENTER

(also known as <u>Harlem-East Harlem Drug Treatment Program</u>)
A project administered by Addicts Rehabilitation Center in the Harlem-East Harlem Model Cities Neighborhood to help addicts get off drugs through a comprehensive treatment program from detoxification through job placement, thus reducing crime in this area by reducing the number of addicts who steal to buy drugs. Project elements include hospital detoxification; a crisis intervention center open 24 hours a day, 7 days a week; two residential therapeutic communities; and aftercare including vocational training and job placement.

ALTERNATIVES TO DETENTION—HRA

The project provides a non-secure facility for children as an alternative to a detention facility, avoiding removal from a home environment. Boarding Home Program component utilizes private homes. These homes will serve younger children who need a one-to-one relationship with a parent or parent substitute. Program social workers make home visits and act as a liaison with boarding home parents. Group Homes component cares for a number of severely delinquent children at the same time, with social and part-time recreation workers assigned. This program involves older children more independent of parental ties and who respond favorably to group living; each home is assigned House Parents.

ALTERNATIVES TO DETENTION—PROBATION

The project provides day and evening counseling and referral, services to children and families to resolve problems while keeping the children out of detention facilities. This is meant to reduce the workload of the judicial system and avoid establishing or strengthening the self-image of the child as a delinquent.

In the Pre-court Intensive Services component social and community workers "provide direct services to children and their families including referrals to health, housing, social and other agencies."

The Day and Evening programs components provide "counseling, educational services and recreation programs." The design calls for the older children to "receive individual and group counseling with special emphasis on vocational counseling and employment related problems," as well as "being enrolled in a structured evening program."

The Supervised Detention Release Program component has a community worker making daily visits to each child's home to be informed of the child's activity, to get appropriate assistance through referrals to other agencies; and to alert the court, if necessary, to the need to reconsider the child's status on predisposition parole.

INDEPENDENCE HOUSE

A project sponsored by the YMCA in conjunction with the Youth Services Agency. Its voluntary residential program attempts to provide participants with alternatives to anti-social and criminal activities, and to assist them in shaping a new life style, through the provision of psychological, educational, and vocational counseling in a self-help atmosphere. Participants are to be 17-20 year old males who have completed Reformatory sentences, been released from the Adolescent Remand Shelter, or referred by YSA.

LEGAL PROPINQUITY

A project to implement a program of legal intervention for a selected population of youth in the East Harlem Community, to ensure the best possible legal defense, and also to provide a full program of rehabilitation services for those involved in the criminal justice system. Project streetworkers, assigned to Manhattan Criminal Court, Youth Part, work with Legal Aid attorneys and additional streetworkers at the community level to provide back-up rehabilitation services.

MORRISANIA YOUTH SERVICE CENTER

(also known as Morrisania Legal Assistance for Youth)
   A project to provide competent legal assistance to youth of the Morrisania community who have had encounters with criminal justice institutions, or who, through drug abuse or other activities, seem ripe for such encounters. It provides a variety of follow-up and rehabilitative services to these youth. During the second year of the project, the Morrisania Center intensified service delivery and streetworker follow-up, strengthened their relationship with Legal Aid, initiated a bail reduction procedure, and developed services for the incarcerated client.

NAACP PROJECT REBOUND

(also known as Restoration Opportunity Center)   .
   A project operated under the auspices of the NAACP, to provide the following services for 100 ex-offenders on an intensive level and for 100-200 ex-offenders on a transient immediate-need level: individual and group counseling; job development and placement services with follow-up services for at least three months after job placement; referral by counseling staff to community agencies for supportive services; financial assistance at an average of $25 per client for 100 clients for emergencies and expenses incidental to employment; and an educational component to prepare at least 50 participants for the high school equivalency diploma.

NEIGHBORHOOD YOUTH DIVERSION

   A project to divert youthful misdemeanants (ages 12-15) who reside in the East Tremont area of the Bronx from the criminal justice system to a community-based service center. The youngsters received counseling from trained community "Advocates" and were provided with comprehensive rehabilitation services. The program has also worked with others to develop a mini-school and a short-term residence. The Community Forum, which mediated disputes, included cases referred directly by the school and adjudicated cases referred for investigation to the Office of Probation by the Family Court.

PROBATION—URBAN LEAGUE

A project administered by the New York Urban League and the New York Office of Probation to develop a model probation program. The project was designed to utilize five Probation officers, out-stationed in Harlem to supervise the delivery of services to 500 probationers, aged 14-21, by Urban League Streetworkers. The program included 28 days of exposure to work and education opportunities in the city, 28 days of outdoor survival activities outside of the city, and placement in a school, street academy, training program or job. The project also offered full medical and counseling services, as well as role models and the use of peer-group pressure to motivate youth towards a constructive future.

PROJECT BYCEP

A project administered by the City's Youth Services Agency to provide youth at the Adolescent Remand Shelter with counseling and other services, referral to service agencies in their community upon release, and follow-up in the community to ensure provision of educational and vocational opportunities and assistance with other personal needs. Based upon project experience and evaluation reports, the program focused on the following: more immediate post-release contact with youths, immediate post-release referrals to drug rehabilitation programs when needed, a remedial tutoring program, job counseling and orientation, and a joint effort with Independence House.

PROJECT MANHOOD

A project to provide employment, training and education to ex-offenders. The population, both male and female, are probationers, parolees, and those released from Federal, State and city institutions. The project was under the jurisdiction of the Manpower Career Development Agency. The project emphasized vocational opportunities; counselors and follow-up workers assist participants in gaining other needed supportive services, e.g., mental health, educational, and court-related services.

PROJECT SECOND CHANCE

A project administered by the Brooklyn Businessmen's Committee to provide jobs for persons released from Federal, State and local institutions returning to Brooklyn. Before release, program personnel interviewed, gave aptitude tests, determined job motivation,

provided counseling and determined acceptability for job placement.
It was hoped that at least 300 jobs for each funding period would be
assured through the committee and community businesses. Counseling
services are available to participant and family.

PROJECT SHARE

A project administered by the Hudson Guild to offer a program
of 10-week cycles on a yearly basis plus follow-up, of personal
counseling, remedial education, and help for employment-seeking
to ex-offenders in the Chelsea area of Manhattan. Male and female
participants (young adults) are screened and recruited from both
State and local institutions. A small residence for participants with
no place to live has been included until permanent housing can be
secured.

PROTESTANT BOARD OF GUARDIANS

A project, sponsored by the Protestant Board of Guardians, to
offer counseling and rehabilitation services to youth aged 7 to 17 who
have had encounters with the juvenile system. PBG provides short-
term (60-120 day) crisis intervention, family aid and counseling and
long-term referral services to youngsters who meet age requirements,
reside in the Central Brooklyn Model Cities area, and who are referred
to the Guardian program from Probation Intake, Family Court judges,
or the Police Department's Youth Aid Unit. In all cases PBG will
have to report back to the appropriate agency within a fixed time to
assess the current situation and to recommend extension of the
period of supervision, dismissal of the case, or further court action.

VERA SUPPORTIVE WORK PROGRAM

A project under the auspices of the Vera Institute of Justice to
assist ex-addicts and ex-offenders in the development of socially
positive behavior through a program of supportive employment in
the public and private sector. All work projects are to utilize the
concepts of group employment, on-site employment counselors,
specialized employee training and orientation, graduated performance
demands, performance feedback, and supportive services. The goal
is to have each employee move on to conventional, non-supported
employment.

VOI-BRONX COMMUNITY COUNSELING

A project, operated by Volunteer Opportunities, Inc. in the south
and east Bronx, to divert children, youthful offenders and adults from

courts and prisons, thus easing the burdens on the criminal justice system; to develop within the Bronx community the capability for assisting in the rehabilitation of offenders and for community involvement, to develop socially positive attitudes and behavior in offenders, thus reducing recidivism.

YOUTH COUNSEL BUREAU

A project administered by the Youth Counsel Bureau (YCB) to provide supervision, counseling, support, and referral services to youth falling into three categories: 1) first offenders arrested for violations or minor misdemeanors, 2) youth who have had charges against them dismissed by the courts or a grand jury and who are recommended to YCB by an assistant DA or other court personnel, 3) youth who have not been charged with a crime, but who have been referred to YCB for assistance and counseling by parents, school personnel, lawyers, police or other concerned persons. The City of New York, in an effort to upgrade services to client youth, decrease recidivism and avoid further congestion of the court calendar, has increased YCB's capability by providing additional supervisory, casework and clerical support. One supervisor was assigned to the development of specific in-service training programs for new and experienced YCR staff.

BIBLIOGRAPHY

Act of September 7, 1974, P. L. 93-415, Title V, §541, 88 Stat. 1142.

Andenaes, Johannes, Punishment and Deterrence (Ann Arbor: University of Michigan Press, 1974).

Antunes, George, and Hunt, A. Lee, "The Impact of Severity of Punishment on Levels of Crime in American States: An Extended Analysis." Journal of Criminal Law and Criminology 64 (1973): 486.

Bailey, William C., Martin, J., and Gray, Louis, "Crime and Deterrence: A Correlational Analysis." Journal of Research in Crime and Delinquency 11 (1974): 124.

Cahill, Kevin M., "Report to the Governor, Governor's Panel on Juvenile Violence," Albany, New York, January 5, 1975, pp. 31, 32.

Cochran, W. G., "Comparison of Methods for Determining Stratum Boundaries." Bull. Int. Stat. Inst. 38, no. 2 (1961): 345-58.

Cochran, W. G., Sampling Techniques, 2d ed. (New York: John Wiley and Sons, 1963), pp. 128-33.

The Consolidated Laws of New York—Annotated, vol. 39—Penal Law, pts. 1 and 2 (Brooklyn, N. Y.: Edward Thompson, 1944).

Dalenius, T., and Hodges, J. L. Jr., "Minimum Variance Stratification." Journal of the American Statistical Association 54 (1959):88-101.

Declaration and Purpose, Law Enforcement Assistance, Act of June 19, 1968, P. L. 90-351, Title I. §100; 82 Stat. 197.

Declaration and Purpose, Law Enforcement Assistance, Act of August 6. 1973, P. L. 93-83, § 2, 87 Stat. 197.

Ehrlich, Isaac, "The Deterrent Effect of Criminal Law Enforcement." Journal of Legal Studies 1 (1972): 259.

Fishman, Robert "A Proposal for Individual and Comparative
    Evaluation of Diversion Projects for the Criminal Justice
    Coordinating Council." May 15, 1971, proposal at the Mayor's
    CJCC, New York City.

Friedman, Lucy N. , and Zeisel, Hans, "First Annual Research
    Report on Supported Employment," Vera Institute of Justice,
    1973.

Gibbs, Jack, "Crime, Punishment and Deterrence." Social Science
    Quarterly, 48 (1968): 515.

Heinz, Anne M. , Heinz, John P. , Senderowitz, Stephen J. , and
    Vance, Mary Anne, "Sentencing by Parole Board: An Evaluation."
    Journal of Criminal Law and Criminology 67 (1976): 1.

Kozol, Harry L. , Bowcher, Richard J. , and Garofalo, Ralph F. ,
    "The Diagnosis and Treatment of Dangerousness." Crime and
    Delinquency 18 (1972): 371.

Lipton, Douglas. , Martinson, Robert. , and Wilks, Judith, draft of
    "Treatment Evaluation Survey," (1971): 54.

Lipton, Douglas, Martinson, Robert, and Wilks, Judith, The
    Effectiveness of Correctional Treatment: A Survey of Treatment
    Evaluation Studies (New York: Praeger, 1975), pp. 4, 5.

Martinson, Robert, "What Works? Questions and Answers About
    Prison Reform," The Public Interest 35 (1975): 25.

Martinson, Robert, "California Research at the Crossroads."
    Journal of Crime and Delinquency (1976): 184.

Morris, Norval, The Future of Imprisonment (Chicago: University of
    Chicago Press, 1974), pp. 59, 66.

National Criminal Justice Information and Statistics Service, LEAA,
    "Crime in the Nation's Five Largest Cities," April 1974.

New York 1975 Sessions Laws, Ch. 878, § 3, 16.

New York State Commission of Investigation, "The Criminal Justice
    System in the City of New York-An Overview," November 1974.

New York Times, January 27, 1975.

New York Times, February 11, 1975.

New York Times, February 21, 1975, p. 37.

New York Times, August 10, 1975, p. 1.

Partridge, A. , and Eldridge, W. , The Second Circuit Sentencing
    Study: A Report to the Judges of the Second Circuit, Federal
    Judicial Center, August 1974.

Penal Law of the State of New York, 1973-1974 (Binghamton, N. Y. :
    Gould Publications).

Sellin, Thorsten, and Wolfgang, Marvin E. The Measurement of
    Delinquency (New York: Wiley, 1964).

Tittle, Charles R. , "Crime Rates and Legal Sanctions." Social
    Problems 16 (1969): 409.

Tittle, Charles R. , and Logan, Charles H. , "Sanctions and
    Deviance: Evidence and Remaining Questions." Law and
    Society Review 7 (1973): 371.

Tullock, Gordon, "Does Punishment Deter Crime?" The Public
    Interest, 36 (1974): 103.

Twentieth Century Fund, Fair and Certain Punishment (New York:
    McGraw Hill, 1976).

van den Haag, Ernest, Punishing Criminals (New York: Basic Books,
    1975).

Vorenberg, John. , and Ohlin, Lloyd, "Draft of a Proposal for the
    National Institute of the LEAA for the Evaluation of the
    Addiction Research Treatment Center (ARTC) in Brooklyn,
    N. Y. ," 1971.

Vorenberg, James, "Against Mandatory Minimum Sentences." New
    York Times, December 22, 1975, p. 29.

Wenk, Ernest A. , Robison, James O. , and Smith, Gerald W. , "Can
    Violence Be Predicted?" Crime and Delinquency 18 (1972):
    396.

Wilson, James Q. , "Lock 'Em Up and Other Thoughts on Crime."
New York Times Magazine, March 9, 1974, p. 11.

Wilson, James Q. , Thinking about Crime (New York: Basic Books,
1975).

Wolfgang, Marvin E. , Figlio, Robert M. , and Sellin, Thorsten,
Delinquency in a Birth Cohort (Chicago: University of Chicago
Press, 1972).

Zeisel, Hans, deGrazia, Jessica, and Friedman, Lucy, "Criminal
Justice System Under Stress: A Study of the Disposition of
Felony Arrests in New York City," Vera Institute of Justice,
August 1975.

Zimring, Franklin E. Perspectives on Deterrence, U. S. Department
of Health, Education, and Welfare Publication no. (ADM) 74-10
(Washington, D. C. : Government Printing Office, 1973).

Zimring, Franklin E. , and Hawkins, Gordon J. Deterrence (Chicago:
University of Chicago Press, 1973).

ABOUT THE AUTHOR

ROBERT FISHMAN is an independent consultant in the evaluation of programs in criminal justice, manpower training, remedial education, and mental retardation. Mr. Fishman planned the criminal justice evaluation project at the Vera Institute of Justice and directed the project from its beginning in 1971 to completion in 1975 at the Graduate Center and Research Foundation of the City University of New York.

As research director of the Kentucky Department of Child Welfare and, subsequently, of consulting firms in the private sector, Mr. Fishman conducted, from 1964 to 1970, evaluations of a variety of programs. Sponsors of these evaluations have included the U. S. Departments of the Interior, Labor, Health, Education, and Welfare, and the Office of Economic Opportunity.

Mr. Fishman received his M. S. degree in psychology from the University of Kentucky in Lexington, Kentucky.

THE EFFECTIVENESS OF CORRECTIONAL TREAT-
MENT: A Survey of Treatment Evaluation Studies
                         Douglas Lipton,
                         Robert Martinson,
                         and Judith Wilks

ISSUES IN CRIMINAL JUSTICE: Planning and
Evaluation
                         edited by Marc Riedel
                         and Duncan Chappell

PRISON WITHOUT WALLS: Report on New York Parole
Citizens' Inquiry on Parole and Criminal Justice, Inc.
                         Foreword by Ramsey Clark
                         Preface by David Rudenstine

PRISONER EDUCATION: Project Newgate and Other
College Programs
                         Marjorie J. Seashore,
                         Steven Haberfeld,
                         John Irwin,
                         and Keith Baker

*PUBLIC LAW AND PUBLIC POLICY
                         edited by John A. Gardiner

TOWARD A JUST AND EFFECTIVE SENTENCING
SYSTEM: Agenda for Legislative Reform
                         Pierce O'Donnell,
                         Michael J. Churgin,
                         and Dennis E. Curtis

BARGAINING FOR JUSTICE: Case Disposition and
Reform in the Criminal Courts
                         Suzann R. Thomas Buckle
                         and Leonard G. Buckle

*Also available in paperback as a PSS Student Edition